Home Is Where the

Ecology Is

Home Is Where the
Ecology Is

Written and Illustrated
by Rohit Bangay

Book design by Publishing Push

ISBNs:
Paperback: 978-1-80227-677-0
eBook: 978-1-80227-678-7

Contents

Contents

Introduction

Nature is all around us and not only that, but we are part of it. I find it difficult to understand why some may think of humanity as somehow separate from the rest of the animal kingdom. I am currently studying to become an ecologist, simply because I love nature. I tend to live in a somewhat 'isolated' way, in the social sense, I like my own company, I generally don't go out and meet people very often, but I do go out to look to for birds, butterflies, spiders, trees, flowers, anything I can spot. No matter where I go, whether that's into the garden, fields, or woodlands, or even when looking into my pond, I can see species that are working with and against each other, competing for various resources in order to survive. There are so many different things to see, so many organisms that are on our doorstep that many of us fail to realise are there, there is a remarkable abundance of life around us. This is where the premise for my book came about.

What is out there? How many times have you looked out of the window of your home, office, car, bus, wherever you may be and asked yourself this question? Or have you spoken to older generations and asked them what it was like before, what were the animals they used to see before phones and the internet took over the world and diverted our attention? I began monitoring my garden in the summer of 2016 and the local fields in late 2018. I started with birds simply because they happened to be the main group of species I saw most often, and I didn't have much knowledge about any other species at the time. I bought a digital camera, a relatively cheap one as cameras go, and every time I spotted a bird in the garden, I'd take a photo. I kept a word document which contained a list of all the species I found per month,

I looked up the Latin names of each species, which is extremely helpful because Latin names are universal whereas common names in the UK for a specific species may go by another alias in another region or country. By the end of the following summer, I had identified well over 100 species, where my focus had shifted to predominantly insects. What I realised is that there are a tremendous number of processes occurring between a huge array of species just in our gardens. A pot with some soil and a plant can kickstart any number of endless interactions.

What I also found was an aspect of life that I could maintain an engagement with. Its somewhat strange to realise that I generally feel isolated around people when compared to being in a seemingly 'empty' field. Its safe to say that with the knowledge I have gained and the things that I see when in and around nature, there's no doubt that I'm engaged with the environment I happen to be in, although no words are being spoken, there is still a large amount of communication occurring. Just as plants emit volatiles when under attack through herbivory, attracting various predatory insects, a Kestrel *(Falco tinnunculus)* or a Fox *(Vulpes vulpes)* 50 metres away can pick up on my presence and decide for itself whether to stay or go. Ecological interactions are what I am interested in, how do species coexist with each other, how do their actions affect the environment, how are abiotic and biotic factors causing changes throughout the seasons temporally and spatially? I hope I'll have a lot more knowledge about these ecological aspects over time. The world is a lot more interesting once you pay more attention and engage with it.

In this book, I have picked out species that I've spotted in my local area of Heston, a small village located in the London Borough of Hounslow. I wanted to focus on Heston because its the area I grew up in. My recordings have been acquired from both our garden and the local fields. My illustrations are not meant to be exact in terms of colour, size or form but all have a resemblance to the species portrayed. All photographs are from my old (and slightly battered) DSLR as well as some 35mm film photos. I want to be able to show that in a relatively small local area, the abundance of biodiversity can be astounding if one only knows where and how to look at the natural world. I'll try and give some pointers throughout the book on what I believe to be helpful in terms of spotting species as well as times of year to see specific species, along with what I find to be interesting about various species and their ecologies. This book is a very personal account based upon my own observations and reflections. There are two distinct parts to this book, the first focuses upon the garden, and the second part focuses on the fields. Each of the habitats are distinctive in size, topography and species richness of both flora and fauna. There are tons of species that I have yet to come across and I must state that this book should in no way be considered as a comprehensive list of what is in the area, its purely observational!

We must not forget that we are animals and part of a natural process; our behaviours, what we know, learn and experience are natural processes. I tend to respond to my instincts; I try to listen to that ever-present inner compass. I respond to my gut daily, when I decide to go for a walk, when I decide to step into the garden to look into the sky or to close my eyes and listen to the birds, a distant Chiffchaff *(Phylloscopus collybita)* in April newly arrived in a local field, or a Wren *(Troglodytes troglodytes)* during the dawn chorus. In a time where technology is advancing and evolving at a dizzying rate, its the natural environment in my immediate surroundings that helps me to focus on the aspects of life that are most important to me.

A Wren looking up at a Stonechat *(Saxicola torquata)*.

Part One: The Garden

For many people I imagine that a garden is a mini oasis, where you can relax, grow vegetables and plant flowers to sculpt your ideal garden. In terms of the environment and creating an ecosystem, gardens are extremely important as they harbour numerous species, across various taxa, ranging from bacteria to fungi to insects to birds to mammals. Gardens can act as natural corridors which allow the movement of organisms such as newts, frogs, birds, bats, hedgehogs, as well as many species of butterfly and moths between and across various areas. Sadly, in Heston, many front gardens as well as back gardens have been lost within the last 20 years or so. I have seen many trees cut down and many garden spaces concreted over for spaces such as garages, buildings and conservatories. These areas are not just losses in terms of green space, but it is also detrimental to the species that once relied on them. Hedges which act as shelter for various birds as well as foodplants for an array of insects have been lost. If conversion of green space is an absolute must, its extremely important to retain some plants for wildlife, even if it means having a small patch of weeds. Weeds are considered by many as unnecessary, but they are extremely beneficial for many insect species which are typically monophagous as well as pollinators, they can also be very beautiful when in bloom. A few wildflowers which are commonly considered as weeds are Clovers (*Trifolium* spp.*)*, Birds Foot Trefoil (*Lotus corniculatus*)*, Daisies, Buttercups, Dandelions and Thistles. Each of these wildflowers are great for Lepidoptera (Moths and butterflies) and Coleoptera (Beetles) along with many other insects and their predators.

Having a garden is a great thing, when I was younger me and my brother would play endless hours of football in the garden, and my Dad would get angry every time we left some flower heads lying around, due to our lack of shooting accuracy (sorry Dad and flowers!). Eventually we stopped playing football, simply because other aspects of life took over and playing football with a tennis ball became more difficult. Since then, the garden has always been a place for me to relax, to sit and look up at the skies during the warm summer evenings, listening to Swifts *(Apus apus)* screeching from above. I used to try and keep an eye on the Swifts flying until they flew so high that they appeared to dissolve into the sky. Whether I was coming home from stressful days at work or coming home from University I would head straight for the garden and instantly feel calm.

The vegetable patch at the back of the garden where many insects would visit during the summer months.

The garden during the summer. The apple tree on the right was a favourite place for a number of birds.

It is no wonder then that when I decided I wanted to learn more about the natural world I headed straight for the garden. Keeping track of what I saw in a word document was essential because I wanted to understand the timings of species that I saw in relation to the season. Some organisms appear all year round whereas others only appear during certain months of the year. There are also patterns within the day where species may appear only at a certain time. I was not expecting a great deal of wildlife simply because I naively thought I had already seen what there was to be seen in the area, I grew up spending tons of time outside so I must have noticed what was around me right? I was completely wrong, until I really started paying close attention to the environment, I realised I had missed a tremendous amount of wonderous life.

The first moth I ever caught (with the use of a cotton bud tub) was this individual, an Old Lady *(Mormo maura)*.

The Garden: Winter
(December, January, February)

Winter is usually a time when its nice to be snug indoors with a hot drink and looking out of the window, but these last few years have been a little strange in terms of how mild it has been. This is a bad sign for many trees and plants that may need a cold period of vernalisation to essentially wake up for spring and promote new growth. Insects may also start to emerge earlier from diapause, mismatches in timing of phenological events between plants, insects and birds is extremely important and can have massive effects on the survival of certain species.

In terms of monitoring, the low hours of daylight along with cold temperatures makes winter the most difficult time of year for finding species in the garden for me, you may have better luck! Many insects are firmly in a state of diapause hidden away and some insects may be overwintering as adults such the butterfly, Red Admiral *(Vanessa atalanta)*, which is likely to be sheltering in a garage or in a disused plant pot. In spite of the harsh conditions, there are organisms to be found.

December

December has, for the last few years, been the month with the lowest number of species that I've been able to find in the garden. A majority of the plants are dormant which means no foliar feeding by insects, and everything just looks grey and muddy. A plant that does add colour is Cotoneaster, its bright red berries may be inedible to us but they are readily eaten by many different birds including Blackbirds and Thrushes (Turdidae).

A source of food is a massive attraction for many birds during wintertime, fully stocked birdfeeders can be rapidly diminished during this season, but its worth keeping them stocked up for the variety of species that do visit. The garden during winter is a great place for seeing birds feeding. In Heston it appears that the birds consistently found in the garden at this time of year are; Robin *(Erithacus rubecula)*, Great Tit *(Parus major)*, Blue Tit *(Cyanistes caeruleus)*, Coal Tit *(Periparus ater)*, Blackbird *(Turdus merula)*, Woodpigeon *(Palamba columbus)*, Dunnock *(Prunella modularis)*, Wren *(T. troglodytes)*, Magpie *(Pica pica)* and the Feral Pigeon *(Columba livia domestica)*.

The Wren is a lovely bird, easily identifiable due to its tail often being cocked upwards, along with its distinctive bird song, it is also one of the smallest birds in the UK. From my observations it appears to prefer being concealed within the branches of trees, shrubs and thorny hedges, its movements are quick and direct, a trait shared by Coal Tits and Blue Tits. Wrens predominantly forage for caterpillars, insects located under leaves or spiders that they pick off quickly. They are early risers and can be heard before they are seen, for such a small round being, it can produce an extremely loud and high-pitched bird song. I'll take the sound of a Wren waking me up over the sound of aeroplanes beginning their descent into Heathrow any day of the week!

The Robin is easily the most recognisable bird in the UK. In a poll based on choosing a national bird for the UK, the public voted the Robin as being the number one candidate for this title. Its synonymous with Christmas and is a species that is widespread across the country. People love Robins, they are full of character and add a bright red dash of colour to cold, winter days. They also have a lovely bird song which they sing loudly from the tops of trees.

A Robin looking extremely round and fluffy during a cold winters day.

On particularly cold days Robins will fluff their feathers to increase insulation of air around them to keep warm. Bird song is extremely important to many birds but in the case of the male Robin, it signifies to competitors (other male Robins) of their presence and area of territory, females will also do the same[1]. Robins are fierce competitors and can show intense aggression which is a characteristic that often goes overlooked. They are a small fluffy bird, what damage can they do? Well, in fact some mortalities are caused by injuries sustained during fights over territory.

One of my favourite birds that is often in the garden during winter months is the Dunnock. A small passerine, it spends a lot of time foraging on the ground underneath feeders, hoovering up any seeds that have been dropped from above, although when the birdfeeder is vacant they will also feed directly from it. Unassuming, Dunnocks hop around seemingly unafraid of larger birds such as Woodpigeons and Blackbirds. During the dawn chorus I can often hear them singing from the top of a tree. I have seen many people misidentify Dunnocks as House Sparrows *(Passer domesticus)*, but they are fairly easy to distinguish once you know what to look for, for example, their beaks are clearly different along with their head shape and plumage. Behaviourally, if you do happen to see a small brown bird hopping about on the ground, searching for seeds its more likely to be a Dunnock than a House Sparrow, and if its tiny, fairly round, with a cocked tail and brown its likely to be a Wren.

What I really like about December is the diversity in the appearance of Feral Pigeons. I find their iridescent feathers to be extremely pretty, and I generally like pigeons. They tend to clean up the area underneath the bird feeder. I have a Squirrel proof birdfeeder which I find to be effective, although it does seem that young Common Brown Rats *(Rattus norvegicus)* are able to climb onto the birdfeeder and once they are able to retrieve food, they tend to finish it all. The largest bird I have managed to see on the bird feeder is in fact a Starling *(Sturnus vulgaris)*.

Beautiful colours of iridescent feathers on the neck of a Feral Pigeon in the garden.

The Woodpigeon is another favourite of mine, I have spent many hours watching Woodpigeons in the garden, they're full of character, waddling about, sometimes jumping when faced with a step. I find them to be incredibly interesting, they tend to look at the birdfeeder, trying to figure out, what I perceive them to be thinking, 'how do I get there?', they're too heavy and large to perch on the birdfeeder but that doesn't stop them from walking along the wooden fence, jumping onto the apple tree branches closest to the birdfeeder, and trying to stretch and balance at the same time, to get to the bird food. They rarely succeed but they don't go hungry because other smaller birds come along and cause lots of seeds to fall which the Dunnocks, Pigeons and Rats are all too happy to eat.

The wet and rainy days are great for the Blackbirds, which visit the garden and find their fair share of worms that have been forced to emerge perhaps due to waterlogging. I am a little annoyed with myself for not understanding soil organisms better, particularly worms as they are such an integral part of the rhizosphere and soil systems. Favourable edaphic conditions are required for optimum and healthy growth of flora. Worms have a pivotal role in the food chain and are detritivores, collectively they consume a large abundance of dead plant material, fungi and other types of organic matter. Due to their movement within the soil they act as an organic plough, turning the soil and thereby enhancing aerobic conditions for further decomposition of organic material by various organisms within the soil, worms also have an important role in dispersing and releasing nutrients within the soil as they drag leaves underground which they consume and later excrete[2].

I find December to be a focused month in terms of monitoring in the garden, what I mean by that is, due to the lack of organisms that I see, it gives me more time to focus on a small number of species and to understand their patterns and behaviours. These can include intraspecific or interspecific interactions. For example, a pecking order seems to exist at birdfeeders, certain species chase away others if they are trying to protect a territory or the food source (e.g., Robins chasing off intruding Robins and other passerines). On the ground, large Woodpigeons tend to dominate the area, and I often see them spreading their wings and charging at other Pigeons in the garden.

Underneath our apple tree it appears that Rats have a made a home and generations have lived there for a few years now, the constant source of food and the water source of the pond makes our garden the perfect place for them to live. The Rats and Pigeons appear to tolerate each other with no real aggression, there appears to be more of a sense of caution than anything else. I personally don't mind Rats, they're extremely clever and help aerate the soil underneath the trees and plants due to their burrowing behaviour. The Pigeons also pay no mind to the smaller passerines. I believe the Pigeons use the passerines, after all, the Pigeons wouldn't be able to retrieve any food from the feeder without the help of the smaller birds. Dunnocks are seemingly unflappable, and quietly go about their business whilst foraging. Dunnocks are omnivorous and eat both seeds and insects, the lack of insects in winter forces them to feed on seeds. Goldfinches *(Carduelis carduelis)* feed from the Niger seed feeder, which is different to the regular birdfeeder, the Goldfinches tend to be ignored by the other bird species, probably due to the other birds not feeding on Niger seed, and the Goldfinches are left to squabble amongst themselves.

During December 2018 I ran a small survey observing the number of bird species in which a resident Robin had reacted aggressively to, and I found that Robins chased away five species of birds that were using the birdfeeder (Great Tit, Blue Tit, Coal Tit, House Sparrow and Dunnock), aggressive tactics included physical lunges along with consistent chasing and driving away of individuals. The most tolerant species at the birdfeeder was the Great Tit which shared space at the bird feeder with Blue Tits, House Sparrows and Dunnocks. Overall, in a vast majority of cases individual species appeared to prefer to feed either with conspecifics or leave when other species arrived.

One of the many moments a Robin was doing its best to defend its territory from other passerines, in this case a House Sparrow.

I have always enjoyed seeing Goldfinches as I love their colourful plumage along with their chirpy lyrical song as they fly in small flocks overhead. I rarely used to see them in the garden, but this was due to the lack of suitable food such as Niger seed. These are readily available from various stores and its an easy way of attracting Goldfinches into the garden. If you own a medium-large sized garden, then planting Teasel is a good plant for Goldfinches as they feed on the seed heads. Greenfinches (*Carduelis chloris*) will also feed on Niger seeds and perhaps if you're lucky you can attract Bullfinches (*Pyrrhula pyrrhula*). I have not yet seen any Bullfinches but hopefully one day I'll be eagle-eyed enough to spot one. Goldfinches are now, along with Robins, the first to arrive in the garden at dawn.

The defining colours of a Goldfinch, black, yellow and red.
Males tend to have a larger area of red on their face in
comparison to females, whereas juveniles lack red colouring.

On a couple of occasions, I have managed to see both a Blackcap
(Sylvia atricapilla) and Goldcrest *(Regulus regulus)* in the garden.
Blackcaps are beautiful birds, the males have a black cap, hence the name,
whereas the females and juveniles, confusingly, have a brown cap, but at
least it makes the them easy to distinguish. I have seen them at various
times of the year in the garden but predominantly in winter and spring.
Most Blackcaps are thought to migrate to the British Isles from various
places, but some populations appear to overwinter due to milder winters
in recent years. This also allows Blackcaps to venture further northwards
as average temperatures become milder across the country.

The increase of birdfeeders in households may also add another
element for the increased survival for Blackcaps. If food is readily
available from birdfeeders, then Blackcaps can use their energy

efficiently by feeding from a reliable source. Interestingly research has indicated that overwintering Blackcaps in the UK may drive evolution within the species as migration is genetically determined, therefore overwintering Blackcaps may evolve differently to migrating Blackcaps that arrive from various places in Europe[3]. Evidence supporting this theory can be attributed to changes in bill morphology in overwintering Blackcaps which appear to be thinner and longer than other European Blackcaps, perhaps due to the availability of different types of bird seed in feeders[4]. A great website for adding your sightings is the Woodland Trusts 'Nature's calendar' website, there you'll be able to submit sightings of specific species and also see current data on where sightings have been recorded around the United Kingdom.

Similar to Wrens', Goldcrests feed on insects and spiders. I find them to have similar jerky movements to Wrens and Coal Tits and in my case, I have found it very difficult to get a clear photograph of them. They are extremely agile and have great dexterity when it comes to manoeuvring within branches of shrubs and trees to find their prey. Goldcrests and Firecrests *(Regulus ignicapillus)* are recognised as being the smallest birds in Britain.

Goldcrest searching for invertebrates to feed on.

An aspect of all these birds' morphology is their ability to blend into the surrounding environment. The colour patterns of many birds contain various shades of green, blue, yellow, grey, brown and beige. This cryptic camouflage can help in concealing them from predators. When in amongst foliage it can be extremely difficult to accurately identify a bird based on its plumage or appearance, being able to discern species from the sounds they produce can be extremely helpful, especially as what happens often is birds will fly away before you get close enough to have a clear view of them. For this reason alone it can be a good idea to purchase binoculars.

Its important to understand that species need ways of being able to recognise each other and in birds this can be through birdsong as well as plumage. Even though we may see birds in a certain way based upon their appearance and colour, this isn't analogous to the way in which birds see each other. Birds have tetrachromatic colour vision which means they can visualise a greater range of colours at different wavelengths[5]. This makes it possible for birds to see ultraviolet light, therefore, plumage may appear completely different to a bird in comparison to our visual perceptions. Its important to realise that the world around us is not rigid or similar in the way it appears to all organisms, many other organisms possess traits which enhance detection of specific elements of the environment, to which humanity is unaware or physically incapable of sensing. This is why I feel its imperative to try to understand the species around us and the ways in which they are adapted to sense the environment.

Great Tit splendidly camouflaged against the background, within the branches of an apple tree.

Goldfinch plumage matching its surroundings. Despite its striking appearance it can be difficult to spot.

Although many insects may be overwintering and in a state of diapause, I have been able to find a couple of Moths that are flying as adults during the winter, these are the Winter Moth *(Operophtera brumata)* and the non-native pest species, Light Brown Apple Moth *(Epiphyas postvittana)*. As insects are ectothermic (cold blooded) its difficult for many species to be active as adults during cold periods of the year, but some species have adapted to thrive in such conditions.

A Winter Moth attracted to my light trap, a species well adapted to cold conditions.

Although the days of December are generally cold and the garden can appear to be empty in terms of flowers and vegetation, its an ideal month for birdwatching, particularly if you are just beginning to get into the habit of species monitoring. December has a lot to offer, and birds will be a reliable source of inspiration to keep you engaged with the activities occurring in the garden. December also provides a good reference point to refer back to once it gets to summer, as changes in the garden can be dramatic.

January

Its more of the same in January in terms of garden visitors. A welcome visitor to the garden during January is the Collared Dove *(Streptopelia decaocto)*. I tend to see them in pairs, with one never being far away from its partner. Much like the Magpies that always seem to be around, perched at the top of trees or chimneys, keeping a watchful eye on the happenings of the gardens beneath them. Collared Doves are smaller and slenderer in comparison to Woodpigeons. Their cooing is also very distinctive and can be heard throughout the day although I often hear them in the morning. The appearance of Collared Doves in the garden is sporadic and although I see them mostly during the winter and spring months, they can be present at any time of year.

Collared Doves below the birdfeeder, looking for seeds.

Grey Squirrels *(Sciurus carolinensis)* always seem to appear when there is nothing else around, they seem to follow a specific route when entering the garden, not just running around haphazardly but their movements are direct. I'll see a Squirrel jump from a tree branch, onto a shed, across a fence, down onto another fence, onto the apple tree and on to the birdfeeder. Squirrels can also appear in the garden at any time of year, but again, I see them predominantly in winter and spring, during early morning.

Long-Tailed Tits *(Aegithalos caudatus)* are a rare visitor to the garden and appear at seemingly random times of the year although in winter, the lack of invertebrates can cause them to gather at feeders or fat balls in gardens. They travel in small flocks in Heston and will have the odd Blue Tit or Coal Tit flying alongside them. I find these birds to have a very distinctive call, a very high pitched 'seep' sound. Their long tails as well as plumage makes them easy to distinguish from the other Tits.

Long-Tailed Tit on an Oak *(Quercus* spp.) in winter.

I find that fungi are often overlooked, especially in terms of monitoring, but they play a key role in the natural world and are major components of ecosystems across the entire globe[6]. Fungi associated with plants, can be classified into different types;

- Mycorrhizal – includes arbuscular mycorrhizal fungi and ectomycorrhizal fungi, these typically associate with the roots of plants and trees.
- Endophytic – these fungi are located within plant tissues but often do not show any type of negative affect upon the plant.

Other types of fungi are saprotrophic, which typically break down dead or decaying matter in order to obtain nutrients and carbon that may be stored within them. These materials are usually in the form of leaf litter or logs which is why during autumn and winter you may find many fungi on a deciduous woodland floor where leaf senescence has produced a colourful carpet of leaves for fungi to degrade. The mushrooms we might see in a park or on our lawns are mushrooms that are typically formed from ectomycorrhizal fungi or saprotrophic fungi and these fruiting bodies act as beacons in which to release their spores for sexual or asexual reproduction. In plant-fungi mutualisms the fungus benefits from the plant through acquisition of carbon from photosynthesis, in return, the plant benefits from an increased uptake of nutrients from the soil via the fungi, these nutrients include nitrogen and phosphorus when available, but also increased water absorption, these mutualisms can even help plants adapt to the effects of climate change[7]. Not all interactions between fungi and plants are mutualistic and some fungi may be parasitic, benefitting through negative interactions with their host. This typically means that the fungus is feeding from the plant without providing any nutrients in return causing a reduction in health of the plant, and can result in disease, this occurs with many crops[8]. The use of fungal pathogens may be an effective way of combating the proliferation of certain invasive plants[9].

Old mature specimens of Sulphur tuft.

19

Gardens can be great for finding fungi and you may see them pop up from time to time on the lawn. In January 2019, I was able to identify two types of common fungi in the garden Crystal Brain Fungus *(Exidia nucleata)* and Sulphur Tuft *(Hypholoma fasciculare)*. Crystal Brain Fungus was found on a log pile and can be described as shiny blobs hence the name, they are spongy in texture and appear to glisten, especially after rainfall. I found Sulphur tuft in the surrounding area of a log pile and the mushrooms first emerged as a tight compact clump before quickly maturing and finally degrading with a darkened centre on the cap and the edges adopted a slightly tinged green appearance. The world of mycology still contains vast gaps in knowledge about their varied interactions with the environment. There are a great deal of opportunities for new discoveries in the world of mycology.

In recent years some plants that are thought to be associated with spring are now flowering in January, for example, White Dead-Nettle *(Lamium album)* and Daffodils can be seen flowering in mid to late January. Daffodils in the garden have bloomed around this time for the last three years. This is considerably earlier than used to be the case in the past. First flowering times of flowers and budburst of trees are both important indicators of the response of plants to the effects of climate change. As temperatures have consistently increased over the last few decades many plants have been advancing their flowering times. This has massive implications for the species that rely on these plants with the potential to rearrange food webs and energy flow within ecosystems[10]. Its easy to be unaware of the environmental changes from year to year as other aspects of our lives grab a foothold and end up taking priority but there are important details and events occurring in our gardens that are essential to understanding various processes in the environment.

Citizen science is a major advantage when obtaining data over a large scale as well as over long-time scales. Trends and patterns can be discerned from long term studies that would otherwise not be comprehensible at a shorter scale. One of the key characteristics when monitoring is having a high degree of patience. I, along with millions of others, have spent endless hours in nature searching and watching, trying to spot something not seen before, or perhaps see an unnoticed behaviour of a certain species. Birdwatching is a perfect example of this, places such as the Wildfowl and Wetlands Trust in Barnes is hugely popular amongst birdwatchers with various hides scattered across the site where many people spend their entire day trying to catch a glimpse of rare species such as a Bittern *(Botaurus stellaris)* or iconic species like the Kingfisher *(Alcedo atthis).* When looking out at the garden from inside your home, its essentially the same as being in a hide.

During wintery days it can be worthwhile to look at how birds fly against strong blustery winds and the way in which some birds use the currents to aid their flying. Pigeons can fly at high speeds; they must be fast and agile to prevent being predated by hawks and falcons and on many occasions I have seen pigeons flying at tremendous speeds across the sky on gusty days. The Corvids (e.g. Crow, Jackdaw, Magpie, Jay, etc) often try to glide with the wind, but in many cases I have seen Jackdaws and Crows being redirected into the opposite direction due to extremely high winds. It has been suggested that birds are able to detect changes in atmospheric pressure and hence be able to respond early to incoming storms or bad weather[11] this makes sense considering storms may be life threatening to birds. Another physiological aspect of passerines is their ability to perch on branches with a tight grip, this is due to an involuntary reflex, thus passerines can conserve energy when perching[12].

Back in 2017, I decided to make a small pond at the back of my garden, I thought it'd be helpful for the birds to have a water source. Each winter the pond freezes over so if you happen to have frogs dwelling at the bottom its important to keep at least part of the pond surface from being completely frozen solid as oxygen transport into the pond can be rapidly reduced, this could potentially kill various organisms in the pond. Creating an opening will give organisms a way out. A small floating ball or a few ping-pong balls are effective at stopping small ponds freezing over completely. I have not yet had any frogs in my pond, but fingers crossed, maybe one day they will find their way to it.

In time, January may become a month where typical February/March spring events become observed consistently, particularly in southern UK where average temperatures are warmer than in the North. With signs of many plants emerging earlier from winter dormancy this may cause insects and other organisms such as fungi to emerge earlier. January can show signs of new life emerging in the form of plants.

February

February is the month where everything in the garden begins to perk up. A number of flowers are in bloom and budburst of some trees are occurring. The weather in February in the last four years that I've been monitoring has been extremely variable and each year has been relatively different in terms of species I've seen. Most of the birds I see during December and January are still making appearances in the garden but there is also the odd newcomer.

Goldcrests are still shifting about amongst the shrubs and trees looking for invertebrates but another bird that seems to make its way into the garden around this time is the Chaffinch (*Fringilla coelebs*). Chaffinches are extremely pretty birds, and display sexual dimorphism, the males have a red breast and chalky grey crown whereas the females are predominantly an olive green. They tend to be similar to Dunnocks in terms of their foraging habits by feeding on the ground rather than at a feeder.

Male (red) and female (olive green) Chaffinch feeding on the ground in 2018. There is a clear difference in the colours of their plumage.

A possible reasoning behind this sexual dimorphism could be due to the feeding habits of female Chaffinches which spend more time on the ground compared to males, being in the open increases the risk of predation for females and so having a cryptic plumage which matches foliage would be advantageous in concealing their presence from potential predators[13]. Although its one of the most common birds in the UK, I tend not to see them often in the garden or generally around Heston, so it always makes me happy to see them when they do appear. For me, seeing birds which only appear occasionally is like seeing old friends.

Late February in 2018 was extremely cold due to the 'Beast from the East' which brought cold weather from easterly winds, as well as periods of snow. In terms of my own monitoring, this month happened to have the highest bird species diversity compared to milder February's of 2017, 2019 and 2020. Cold conditions are likely to have caused a decrease in insect abundance and therefore many birds may have had to compensate for this lack of optimal food by visiting feeders instead. By providing bird food during cold periods, the probability of survival for birds during these times can be increased and may also help to attract some uncommon visitors to our gardens.

A group of House Sparrows making the most of the food available during a cold and snowy February in 2018.

Before the weather became colder that same month, I purchased a Robinson trap to monitor my garden for moths. Its probably the best purchase I have ever made in terms of species monitoring. I decided to buy one due to the recommendation from a friend (thanks Alan), I also volunteered in the Wildlife Garden at the Natural History Museum, where I was able to help with moth surveys, I saw the diversity there and wondered what I might have in my own garden. Along with the trap I also bought a reference book as there are approximately 2,500 moth species in the UK alone. Reference books are the way to go when it comes to identifying species, they are extremely useful and are essential to any naturalist irrespective of expertise, you never know when you may come across something new. Its also helpful to thumb through the book just to get yourself familiar with species. Most of my reference books are predominantly based on birds and Lepidoptera and I would not have learned as much as I have about specific species and general ecology without them.

Oak Beauty, the first moth I ever caught in a Robinson trap.

The ultraviolet light of the Robinson trap bulb attracts moths towards it, and egg boxes within the trap provide a place for the moths to climb under and wait until they have been released. Ever since I began, two species have always appeared in February, the Common Quaker *(Orthosia cerasi)* and Hebrew Character *(Orthosia gothica)*. Interestingly, February 2020 produced the lowest abundance of both species to date as well as the smallest individuals I have seen compared to previous years. Ecologically, there are a number of reasons as to why this might be the case; firstly, climate change, its predicted that as temperatures increase species may evolve by reducing body size[14], a larger surface to volume ratio in smaller bodies allows heat to be lost at a faster rate, secondly, foodplants of the insects may not be of high quality resulting in smaller individuals. In an area where many gardens and green spaces have been lost its likely that the number of available foodplants have also perished. In terms of abundance, 2020 may have been a good year for predators of these moths such as parasitic wasps which can parasitise larvae of numerous insects, thus reducing their overall abundance. Its a nice feeling being able to predict when certain species will arrive in the garden and it also allows me to understand phenological patterns better. This facilitates more efficient and effective monitoring so I can spread my focus across all aspects of nature. If I know that a species is not going to appear until an approximate time, then this allows me to shift my focus onto species that are present. To get to this point requires lots of time and patience.

Left - Common Quaker, Right – Hebrew Character

The Marmalade Hoverfly *(Episyrphus balteatus)* may also begin to appear in milder February's. There are many species of Hoverflies, and they are extremely diverse in form. It is not only bees and butterflies that are pollinators but Hoverflies, various beetles (Coleoptera), flies (Diptera) as well as moths are also key pollinators, and their presence should be promoted through the planting of various wildflowers.

Another predictable aspect of February is the arrival of Smooth Newts *(Lissotriton vulgaris)* into ponds and other water bodies. A Smooth Newt found its way into my pond in February 2020, which was the first time I had seen an adult Smooth Newt in the garden. As with most amphibians, Newts require water in which lay to their eggs to prevent them from drying out. Smooth Newts are the commonest

Newts in the UK and during the breeding period, males have a lovely crest that runs along much of their body which distinguishes them from the relatively plain females. Being amphibious means that they can also live terrestrially. When submerged underwater, they will prey upon various organisms in ponds such as pond snails, insect larvae and even frog eggs or tadpoles. What I have found is that Smooth Newts tend to stay motionless unless disturbed where they then swim off into the deeper depths of the pond or into some underwater foliage and they are most active between dusk and dawn, so going out at night with a torch can be the best way to see them.

A male Smooth Newt at the shallow end of my small pond.

I find it amazing to be able to find a Smooth Newt in the pond simply because there are not a great deal of water bodies or ponds in the surrounding neighbourhood that I am aware of. The closest large water body being that of the lakes in Osterley Park, which is at least one mile away.

Other organisms which appear to become increasingly active as temperatures rise in February are spiders. These arachnids are probably not high on the list of people's favourite animals as arachnophobia is common amongst many, which is a shame because they are amazing organisms. With the adaptation of spider silk and the ability to spin various types of webs, spiders are incredibly successful and diverse. Hunting techniques differ between species, and they can be found in almost any habitat, including under water! The UK is host to around 650 species and accurate identification can be extremely tricky.

I used to be extremely wary of spiders as a child, their unpredictable movements from still to lightning quick had me on edge whenever I would spot one, especially if it happened to be in my room, but after years of catching spiders around the house with my trusty Cotton Bud Tub and spending a lot of time watching them in the garden, I have grown to appreciate them and their distinctive habits. Many species of spider tend to hide away during the winter and being ectothermic they will slow down and become less active during this period. Spiders are extremely helpful in terms of pest control by collectively consuming large quantities of flies and other organisms, imagine all the flies that would be around if not for spiders! If you happen to find a spider in your home, its best to leave it as the cold outside is likely to cause it to freeze to death. If you must remove it then place it in a sheltered area or even in a shed or garage if possible. Mild temperatures and bright sunny days in February 2019 uncovered the presence of various spider species including the Cellar spider *(Pholcus phalangioides),* House Spider *(Tegenaria domestica),* Zebra Jumping Spider *(Salticus scenicus),* Crab spider *(Misumena vatia),* Nursery Web Spider *(Pisaura mirabilis)* and Noble False Widow *(Steatoda nobilis).* Out of these spiders, Cellar spiders and Noble False Widows are the only species I tend to see all year round, House Spiders will be tucked away until its time to find a mate.

A number of these spiders are not native to the UK and this may negatively change the dynamic of native species distributions due to being outcompeted or even predated upon by non-native species.

Spiders are cannibalistic and will consume members of their own species as well as others. Many times, I have found House Spiders that have perished after being caught and consumed by Cellars spiders.

Zebra Jumping spiders are so called due to their black and white appearance as well jumping ability which they use to ambush their insect prey, they are active hunters and can jump many times their body length and have 8 eyes which allow for extremely accurate vision. These spiders are generally very small, and this species is approximately 5mm in length. I find their movements to be quite robotic as they twist and turn and shift position constantly before leaping a couple of inches to another area.

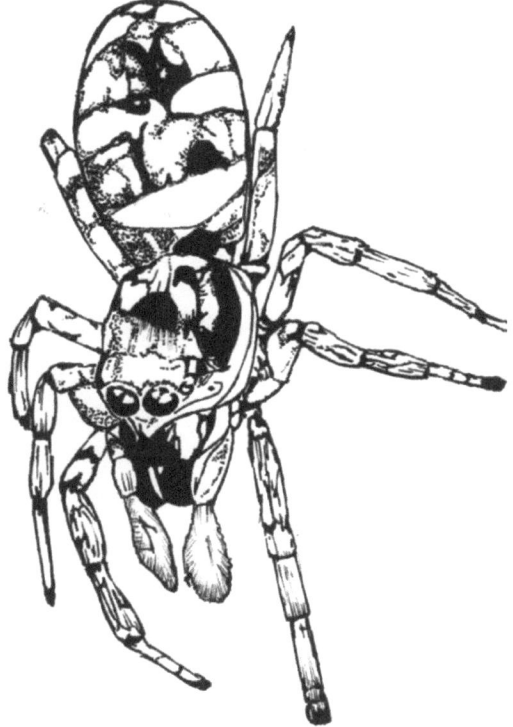

The Noble False Widow is thought to be a non-native species and appears to be extremely well adapted to a variety of conditions, including indoors as well as outdoors. For years we have had a number of False Widows in our garden, and they seem to be active every night resting on their webs. The fact they are so well adapted and can tolerate cold conditions, they may have a pivotal role to play within the ecosystem in which they inhabit, this also means increased competition for space and food with native spider species such as the Missing Sector Orb Weaver *(Zygiella x-notata)* which seem to occupy a similar niche.

Noble False Widow suspended on its web at night
in February 2019.

The silk that's used for construction of webs of these spiders is extremely strong and sticky and is probably why I have been able to observe these spiders capture insects such as bumblebees, wasps, moths, and butterflies. It also has been recently discovered that this species is capable of catching and preying upon bats[15]. This species displays clear sexual dimorphism with females being larger than the males. During daylight, the spider remains hidden and rushes out when its prey comes into contact with the web. Vibrations from prey struggling in the web are detected by the spider and instigates its movement. The spider then cocoons its prey at a rapid rate with sheets of silk and once sufficiently wrapped, a venomous bite paralyzes and liquifies the internal material of the prey which allows the spider to feed upon it.

February is another great month for monitoring birds but there are also insects starting to emerge, predominantly moths and it can be an appropriate time to start moth trapping. Its also a time to start taking note of the plant species that are beginning to grow and flower. Temperature can be a key component in determining whether you'll find certain species or not, as the cold snowy period of 2018 showed, bird activity in our gardens can increase but conversely, if days are warm then that will increase the likelihood of seeing more insects. A very variable month in terms of weather and climate, February is great for keeping your senses alert.

Winter Summary

Winter is a great season for witnessing changes in climatic conditions, it is also a good season for observing how species diversity increases gradually as the season progresses into spring with the arrival of insects and amphibians as well as budburst of trees and blooming of early spring flowers. Although the days are short in mid-winter observations of the garden can still be made and something as simple as watching a birdfeeder for a specific amount of time per day can provide an important insight into the interactions occurring between species. Although the garden and the general outdoors may look static and quiet during the winter there are still many processes occurring and the more time dedicated to exploring the environment the more that will be uncovered and understood. Its always worth remembering that not all the species on the planet have been discovered and identified so there is always a chance of coming across something that is 'new'.

If you are interested in monitoring species in your garden then I believe winter to be the easiest season to begin with due to the relatively low numbers of species you're likely to witness, in comparison to the other seasons, this can be helpful as you are unlikely to be overwhelmed with information and you can become familiar with species that appear often (e.g. birds), although it should be noted that it depends on where you live and the structure of your garden, if your garden is really big and hosts a large pond and/or a range of plants and habitats, then you may find high species diversity irrespective of season.

Tips for beginning Garden Monitoring

- Invest in a Camera/binoculars, this will help with identification.
- Install a birdfeeder into your garden to attract birds. Be sure to clean it regularly to reduce risk of infection amongst birds.
- Keep a log of species identified (word and excel) and learn the Latin names of common species.
- Think about long-term monitoring. Pay attention to flowering times.
- Become familiar with a species of interest.
- Purchase a couple of reference books to help with identification.
- Submit findings to relevant websites e.g. Woodland Trust.
- Check the NBN Atlas to find out what wildlife has been recorded in your area.

Common Name	Latin Name (Species/genus)	Family
Robin	Erithacus rubecula	Muscicapidae (Old world flycatchers and chats)
House sparrow	Passer domesticus	Passeridae (Old world sparrows)
Blackbird	Turdus merula	Turdidae (Thrush)
Mistle Thrush	Turdus viscivorus	Turdidae (Thrush)
Crow	Corvus corone	Corvidae (Crow)
Jackdaw	Corvus monedula	Corvidae (Crow)
Magpie	Pica pica	Corvidae (Crow)
Great Tit	Parus major	Paridae (Tit)
Blue Tit	Cyanistes caeruleus	Paridae (Tit)
Coal Tit	Periparus ater	Paridae (Tit)
Long Tailed Tit	Aegithalos caudatus	Aegithalidae (Long tailed/bushtits)
Goldfinch	Carduelis carduelis	Fringillidae (Finch)
Chaffinch	Fringilla coelebs	Fringillidae (Finch)
Greenfinch	Carduelis chloris	Fringillidae (Finch)
Wren	Troglodytes troglodytes	Troglodytidae (Wrens)
Goldcrest	Regulus regulus	Sylvidae
Blackcap	Slyvia atricapilla	Sylvidae
Dunnock	Prunella modularis	Prunellidae (Accentors)
Pied Wagtail	Motacilla alba	Motacilladae
Swift	Apus apus	Apodidae (Swifts)

An example of the spreadsheet I created to keep track of what I find. Looking through the list often can make it easier to remember Latin names, and the sorting capabilities of Excel adds flexibility to how you want to classify and arrange data.

The Garden: Spring
(March, April, May)

Spring is when everything begins to look more colourful and lusher as more and more flowers bloom and growth rates of plants rapidly increase. The days are longer than previous months and temperatures are somewhat pleasant, although the weather may still be unpredictable and cold periods may still linger on well into March or April (as in 2018). The world of invertebrates becomes much more noticeable and some migrating bird species make an appearance. Spring is the time to be IN the garden and not just view it from indoors. Various bird species will be looking for suitable places to breed and biodiversity within the garden appears to increase with each passing month. Much time may be spent looking at reference books during this time but as the days pass and you become more enveloped by the nature around you, it becomes easy to remember what you have read.

March

One of the key species I look out for during March in the garden is the arrival of Queen Buff-Tailed Bumblebees *(Bombus terrestris)* which are beginning to emerge to find a suitable spot to set up base and start a new colony. Buff-Tailed Bumblebees are the classic large, tubby looking bee, they are in fact the largest of all bees in the UK. The Queen is large and has a buff-coloured tail, which contrasts to workers and drones which have a white tail, this can make it difficult to discern whether the bee is a Buff-Tailed Bumblebee or a White-Tailed Bumblebee *(Bombus lucorum)* which is a separate species. I often find

Queens basking in a sunny spot in the garden after emergence. Buff-Tailed Bumblebee Queens usually build a nest underground within the soil, burrows of a range of mammals may even be used, I have seen many bees inspecting old rat burrows in search of a suitable area to start a colony. For the last four years I have seen Queen Buff-Tailed Bumblebees in the garden in March, it has been one of the most consistent species in terms of timing of appearance.

Queen Buff-Tailed Bumblebee carrying phoretic mites.

Bees are fascinating organisms, and the UK is home to approximately 270 species, these are predominantly solitary bees which are not part of a colony unlike Bumblebees and Honeybees (*Apis* spp). I find bee identification to be extremely difficult, especially amongst smaller mining bees as there are often only subtle differences between species, there are also bee mimics which aren't actually bees but flies! Even trying to discern a worker bee (female) from a drone (male) can be difficult for me but I find these challenges of identification fun because it is a constant learning process. Insects in general are great for sharpening identification skills as they are extremely diverse and can show various forms even within a species. Being able to find key characteristics for species identification is a necessity.

Other bee species that I have seen emerge in March are the Red-tailed Bumblebee *(Bombus lapidarius)* and Honeybee *(Apis mellifera)*, these species will typically form colonies. Another insect which can build a colony is the Common Wasp *(Vespula vulgaris)*. Common Wasp Queens can also emerge around this time of year and behave in a similar way to a Queen Buff-Tailed Bumblebee, with searching flight, moving swiftly from one place to the next in search of a cavity in which to build a nest. Wasp Queens are more robust and longer than a standard Wasp. Wasps are fearsome predators and have large powerful mandibles with which they bite their prey. I have seen Wasps bite off the wings of their prey (e.g., flies and moths) before carrying away the wingless body. Brutal!

Frontal view of a Common Wasp. Notice the large powerful mandibles used for slicing through exoskeletons.

Social behaviour within the Order Hymenoptera is common amongst a range of species including bees, wasps and ants. Within these colonies there is a hierarchical structure, using Honeybees as an example, at the top is the Queen, the Queen is larger than all other individuals of the colony, she is capable of laying thousands of eggs, many of which are fertilised which become female worker bees and unfertilised eggs which become male drones. This method of reproduction is found in each of the families within Hymenoptera. Interestingly, members of the colony do not have the same roles, and their jobs within the hive can change throughout their lifetime, this is especially true of the workers[16]. The main purpose for male Honeybees (drones) is to be able to mate with other Queens from other colonies. The rest of the duties are left to the workers (females). These duties include;

- Defending the hive
- Feeding the Queen and larvae
- Maintaining temperatures within the hive
- Foraging for nectar and pollen
- Keeping the hive clean

A good way of sharpening your eyes for bee identification is being able to notice the differences between females and males, there are physiological differences between both. Sometimes these differences are very subtle such as size disparity or a difference in roundedness of abdomens but over time it becomes easier and its quite satisfying being able to determine such small characteristics.

Wasps that are often overlooked are the Ichneumonids (Parasitic Wasps), these are not your typical black and yellow Common Wasps, they have a very different appearance in terms of morphology and can also differ in colour. They can vary greatly in size between species and be extremely specialist in terms of hosts. Parasitic Wasps are amongst the most diverse group of organisms, yet they have been largely unresearched with many species likely to not have been identified yet. Therefore, there is massive scope for acquiring new and previously unknown information about these organisms. In each of the last three years I have found parasitic wasps in my moth trap belonging to the genus *Ophion*. These wasps are active at night and can be attracted towards light traps even during relatively cold nights. This species is capable of stinging humans, so it is best to leave these individuals alone to avoid any risk of pain. I find identifying these wasps extremely difficult and have often resorted to online forums or websites to compare images. Resorting to the internet can be really helpful for species that have distinctive traits but sometimes photographs are not enough and specialist equipment and the actual specimen is required for accurate identification.

Being parasitoids, these wasps will either lay eggs within a host (endoparasitoid), which will feed off the living tissue of the host, or eggs will be laid on the external surface of a host (ectoparasitoid). Parasitism is extremely common in the animal kingdom across various taxa and is an effective lifestyle, however gruesome it may be. In order to be an effective parasitoid these wasps need specific adaptations to locate a host as well as to sting and lay its eggs.

Parasitic Wasp *(Ophion* spp.) with a striking orange body, large eyes and predominantly clear wings.

Another insect which is associated with spring is the Bee Fly *(Bombylius major)*, these flies are furry insects which typically look like bees at first glance but on closer inspection its clear that they are not bees. They are in fact harmless bee mimics and do not possess a sting. I often find Bee Flies flying from flower to flower, feeding on nectar. They will often bask in the sun on hot, sunny days and are quick to react to movement when approached. The eggs of Bee Flies are parasites of bee nests, where they feed on larvae. Being a bee mimic may help them to deter predators and can allow them to get close to bee nest entrances where they can deposit their eggs. Although Bee Fly larvae are parasitic, as adults they are effective pollinators and so their presence should not be discouraged.

Bee Fly basking in the sunshine, it has a triangular appearance and a large proboscis which it uses to feed on nectar. Being part of the Order Diptera, Bee Flies only have two wings whereas bees (Order: Hymenoptera) have four. Also, features such as eyes, antennae and legs of Bee flies differ to that of Bumblebees.

The number of insects present throughout March is a large increase from preceding winter months. On warm sunny days butterflies such as Peacock *(Inachis io)* and Red Admiral may be seen flying in search of flowers or basking on the ground. Both butterflies are common and widespread and can overwinter as adults. The numbers of the other half of Lepidoptera, moths, also increase in species richness during March.

Moth species I have found during March include the following;

- Hebrew Character *(Orthosia gothica)*
- Chestnut *(Conistra vaccinia)*
- Common Quaker *(Orthosia cerasi)*
- Clouded Drab *(Orthosia incerta)*
- Oak Beauty *(Biston strataria)*
- Brindled Beauty *(Lycia hirtaria)*
- Twin Spotted Quaker *(Anorthea munda)*
- Light Brown Apple Moth *(Epiphyas postvittana)*
- Plume Moth *(Emmelina monodactyla)*

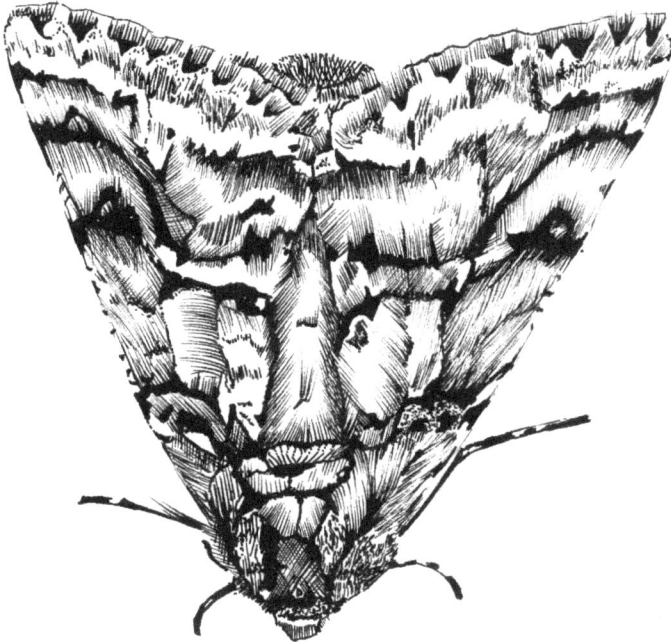

My interpretation of a Brindled Beauty, it has lovely patterns on its wings.

The exciting aspect about the increase of life and emergence of various species is the interactions that take place between them. An interaction between two or more species can be classified into one of the following;

- Predation
- Competition (Interference, Scramble, Exploitative, Apparent)
- Symbiosis (Mutualism, Commensalism and Parasitism)

Predation is where an organism consumes another organism, this is necessary for the survival of species but also in many cases for the longevity of prey populations. Predation is also a key component of food webs and energy flow between various trophic levels. The amount of energy available for predators decreases at each increasing trophic level, this is due to energy being transferred to heat through metabolism and released into the environment. Although food webs and links between organisms may be extremely complex there are only a small number of trophic levels that can be sustained, this is generally around four trophic levels[17].

Shieldbugs are part of the Order Hemiptera (True Bugs), they are also known as Stink Bugs. All Hemiptera have sucking mouthparts from which they ingest their food, examples of Hemipterans include Aphids, Crane Flies, Froghoppers as well as many other species. The shape of a Shieldbug is likened to that of a Shield hence the common name, but in terms of the name Stink Bug, that is due to a defensive physiological trait that these insects implement in order to protect themselves from predators, or when they appear to be threatened. If you happen to disturb or touch a Shieldbug, you may find yourself smelling something in the air that is not very nice!

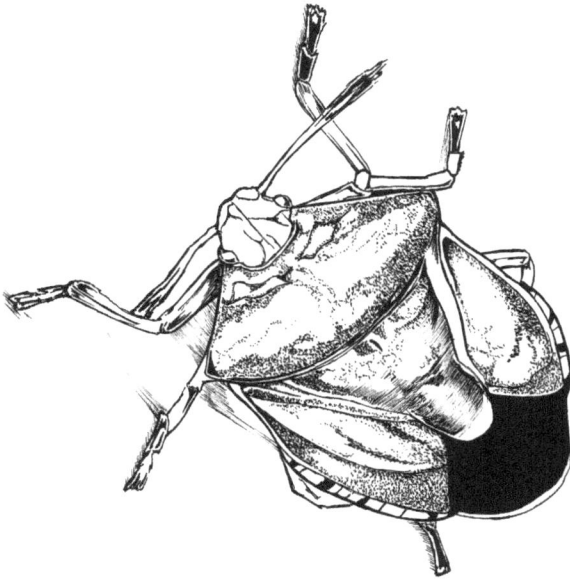

The Common Green Shieldbug *(Palomena prasina)* is often found in gardens.

Ladybirds (Coccinellidae) are Beetles (Coleoptera). They are usually welcomed by gardeners due to their ability to control garden pests such as aphids (Hemiptera), in some cases people may even buy Ladybird larvae to help control aphids in their gardens or greenhouses to protect their plants. Ladybirds are predators both as larvae and as adults. Their bright colouring is a good example of aposematism. Aposematism is the ability of an animal to display colouration which indicates to their predators that they are either; dangerous or extremely distasteful. In the case of Ladybirds, they appear to be avoided or ignored by some species of spiders as a prey item due to their distastefulness, although I have seen European Garden Spiders *(Araneus diadematus)* catch and consume Ladybirds.

Entomology is the study of insects and explores every aspect of their being such as morphology, physiology, phenology, ecology, natural history along with several other aspects. First things first, insects are essential! They are important pollinators for many flowers as well as crops, honeybees are utilised for their honey making abilities and are of huge economic importance, in terms of crop protection, natural enemies of crop pests are used as natural biological control to help maintain pest numbers and reduce crop damage. Insects are food for many organisms without which they would otherwise perish. Birds of prey as well as bats will regularly feed upon insects, for example the diet of a Little Owl *(Athene noctua)* can be predominantly insect based if small mammals are not available or in low numbers. Many passerines rely on an abundance of caterpillars during the breeding season to feed their chicks. A loss of insect abundance can have devastating effects on chick survival[18]. Insects are fascinating organisms, the range of colours, body shapes, feeding strategies, life cycles, behaviours and so on, is mind boggling. There are still so many amazing characteristics, mechanisms and behaviours of these organisms to be explored and understood. There are many species present in our gardens and most of the 300+ species I have documented within my own garden are predominantly insects.

Due to their size, interactions involving insects will likely be on a small scale, unless you happen to find a group of swarming bees. Insects will be found on plants, flying at head height, running along the ground or barks of trees and scurrying around under rocks or logs so you will need to be proactive in searching for certain insects. With flying insects, a butterfly net can be handy, but I tend to just try and follow an insect visually until it slows down its movement, and then I approach it. I find that some species often return to the same spot, so if you happen to disturb them and they fly away chances are that they'll come back shortly afterwards, although in many other cases the insects fly away into the distance. Again, try and hone your senses to work with what is around you. I feel its extremely important to change and adapt visual perspectives when exploring nature, to not become fixated and comfortable at viewing the world from normal walking head height but also to crouch down and see what is beneath you or look at the treetops to try and spot something. Most encounters with wildlife are of course down to a certain degree of chance but those chances can be increased if you become more adventurous and adaptable in your ways of interacting with the environment.

In terms of birds in March, garden observations may become increasingly interesting. If conditions are favourable such as warm and stable weather with many flowers blooming and a high number of insects, some birds may begin to breed during this month. This was the case in the garden in 2017 for a pair of Blue Tits and for a pair of Robins in March 2018 and 2019. Even if the weather turns out to be cold, windy, and snowy, as it was for a few days in March 2018, there is still a lot to see. Bird species diversity has always been highest during March in my garden. The birds fly in for food as well as for garden inspections for potential nesting sites. During a snowy period in March 2018, many birds came to the garden to feed on the bird feeder and a few times I saw up to ten species all feeding within a 3-metre area. This happened to be the only time I ever saw that many different species together in the garden without any type of obvious conflict, even the Robin was seemingly indifferent to the presence of other species. The harsh weather of that period must have made feeding difficult and therefore the birds had to resort to seeds from feeders.

Nesting for birds can be a dangerous task especially when eggs or chicks are available for other species to consume. A nest predator is the Common Rat, they are omnivores which will predate young birds and eggs, in 2019 the Robins had abandoned their nest of three eggs after Rats had been climbing up a trellis which happened to be where the robin nest was situated. Robins will abandon a nest if they become disturbed, the incubation period is extremely important, and Robins are extremely sensitive to disturbance during this time. Its an eye opener being able to view these types of interactions because its another reminder that even the animals we see on a day-to-day basis, that we are extremely familiar with, also lead extremely tough lives in which they have to contend with various dangers to survive and produce a new generation. Robins will nest in a variety of spaces but usually they are in well-hidden areas such as within a bushy climber or sheltered cavity. Their nests are open cup shaped; this may be partly the reason as to why chick mortality of Robins is high; many are predated or nests can be easily destroyed by bad weather.

Interacting with nature does not just mean observing it and monitoring but it also involves actively trying to help it to function more efficiently to promote more life and diversity. One way in which to do this is by building suitable nest boxes for various birds. Open fronted nest boxes are readily used by Robins and have proved to be a trusty choice for residency in my garden. Open fronted nest boxes provide increased shelter and protection from the weather. If you do decide to build your own nest box, be sure to use untreated wood as chemicals may have a negative effect on wildlife, chemicals leaching from the wood may also run off onto other surrounding organisms as well as into the soil. The other types of nest box that are common within gardens is the classic nest box which has a circular opening to allow birds to fly in and out. The width of the entrance will determine which birds can nest in there, it is therefore key to know what species of bird will be able to use the box. From my experience Great Tits and Blue Tits can both use a nest box with an entrance diameter of 30mm.

Great Tit perched upon a neighbours' Elder tree *(Sambucus spp.)*, where old branches have been encrusted with lichen.

Location of the nest box is also of great importance, each of our three nest boxes face the same direction, Northeast, this allows protection from south-westerly winds as well as providing sunlight for part of the day. Height is also important, just under the eaves of our house we have a nest box containing three compartments. My brother built it nearly 20 years ago and it has been continuously used by House Sparrows and on occasion, Great Tits. The open fronted nest box is located just under two metres from the ground hidden within a climber and the classic nest box is around three metres high against a wall in the open, although it has only been used twice in four years. Studying Ecology involves a lot of patience, trial and error. Some things work and other things don't but all outcomes should be acknowledged and analysed to understand why something is successful and why it isn't, this is so amendments can be made to try and produce a positive outcome.

Female Blackcap perched on our apple tree in March 2018.

March can be a great month for observing courtship behaviour in Robins. The female will be flapping her wings whilst perched in sight of the male where it will approach the female and feed her. The Robin pair will establish and maintain a territory by chasing away any intruders.

Throughout March, activity in the garden continues to steadily increase, more moths emerge, plants begin to grow, and flowers begin to bloom. A range of birds will visit, as many may be migrating from one area to another, but many will also be scouting areas for suitable places to nest. Our gardens are extremely valuable to birds as a place for raising chicks and so its good to be mindful of this, disturbance can drive birds away from their nest so be prepared to give a little space to nesting birds during the spring period.

April

April is a time when many plants are becoming established and there is a great surge in garden activity. I have found there to be a lot more moths in April in comparison to the previous months that have been discussed so far. Courtship and mating in birds is often occurring during this month, especially amongst passerines. For the last three years Robins have been nesting in our open fronted nest box and each year chicks are seen or heard during the month of April. As is the case with many passerines, they are born in an altricial state, seemingly helpless, naked, and unable to fend for themselves, therefore they are solely reliant on their parents for food. Caterpillars are hugely important for chicks as they contain essential fluids as well as protein. Seeds and nuts are not suitable for chicks as they can easily choke on them. Bird feeders are good for the adults as they can sustain themselves for their long days of foraging whilst raising their chicks. Having a constant water source is a great attraction for lots of wildlife and its always nice to see birds drinking and bathing although as a side note, I have had to rescue many bees over the years as they can find themselves in difficult situations in the water.

Watching Robins year-round is a really rewarding experience as you can see a clear change in lifestyle as their circumstances shift from maintaining a territory to preparing for the breeding season to raising chicks which then fledge, although the adults remain close to them, providing food for a short period of time before the fledglings are able to fly. Adult Robins are extremely hard-working, and their stamina is remarkable as they make endless foraging journeys from dawn until dusk ensuring the best chance of survival for their offspring. Starlings also breed at this time of year. A pair seemed to have utilised a small opening on the corner of a neighbours roof a few doors down. The chicks can be loud, and I have heard them chirping away from a fair distance. Starlings are pretty birds, their iridescent feathers reflect a range of colours, including greens, blues, purples which shine brightly in the sunlight.

Adult Starling flying from its nest in search of food for its chicks.

Nursery Web Spiders begin to appear with more regularity at this time of year, with the increase of temperature along with an increased number of prey items (e.g., various insects) its likely you'll find these spiders running amongst the leaves of shrubs or tall grasses which are in direct sunlight. I find these spiders to be one of the prettier ones, although many people tend to disagree with me, each to their own! The adults can reach a couple of inches in length and are quite chunky. They have good eyesight and respond to visual movement, there have been many times where I have attempted to get close for a photograph but have only in succeeded in making it run into dense foliage or underneath a leaf.

A female Nursery Web Spider allowing me to photograph it as it basks in the sun.

Hawkmoths are a favourite of mine, largely because of their shapes, colours and large size. A moth I have regularly captured in my Robinson trap during this month is the Lime Hawk-Moth *(Mimas tiliae)*. An incredibly attractive, large bodied species within the Order Sphingidae.

Their shape is very distinctive, and they seem to be unperturbed by my presence. These moths have extremely an extremely good grip and can support their entire body weight with only one leg clinging onto a surface.

Lime Hawk-Moths are variable in their appearance, ranging from green to pink.

The increase of numbers of different moth species in April compared to March may be due to environmental factors such as temperature changes as well as increased plant growth. Moths emerge at a time when there is an abundance of host plants for them to utilise, this enables them to oviposit eggs onto host plants which will provide the best chance of survival for their offspring. The world of Lepidoptera (Moths and Butterflies) is fascinating and there are currently large amounts of research based on the way in which Lepidoptera use pheromones and Volatile Organic Compounds (VOC's) to navigate their way around as well as to elicit significant behaviours such as mating and oviposition[19]. Aesthetically, Lepidoptera are beautiful creatures, even ones which may appear drab in colour, the wing patterning and physical attributes like antennae can be extremely elaborate.

Moths are extremely adept at being able to detect pheromones as the males can have extravagantly shaped antennae. Females will release pheromones from which the males can lock onto and follow, to where their destiny awaits[20]. One of my favourite moths is the Muslin Moth *(Diaphora mendica).* This moth is a good example of how fluffy a moth can be as well as having a long pair of antennae. I usually capture a couple of these moths at any one time, but it always appears in April and is drawn to light.

The extremely fluffy Muslin Moth displaying feathery antennae.

List of moths I've found consistently in April;
Brindled Beauty *(Lycia hirtaria)*
Common Quaker *(Orthosia cerasi)*
Early Grey *(Xylocampa areola)*
Hebrew Character *(Orthosia gothica)*
Light Brown Apple Moth *(Epiphyas postvittana)*
Lunar Marbled Moth *(Drymonia ruficornis)*
Muslin Moth *(Diaphora mendica)*
Pale Mottled Willow *(Caradrina calvipalpis)*
Red-Green Carpet *(Chloroclysta siterata)*
Ruddy Streak *(Tachystola acroxantha)*

Various butterfly species begin to make the odd appearance in the garden. The only consistent visitor being the Holly Blue, a pretty, small blue butterfly which often refuses to show the dorsal side of its wings. I find them basking in the sun on various plants where they can remain still for a lengthy amount of time. Other visitors include Comma *(Polygonia c-album)*, Peacock, Brimstone *(Gonepteryx rhamni)*, Red Admiral, Cabbage White *(Pieris* spp.) and Speckled Wood *(Parage aegeria)*, each with their own specific behaviours and wing patterning. Its easy to forget that the wings are patterned differently on the ventral side of the wings compared to the dorsal side. There can be a lot of variation in wing patterning within the same species.

An insect species I had only just come across in 2020 was the Valerian Sawfly *(Macrophya albicincta)*. In our garden there are quite a few Red Valerian *(Centranthus ruber)* plants which are a common wildflower that you may see on the sides of roads or motorways. The pink flowers are great for attracting a whole load of insects, especially Lepidoptera and Hoverflies. A space should be made for Red Valerian in any garden. Sawflies are part of the order Hymenoptera and can be easily confused for a Parasitic Wasp but the number of segments on their antennae can be helpful in distinguishing them from each other.

Valerian Sawfly, shining in the sun with its black and white legs.

Back to Hoverflies (Syrphidae), more species of Hoverfly are present at this time of year, species include the Drone Fly *(Eristalis tenax)* and Sun Fly *(Helophilos pendulus)*. I often find the Sun Fly basking on logs in the pond. Perhaps looking for a suitable spot to lay its eggs as their larvae are aquatic. The adults have two vertical lines located on the thorax which makes it easy to identify. I always find watching Hoverflies quite hypnotic, their bodies are still as they hover, and their wings beat so fast it seems like they have no wings at all. Their manoeuvrability is something to behold as they dart around from flower to flower.

A Sun Fly, basking on a log in the pond, the two stripes along the thorax help with identification.

For fans of Lilies, the next guest is probably an enemy, the Lily Beetle *(Lilioceris lilii)*. As our Lilies begin to grow every year these bright red beetles appear, mate and the subsequent larvae completely defoliate the plant although flowers have always appeared to be unharmed by the attack. The larvae are very strange looking and look like blobs of wet soil on leaves.

My knowledge of soil fauna is regretfully poor compared to aboveground fauna and so I aim to know more in time. I am aware that there are an endless number of creatures digging around in the soil, some chomping away on fungal mycelium and hyphae, some insects looking for a place to lay eggs, beetles dragging down dead carcasses into the soil to subsequently feed on and predators in search of prey. Within the soil is where I found the species Common Brown Centipede *(Lithobius forfiticus)*. These speedsters can dash through the soil quickly and have modified limbs along the sides of their head which contain venom, which they use to subdue their prey. Around a couple of inches long its likely they would feed on various invertebrates although I have never been able to see one in the act of feeding. I found an individual as I was cleaning out my tiny pond, underneath the lining, running between stones for safety. If I was a soil invertebrate there is no way I would want to come across this species. This species is likely to be active for most if not the whole year.

Common Brown Centipede scouring a log for prey, notice the modified limbs beside its head which are used to inject venom into their prey.

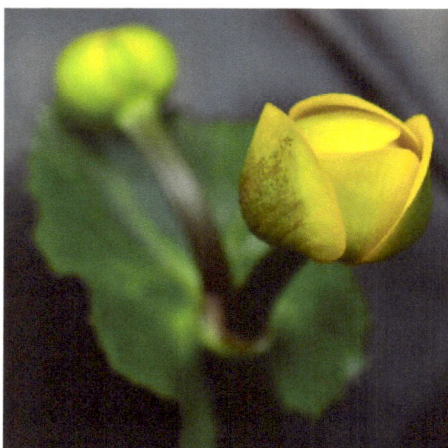

April is a great month for rummaging around in the garden, looking in ponds, under bricks, on bricks, under stones, in the soil, in those parts of a shed which always seem sunny and warm where spiders may be residing, within the plants, between plants, flower heads, and any other places you can think of, there's bound to be life. Days are significantly longer by now and many plants are flowering attracting a whole host of moths and other insects. Marsh Marigolds *(Caltha palustris)* and Water Forget-me-nots are also starting to flower and adds brightness to the pond.

Marsh Marigolds are vibrant pond plants, attracting a large range of invertebrates.

May

By the time May arrives, there is lots of greenery, and the trees have a healthy number of leaves on them. Chiffchaffs can be heard singing away and various bee species are becoming a frequent sight. May is the month for the arrival of Swifts, with their screeching calls and scythe-like appearance. Darting through the skies and then sometimes flying between houses. I find Swifts to be extremely distinctive in terms of appearance and behaviour, their flying habits are erratic, changing direction drastically in the blink of an eye and sometimes appearing to be out of control, I find it impossible to predict which direction they will head towards.

The unmistakable shape of a Swift.

Egg predation is when an organism consumes eggs from a nest, this occurs often and one of the main perpetrators of this are Magpies *(Pica pica)*. I have come across a fair amount of people that have a strong dislike for Magpies because of this. Magpies will often raid the nests of birds such as Robins and Blackbirds among others. The Robins in our garden abandoned their nest which had been raided after a Magpie had figured out where their nest was. Although sad from a human perspective this occurs naturally, and the Magpies also need to survive and raise their chicks. Corvids are extremely intelligent birds with some being capable of self-recognition[21] as well as being able to work out complex puzzles so it can be difficult for many songbirds to raise their chicks out of sight and reach from these birds. The Magpie is easily distinguishable by sound, a somewhat coarse cackle can give it away. Sometimes they will come together in large numbers and perch on top of a house or a large tree for a short while before dispersing back into their pairs. If you see one Magpie,

56

its partner is likely to be close by. A characteristic often overlooked with regards to Magpies are their beautifully iridescent tailfeathers. Numerous shades of metallic blue and green shimmer along their feathers, along with hints of pink and purple. If you ever find a long tailfeather of a Magpie, examine it!

A Magpie showing the faint signs of blue and green of its plumage.

Despite the dangers of nest predation, May has been the most fruitful in terms of seeing fledglings hopping around in the garden. I have seen Great Tits, Blue Tits and Robins fledge during this month in the garden. Robin fledglings are different to their parents in terms of physical appearance. The chicks appear mottled and brown all over. As Robin fledglings are unable to fly very well when they leave the nest, they seek shelter on the ground in amongst shrubbery to conceal their location from predators, they will also remain silent if you happen to get close to them. People often find lone fledglings and feel urged to help but it is often the case that the parents are close by and it is best not to interfere. I always feel a little anxious when I can see or hear fledglings in the garden, the threats of cats, foxes and other birds are always present. The 'grumpy' appearance of fledglings is always quite funny to see!

A Great Tit fledgling at its grumpy best. Taking shelter in the shrubbery of a Loganberry bush.

Sometimes unexplainable things will occur, I managed to find a nest full of dead Blue Tit chicks which did not seem too far from fledging. I noticed a fly making its way into the nest box and realised that's probably not a 'good' sign. The three of them were lifeless and clumped together in their small fluffy moss lined nest, it was sad to see them in that state, they must have perished not long before I found them. There could have been many reasons for their death, perhaps their parents neglected them due to disturbance, perhaps there was not enough suitable food (an often-overlooked aspect of the importance of insects in the food web), maybe infection or disease caused their demise, or maybe there are other causes, either way its something that you're likely to come across if you'll be monitoring your garden for any extended period of time.

The sad moment of realising that none of the three Blue Tit chicks survived to adulthood.

Moths become increasingly abundant during May and one species that appears in May with consistency is the Mint moth (*Pyrausta aurata*). Always a welcome visitor, there are several species of Mint Moth which can be difficult to distinguish from each other. It always seems to appear in May with amazing consistency in our garden, we used to grow mint in the garden so perhaps it was a suitable habitat for generations of Mint Moth, also the volatiles given off by mint must surely be a factor in attracting these moths. The colours of Mint Moths are the attraction, deep reds and purples of the forewings combined with bright yellow markings of hindwings are a lovely contrast. These moths are great to focus on because as they are visible during the day and so there is no need for any light trap equipment (although they are attracted to light too) and they always appear in and around mint plants, with consistency.

The Mint Moth has distinctive colouration and wing patterning. Quite a small moth, it will visit a range of flowers.

Keeping with the topic of moths, Angle Shades (*Phlogophora meticulosa*) consistently appears in my moth trap during this month each year. I've always loved the appearance of this moth; the angular shape and the various subtle colours which are extremely pretty. One time a female had laid her eggs into the egg boxes in my moth trap and so I decided I would try to rear the eggs to adulthood. It was a very rewarding experience as I got to see the various behaviours of the caterpillars as well as the unbelievable transformation from a tiny egg to a caterpillar to an adult moth.

Angle Shades caterpillar munching away on some leaves. The black blob is known as frass which is a term for insect excrement.

The Angle Shades caterpillar had begun to spin a cocoon and pupate. Preparing for adulthood.

In the end a beautiful adult Angle Shades moth appeared from the darkened pupa and was released into the garden. Rearing moths is a great way of understanding the development of a holometabolous insect.

List of moths to be seen in May;
Angle Shades *(Phlogophora meticulosa)*
Brown House Moth *(Hofmannophila pseudospretella)*
Cinnabar *(Tyria jacobaeae)*
Common Swift *(Korscheltellus lupulina)*
Flame Shoulder *(Ochropleura plecta)*
Heart and Dart *(Agrotis exclamationis)*
Marbled Minor *(Oligia strigilis)*
Mint Moth *(Pyrausta aurata)*
Pale Mottled Willow *(Caradrina clavipalpis)*
Setaceous Hebrew Character *(Xestia c-nigrum)*
Shuttle-Shaped Dart *(Agrotis puta)*
Spectacle *(Abrostola tripartite)*
Tawny Marbled Minor *(Oligia latruncula)*
Treble Lines *(Charanyca trigrammica)*
White Ermine *(Spilosoma lubricipeda)*

With a range of flowers in full bloom and warmer sunnier days occurring with increased regularity, more butterfly species visit the garden, particularly Red Admirals, Commas, Holly Blues and Speckled Woods. With an influx of insect species in the garden during this time, it feels like summer is right around the corner. Another insect species that arrives at this time is the European Hornet *(Vespa crabro)*, this giant Hymenopteran can be clearly heard and seen as it flies through the garden, Hornets are important predators of a number of insects, typically those that are considered pests by many, such as aphids, and so can be welcomed into the garden, they will also do the job of pollinating various plants as they visit flower heads to feed on nectar. The Hornet is one species that I have always had difficulty in photographing and have never been able to get a clear close-up photo of one.

In 2020, I was looking outside the window at night and saw these tiny figures in the garden running around, I went outside and realised they were in fact Fox cubs, cute little furry creatures playing amongst the foliage. I set up my camera trap in the garden as I wanted to see if I could get some insight into their behavioural habits. I like how resourceful Foxes are, although I am not too fond of their shrieking in the night, as a kid I used to mistake their sounds for someone being attacked outside. The Fox cubs were never too far from an adult Fox presumably their mother, but they seemed content to rush around within the shrubs and run across the lawn. I managed to capture one of the cubs on video sharpening its hunting technique by catching and killing a small mammal (a mouse or a juvenile rat). As much as Foxes can and do scavenge for food from overloaded bins in the street and litter, they are also great hunters and will utilise the opportunity to use their hunting skills when the opportunity presents itself.

A vixen alongside her cub drinking from the pond during the night. Even with only a black and white image the differences in coat are clear. Without the use of my camera trap, I wouldn't have realised that the Foxes were using the pond so I am glad I have been able to capture these moments.

Activity within ponds can be very high during this period as there are many larvae growing which are subsequently consumed by predaceous larvae, birds and amphibians. Its amazing to see how many different organisms can be found within a small pond, and the tremendous range of forms and structures that each organism has.

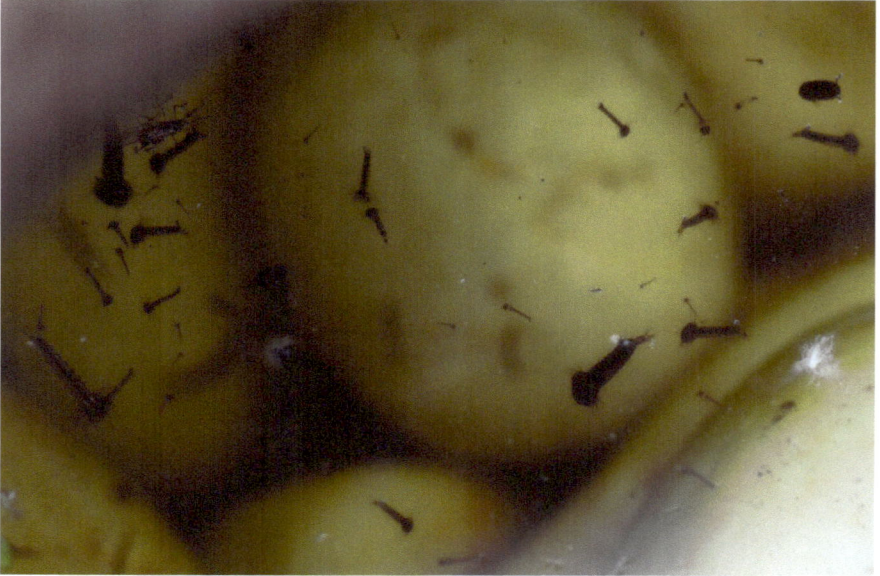

A number of Mosquito larvae, many of which are unlikely to make it to adulthood due to predation.

Pachygnatha degeeri (Long-Jawed Orb Weaver)

What I have noticed over the years is that the edges of ponds can also be great places to look for wildlife. I often see spiders building webs around the edges of ponds or just above the water to exploit the incoming insects that are looking to lay eggs or hunt.

Shifting the focus onto fungi, the Glistening Inkcap *(Coprinus micaceus)* is a saprobic fungus which absorbs nutrients through breaking down dead roots and logs of various broadleaved trees. Seeing a clump of these mushrooms at the base of a tree or woody plant may indicate the tree is dying. The fruiting bodies of these mushrooms can deliquesce within hours and if harvested, the 'ink' can be used to write or draw with! The mushrooms themselves are soft and break easily, the white spots on top of the mushroom are quite distinctive and help in aiding identification.

Clump of Glistening Inkcaps growing at the base of a tree. These two photos were taken two days apart and show how drastically the appearance can change.

May is a time when many birds and mammals are breeding, you're likely to find young birds and Foxes rummaging around, as well as hearing alarm calls of adults and the quiet chirping of fledglings. The garden continues to become busier with activity heading into the summer, and insect diversity continues to increase drastically. Butterflies and moths can be seen more often, frequenting the blooming flowers. By the end of May, the days are long, and temperatures are usually warm, so its a perfect time to be out in the garden documenting everything you can find.

Spring Summary

My favourite seasons tend to be spring and autumn, although every season has its own charm, but I love the progression of life in spring and the changing of colours, going from a lush green to a bright canvas of colour, also its not too hot (which is good for me!). There is an abundance of life that is easily detectable during spring and migratory species (insects and birds) are welcome surprises. Insect diversity rises dramatically from March to May, as temperatures begin to rise, and the hours of daylight increase, more flowers begin to bloom. Pollinators become more frequent, namely Hoverflies, Bees and Lepidoptera. Colours become more vivid with the blooming of flowers alongside the vibrance and iridescence of various birds. The air becomes saturated with a cocktail of intriguing aromas from flowers. Sounds become more varied and pronounced as passerines raise their chicks and fend off unwanted visitors and then in the night, bustles and screeching can be heard from Foxes exploring. I understand life can be busy with work and the many other responsibilities that everyone has, but many of these aspects of nature can be enjoyed with just a small amount of attention. Focusing on these moments can completely change my mood, especially in times of stress. Spring is a perfect, picturesque corridor which leads us into the natural party that everyone's invited to in the summer.

The Garden: Summer
(June, July, August)

I was never a huge fan of summer as a kid, simply because I hated the heat, those warm muggy nights made it difficult to sleep and playing football in the heat of the sun was energy sapping. As I've gotten older, I can appreciate summer more, the long days of sunlight, evenings which used to be football filled have now been replaced with hours of relaxing in the shade, looking up at the sky and listening to the humming sounds of cockchafers flying, birds and other critters scrambling about in the garden. The simple moments where I would be doing everyday things like putting out the laundry and being completely distracted by a butterfly landing on a drying towel or T-shirt, or Ladybirds landing on my arm as I water the plants would always make everything so much more interesting.

The summer is when many plants are in full bloom and the abundance of flowers is at its maximum. This is followed by a dramatic increase in insect activity as they essentially have a buffet of plant material to feed on, not to mention the predatory insects which take advantage of those herbivorous insects. Various mammals pop up and sightings of them become more frequent, such as Foxes, Rats, Mice and Bats. I have finally warmed to the summer, much of this being due to the huge amount of life and natural processes occurring around me of which I was previously unaware.

June

Bird activity during this period is surprisingly varied, during the heat of summer days I rarely saw any birds unless they were trying to cool off by bathing in the pond, having a quick drink or picking off insect larvae for food. Early mornings can be a good time to look for birds in the garden and then again in the evening around 5pm, those were the times when birds would come and feed, predominantly passerines. Greenfinches tend to appear with a fair amount of regularity from this point in the year in our garden. A majority of the time I hear them before I see them, their green feathers help them blend into the trees so they can be difficult to spot. Greenfinches and Goldfinches diminish the Niger seed, sometimes feeding at the same time.

A juvenile Greenfinch, resting after just flying into a window. Thankfully it appeared to be uninjured.

Small groups of Starlings tend to flock to the roof and surrounding trees early in the morning, looking as serious as ever, whilst chattering away with their varied range of sounds. When identifying Starlings,

I find their body shape and flying motion to be extremely distinct. They are also often in groups. Starling murmuration's are famous for being extremely beautiful to witness and are caused by the synchronised movements of many individuals in a large group. Even when in a small group, seeing starlings flocking together is a great show to witness.

Flower heads become fascinating when they are in full bloom. Many flowers will be fully open during the day, but once sun sets, the petals retract, and the flowers close for the night. I have found many insects on flower heads, as they try and get their share of nectar, look for mates or, in the case of bees, to collect pollen. Flower heads can also be dangerous places for insects as many predators lie in wait for their next meal. Spiders are a perfect example of this, the Crab Spider which is an ambush predator, will lie in wait amongst flower heads, front legs cocked to the sides and waiting to clamp down onto its unassuming prey.

This Crab Spider using lavender as the perfect hunting spot, it was amazingly efficient at capturing prey. The bees and honeybees had no chance.

Females of the Nursery Web Spider can usually be spotted carrying an egg sac within its jaws. When females are protecting their eggs, they can be fiercely protective.

Other predators include Ladybirds (Coccinellidae) which thrive on aphids, Coccinellids are a great ally of gardeners which are often bought online to help with pest control in greenhouses. Aphids aren't completely defenceless though; they have 'friends' in the form of ants, where the ants appear to 'farm' the aphids for honeydew in return for the ants' protection against predators. Aphids can also multiply at a rapid rate which is an effective way of maintaining a healthy population, they may also kick out at attackers as well as releasing sticky substances onto the faces of incoming predators. Aphids are important for the ecosystem considering they are consumed by a wide range of predatory insects, these include various types of predatory larvae, beetles, birds and parasitic wasps.

Lots of Black Bean Aphids *(Aphis fabae)* on a thistle, being tended to by ants.

Various ladybird species appear in June, it seems to be the month in which Ladybird diversity and abundance is at its highest. A non-native species, the Harlequin Ladybird *(Harmonia axyridis)* has rapidly increased in numbers within the last 20 years as well as establishing itself across the U.K[22]. This species poses a problem for native ladybirds as they are larger in size, share the same ecological niche and can predate the eggs and larvae of smaller species such as the Two-Spot ladybird *(Adalia bipunctata)*. The decline of native species has been linked to the presence of Harlequin Ladybirds and is likely to continue causing damage to native species without intervention or unless they become controlled by parasitic wasps or other predators that can take advantage of the additional item on their menu[23].

1) H. axyridis spectabilis, 2) H. axyridis succinea, 3) Adalia bipunctata, 4) Coccinella septempunctata, 5) Propylea 14-punctata, 6) Calvia ouattuordecimguttata, 7) Henosepilachna argus

On to another pest! This time we resort back to my fluffy friends, moths, this time in the form of the Box Moth *(Cydalima perspectalis)*, the Box Moth is a non-native species that is native to East Asia. Like the Harlequin Ladybird, it has become well established within the last 20 years and has spread incredibly fast across the U.K, devastating box trees and hedges along the way. This has been a problem for several National Trusts sites due to their use of Box trees (*Buxus* spp.) and hedges on their grounds. This moth is difficult to control as it appears to be resistant to many native parasitic wasps, its able to reproduce multiple times a year (up to 4 generations per year) and also has the ability to overwinter as a caterpillar, so they appear to be extremely well adapted to the U.K. Biological control is difficult to implement without first understanding the ecology of the target species in great depth. Knowing that an organism can predate a target organism is not enough to be able to be implemented as a biological control due to various factors. For example, lets suggest that a parasitic wasp has been found that can parasitise this pest, how would the organism being introduced effect other native species? What if the Box Moth eventually becomes resistant to the control? Would the parasitic wasp be host specific? What if it adapts to parasitise native species? Does the life cycle of the wasp match that of the moth? Does that parasitic wasp have predators of its own that can control it? What if the wasp can carry viruses or contain hyperparasitoids within its own body? These are all questions that must be considered and answered before any type of control can be seriously considered. Its a huge reminder of the complexity and interconnectedness of everything in the environment and with regards to biological control there is never a simple solution. It also outlines why observational studies are so important in understanding the general ecology of organisms.

I have found Box moths in my Robinson trap across various months in Heston which provides evidence of their multivoltine nature but generally they seem to first appear in this area around May/June. As a specimen, aesthetically I find them to be quite pretty, their iridescent wings shine nicely in the sun and the black border around their white wings is quite striking. Two variations of this moth occur, the black and white variation but also a darkened, melanic version.

The two variations of the Box moth.

For any bee lovers or Beekeepers, you may be accustomed to finding the Bee Moth *(Aphomia sociella)*. This moth can be found in nests or hives of various Hymenoptera, especially bees, hence the name. Eggs are often laid at the entrance or inside of hives where larvae will emerge and may feed on a number of resources within a beehive including pollen, wax and even bee larvae, therefore they may not be welcomed by many Beekeepers, but it is an interesting moth species, firstly *A. sociella* is sexually dimorphic in terms of its appearance, although variable, males tend to be brighter and more colourful with tinges of pink and green in comparison to the paler, creamier females. The courtship behaviour of these species is also one of interest as it appears that pheromones along with wing beating from females may induce courtship behaviour in males[24]. There are a lot of processes occurring in nature that we are incapable of sensing or detecting for now. Insects are fascinating!

Now its time to mention a very special moment in time for me, it highlights the spontaneity of life and the importance of observation. When I was first delving into monitoring species, with my excel spreadsheets for logging everything and constant searches in the garden for insects and general wildlife, I kept a keen eye out for butterflies because I like the wing patterning of various species and they are also large enough to be spotted from a fair distance. One afternoon, I happened to be inside, staring out into the garden, it was a sunny day and I was happy to be out of the heat, when suddenly I saw a fluttering object flash in the light for a couple of seconds, which then headed downwards

74

into the grass. Immediately I went into the garden, camera at the ready, and there walking on a blade of grass was a White-Letter Hairstreak *(Satyrium w-album)*, although at that moment I had no idea what it was because I had never seen this species before. I placed my little finger out next to this small butterfly, thinking it would fly away on approach as that's what usually happens, but no, this time this little butterfly walked onto my hand is if was just another part of the landscape, so now this was not just an observation, it was an interaction. After a few seconds it flew away, and I was really happy, first because I had just found a species new to me and secondly because I had interacted with it. After reading about the species and the significance of it, I thought about the whole aspect of monitoring and the importance of being focused on the present. If I had not looked out of the window at that specific moment and not noticed that flash in the sun, I would have never been able to record that sighting. I would be oblivious to this species because to date I have never seen it in the garden again although I have seen them in the fields, but we'll get to that later.

A high priority species, the White-Letter Hairstreak is a small butterfly that is at risk of declining further without its food plant, Elm trees. Easily identifiable as it contains a 'W' located on its hindwing along with white-tipped 'tails'. Adults will occasionally fly to the ground during mornings and early afternoons to lap up nectar from wildflowers. Its a lovely butterfly!

So, what is the importance of the White-Letter Hairstreak, well this species is part of the U.K Biodiversity Action Plan (UKBAP), its a high priority species in terms of conservation and the reason for this is due to its massive reduction in numbers since the 1970's. The causal factor behind their reduction has been attributed to Dutch Elm Disease caused by the fungus *Ophiostoma novo-ulmi,* which decimated tree numbers of Elm (*Ulmus* spp.) across much of the country[25]. This is the butterflies' host plant; without this host it would be very difficult for the species to survive. They appear to be surviving on Elm suckers (shoots which come from roots in close proximity to the original tree) but the effects of Dutch Elm Disease are still prevalent and many Elms die after approximately 10-15 years. After I had first learnt about this species, the next thought in my head was "What do Elm trees look like and where are they?", my tree identifying knowledge was lacking at the time (I am a little better now), so I wanted to know where these food plants for this butterfly were, I had not seen any Elm trees close by anywhere. Once again, all this from noticing something for a couple of seconds. I did eventually find the trees and the likely place the butterfly had come from.

Evidence of a Bark Beetle *(Scolytus* spp.) feeding on cambium underneath the bark. These beetles are vectors of Dutch Elm Disease and pose a great threat to native Elms.

The long days of June means there is a lot of daylight, but nights can be unbearably warm (especially when trying to sleep). Those nights can be great for monitoring species such as moths which also brings along the bats. I was initially pessimistic about bats visiting our garden, simply because of the area being residential and many gardens being paved over, the habitat did not seem accommodating for Chiropterans. Due to the fact I used to help with the odd bat survey at my local park as well as at the London Wetlands Centre, I ended up investing in a bat detector. A bat detector essentially allows us to hear the calls that bats make when they are communicating (social calls) or searching for prey through echolocation. The calls are not within the auditory range of humans hence why its useful to use a bat detector otherwise staring into the dark sky trying to spot a bat can be annoyingly difficult and requires a lot of patience. I personally find it a lot easier to spot bats on cloudy days in comparison to clear nights due to the clear silhouette of bats being visible against a cloudy backdrop. The abundance of food during summer months makes the sightings of bats more likely. Typically, the bats which appear in the garden tend to be the Common Pipistrelle *(Pipistrellus pipsitrellus)* and Soprano Pipistrelle *(Pipistrellus pygmaeus)*, the best frequency for the former around 45Hz and for the latter around 55Hz although it can be difficult to distinguish them in the beginning. Flying patterns appear erratic but most of the time the bats I've seen tend to roam around the same area for a while. The bats I've spotted in the garden appear around an hour after sunset. Depending on where you are and the habitat, timings of emergence can vary. As warm-blooded mammals, bats enter hibernation once temperatures drop low enough for a sustained amount of time, with these increasingly mild winters perhaps bats won't need to hibernate in the future but once it begins to warm up in spring, bats can be seen emerging from roosts. Bats often roost in holes in roofs or under the eaves of houses, bat boxes are also helpful in providing bats with a place to hibernate and roost. It should be remembered that all bats in the U.K are protected and so if you happen to have bats roosting in your roof its best to leave them there.

Hoverflies are part of the order Diptera which are 'True flies', they have one set of wings (two wings) which differs to other insects which have two sets of wings (four wings). The hindwings of Diptera have evolved and ultimately become reduced into physical structures known as Halteres, these are mechanoreceptors which are able to provide sensory information about the positioning of the insects' body as well as providing stability and balance during flight[26]. Hoverflies display what is known as Batesian mimicry, they may be easily mistaken for bees or wasps due to their appearance. A perfect example of this is the Hornet Mimic Hoverfly *(Volucella zonaria)*. As the name suggests, its mimicry is based on the appearance of the European Hornet *(V. crabro)*. The first time I saw one of these Hoverflies, I mistook it for a Hornet because of its size and colouring but these hoverflies are in fact harmless.

Hornet Mimic Hoverfly, a migratory species and the largest Hoverfly found in the U.K.

A pretty species to look out for during this time is the beautiful Large Red Damselfly *(Pyrrhosoma nymphula)*. This species is the earliest of the damselflies to appear in the year, it can be seen from as early as April, but I seem to find them in the garden in June. I had several damselfly nymphs in my pond for a couple of years, the nymphs are predatory and will consume various small creatures within ponds, including midge larvae and mosquito larvae. The nymphs are distinctive in their appearance, their lamellae, which are located at the posterior end, look like three feathery tails and usually have dark markings on them. Damselfly nymphs are quite thin and slender in comparison to their chunkier cousins the dragonflies, which are stockier. For some strange reason it surprised me when I found out that damselfly and dragonfly nymphs can live within ponds for well over a year, considering all the various species found in ponds and the threat of birds which often come and forage on invertebrates, that's a long time to survive. The nymphs are easier to spot at night with the help of a torch when they are more likely to be in open parts of water rather than hiding underneath stones or amongst the leaves of underwater plants.

A Large Red Damselfly nymph in amongst pond plants and algae, almost ready to transform into an adult.

Its helpful to have grasses or tall stemmed plants in your pond as the nymphs require them to climb out of the pond and emerge as adults. Its quite nice to be able to find their perfect casings from which they emerge. I have found Large Red Damselflies basking in the sun on warm mornings, the males appear to maintain a territory and remain in one area.

The bright red and black markings of this damselfly are nice to see in the garden against green foliage.

Pond activity is extremely high in June and Newt efts can be seen emerging from the depths of the pond to the surface for a few moments before returning into deeper waters, although in the case of our pond, deeper waters is about 40 centimetres.

A Newt eft with its gills on full display, the gills will be lost gradually as the Newt matures into an adult.

Common Pond Skaters *(Gerris lacustris)* are voracious predators and will pick up on the slightest vibrations on the water to locate their prey. Pond Skaters are adapted for running on the water without breaking the surface and are usually one of the earliest colonisers of newly built ponds.

Another predator of the waters is the aptly named Backswimmer *(Notonecta glauca)*, this insect is usually found upside down, at the surface of a pond where it sits in wait for prey. Similar to a Pond Skater it detects vibrations in the water to locate its prey. Its hind legs are long and powerful which allow it to manoeuvre quickly in the water. As I have found out many times when trying to photograph this species, when disturbed, a Backswimmer will vanish into deeper water.

Grazers of algae and debris in ponds include Snails, the Pond Snails and Ramshorn Snail (there are many species of both snails). They will slowly sweep across ponds ingesting algae, once established they can produce many eggs and so you'll find a fair amount of these snails in your pond.

A Pond Snail approaching a Ramshorn Snail.

The Cinnabar Moth *(Tyria jacobaeae)* generally appears in our garden during the month of June. As it is drawn to light, I typically capture it in my Robinson trap. The caterpillars are famous for being striking in appearance, they have thick black and orange stripes along their body with long protruding hairs and are often found feeding on the tough weed Ragwort *(Senecio jacobaea)* which can cover grazing fields and pastureland. The moth is aptly named after the mineral, Cinnabar, which is bright red.

The striking appearance of a Cinnabar, the red colouration stands out against a green background.

Migrations are something that most people seem to associate with birds but many other organisms are capable of making long distance journeys across the channel and one of them is the Hummingbird Hawk-Moth *(Macroglossum stellatarum)*. Having plants such as Honeysuckle and Red Valerian will help to attract this species to the garden as they provide lots of nectar, and Red Valerian is also a possible hostplant for the larvae. The multiple times I have seen this lovely moth, it has always been strategically moving from one Red Valerian to the next. It has a long proboscis to reach the nectar of flowers. The wings are blurringly fast, much like a hummingbird. Being a day flying species there is always a chance to see one during the summer months, as powerful flyers they can even be seen during rainy days. They don't appear to be attracted to light so every time I have seen a Hummingbird Hawk-Moth it has from being in the garden. The large size of the moth and the highspeed fluttering of their wings causes them to be audible, I can only describe it as a low drone, but one which is very distinctive.

A Hummingbird Hawk-Moth nectaring from a Red Valerian, the wings beat incredibly fast and are a blur.

Moths to be found in the garden during June;

Bee Moth *(Aphomia sociella)*

Box Moth *(Cydalima perspectalis)*

Broad Blotch Drill *(Dichrorampha alpinana)*

Cinnabar *(Tyria jacobaeae)*

Cypress Carpet *(Thera cupressata)*

Dark Arches *(Apamea monoglypha)*

Green Oak Tortrix *(Tortrix viridana)*

Green Pug *(Pasiphila rectangulata)*

Heart and Club *(Agrotis clavis)*

Heart and Dart *(Agrotis exclamationis)*

Light Brown Apple Moth *(Epiphyas postvittana)*

Light Emerald *(Campaea margaritata)*

Marbled Minor *(Oligia strigilis)*

Middle-barred Minor *(Oligia fasciuncula)*

Mint Moth *(Pyrausta aurata)*

Orange Pine Tortrix *(Lozotaeniodes formosona)*

Riband Wave *(Idaea aversata)*

Setaceous Hebrew Character *(Xestia c-nigrum)*

Shuttle-Shaped dart *(Agrostis puta)*

Small Magpie Moth *(Anania hortulata)*

Treble Lines *(Charanyca trigrammica)*

Turnip Moth *(Agrotis segetum)*

Willow Beauty *(Peribatodes rhomboidaria)*

The Summer Chafer *(Amphimallion solstitialis)* is a beetle which always seems to appear in the garden during this month, they come in groups to fly around my next-door neighbours tree, usually flying around the tops of the tree in the evening as the sun begins to set. They are also attracted to light, and I have been able to catch a couple in my Robinson trap. Similarly, to the Hummingbird Hawk-Moth, these beetles will make an audible humming sound as they fly.

The Summer Chafer with its stocky body, is similar to a Cockchafer *(Melolontha melolontha)* but lacks the elaborate antennae and is also much smaller.

The Common Froghopper *(Philaenus spumarius)* is easily missed in gardens as the adults are small and unassuming, the presence of their larvae are probably more visible due to the foamy secretions they produce for protection from predators as they feed and grow on phloem from plant stems. This foamy substance is sometimes called 'cuckoo spit' due to its appearance. They are able to jump far distances in relation to their body size as well as having large eyes and a general froggy look. The wing patterning is cryptic and they can be difficult to spot depending on the surface they happen to be on.

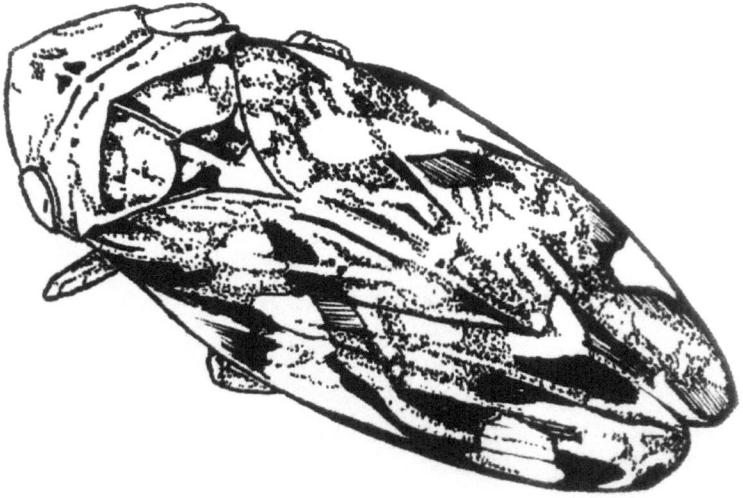

Pen drawing of a Common Froghopper. Powerful legs allow them to jump large distances.

In June, the garden is full of life, in the pond, the trees, the plants, the soil, everywhere you look there is something happening. As the beginning of the truly hot period of summer, June brings about massive changes in abundances of several insects including Moths, Butterflies, Hymenoptera and Coleoptera. Species diversity of moths visiting the garden continues to rise and this in turn brings about the appearance of a number of predatory animals. With warm temperatures and long days, conditions can be good at any time of day for searching the garden for interesting species.

July

The heat is usually intense in July. Numbers of Lepidoptera tend to be peaking during this month in the garden. Lots of flowers are in bloom, many spiders hang around in the middle of their webs during the day and night. All day long the garden is buzzing with wildlife. Birds tend to be quite abundant during this time with various species visiting, continuing to make the most of the pond throughout the day. As schools finish during this month, July can be a very good time for families to explore together and see what they can find. Its usually when the Big Butterfly Count begins too which is always fun, citizen science projects can be extremely useful when trying to figure out where specific species are located across the country as well as exploring which species are most common, and the garden is a great place to start.

Ring-Necked Parakeets *(Psittacula krameri)* visit the garden in order to take over the bird feeder, but thankfully they are too big to fit our on ours and usually fly to a neighbouring garden to make use of their fat balls. Although they are pretty, Ring-Necked Parakeets can quickly finish any bird food in feeders so it might be worth investing in Squirrel proof bird feeders which can stop a number of animals from consuming all the food, such as Parakeets, Squirrels, Pigeons and on occasion, Rats. Small flocks of Tits seem to form around this time and many of them will be found on our apple tree feeding away on small insects, spiders and bird food.

Insects are everywhere during July, there is huge diversity amongst insects and this month is probably the best month to find the greatest number of different species across various families. Diptera, Coleoptera, Hymenoptera, Lepidoptera and Odonata are all abundant and can be seen with regularity. July is usually the time when winged ants emerge from their nests to mate and disperse in huge numbers, typically on the day you've decided to be doing something outside. I often find Blow Flies (Calliphoridae) basking on leaves in sunlight, preening themselves. I like the metallic sheen Calliphoridae have, ranging from green to blue to gold. The maggots of these flies are commonly saprophagous and will feed on rotting material such as plants or carrion and are important in the recycling of nutrients as well as being prey to many predators including spiders, wasps, and birds.

July is a prime time to be running the moth trap. When I first began looking for moths, my equipment consisted of a little cotton bud tub to catch them in, once caught I would photograph them and then release them. Once it gets to dusk some large-bodied moths can easily be seen flying around, some are low to the ground, flying slowly from one flower head to the next and others are extremely quick and busy, darting around at speed. Start with the slow ones! Moths I used to catch with my little cotton bud tub were the Yellow Shell *(Camptogramma bilineata)* and Silver-Y *(Autographa gamma)*, both were fairly easy to catch as they can be considered as slow flyers, as they look for nectar sources. I imagine a torch would help but I was always worried about hassling neighbours and so I relied on my eyes to pick out anything moving.

The Yellow Shell, A vibrantly coloured moth which is readily drawn to light.

A. gamma is named Silver-Y due to the appearance of a "Y" mark on its forewing. The hindwings are a clean white, Silver-Y's are active during the day and so you may not need to wait until dusk to find one. Having a range of flowers in the garden with strong aromas are likely to attract an array of moths. Our garden usually contains an abundance of *Cosmos* spp. (as my Dad loves them), Honeysuckle *(Lonicera* spp.), Sunflowers *(Helianthus* spp.), Cornflower *(Centaurea* spp.) and Giant Oxeye daisies *(Leucanthemum* spp.).

Notice the 'Y mark' located on its wings, the underwings of this moth are white and can be seen while its flying. When viewed from the side this moth displays ridges along its body.

Its time for the tigers to make their appearance! July is the month when a couple of Tiger moths make it to our garden. The two species I have been able to record are the Ruby Tiger *(Phragmatobia fuliginosa)* and the Jersey Tiger *(Euplagia quadripunctaria)*. They are both bold in their appearance, the Ruby Tiger is small to medium sized (around 1 inch in length) with black and red legs and a striped black and red abdomen finished with a pair of dusky red wings. The thorax is also very fluffy!

The Ruby Tiger is one of my favourite moths, I love its colouration.

The Jersey Tiger on the other hand is large and has black and white forewings, whereas the underwings can be yellow or red with black spots. They are one of the most abundant moth species that I find in my Robinson trap. I have seen them flying during the day but they are extremely active during the night and annoyingly, seem to enjoy flying into my face.

Jersey Tigers typically have red and yellow variations.

A moth which is attracted to my moth trap in high numbers during this month is the non-native pest, Oak Processionary Moth (*Thaumetopoea processionea*). Much like the Box Moth, the Oak Processionary was accidentally introduced to the U.K at some point within the last 20 years and has spread rapidly across the country[27]. This moth will strip Oak trees of their leaves, leaving the tree weakened, reducing its ability to fend off diseases and pests. Oak Processionary Moths are also likely to have an indirect impact on native insect species which also feed on Oak trees.

The hairs on the body of the caterpillar can cause skin irritation as well as breathing problems if inhaled. The caterpillars are usually gregarious and form large groups which can be seen along the trunk of Oak trees, the best thing to do if you find them on an Oak is to inform the Forestry Commission who will then arrange for the moths to be destroyed. I fear that these may cause havoc in Osterley Park and surrounding areas where there are many mature Oaks.

Another one of my favourite moths is the Buff-Tip *(Phalera bucephala)*, this moth usually arrives in our garden during July. I've only ever seen this species in my moth trap, as its active at night it becomes attracted to the light of the trap. The first time I saw this moth I didn't realise it was a moth until I looked very closely at it. I thought it may have been a little broken piece of a twig. Its adapted to look like a twig, specifically birch bark, and its an amazing example of mimicry. They are extremely committed to playing the role of a twig and will be unwilling to fly away even when handled.

Perhaps the largest moth that I have ever found is the brightly coloured Elephant Hawk-Moth *(Deilephila elpenor)*. This beautiful pink and yellow moth is another species that is active during the night and will once again be attracted to light. Flowers with strong aromas such as Honeysuckle will also help to attract these species to gardens, as adults will feed on the nectar of the flowers. The first time I saw this moth was once the sun had set and due to its size and the speed in which it flew, I mistook it for a bat. Later during one of my periodic night checks of the moth trap I saw that it was in fact an Elephant Hawk-Moth. With my trusty cotton bud tub, I took the moth inside and had a closer look at it. What surprised me most about this moth wasn't the colouration but the massive size of its eyes. They're extremely large in comparison to other moths and are likely to help the moth spot potential mates. The caterpillar is famous for its incredible mimicry, appearing to look like a miniature snake, although I have never been able to find one yet.

The beautiful Elephant Hawk-Moth with its huge eyes.

Moths that regularly appear in July;
Box Moth *(Cydalima perspectalis)*
Broad-Bordered Yellow Underwing *(Noctua fimbriata)*
Brown House Moth *(Hofmannophila pseudospretella)*
Buff-Tip *(Phalera bucephala)*
Clay *(Mythimna ferrago)*
Dun-bar *(Cosmia trapezina)*
Dusky Sallow *(Eremobia ochroleuca)*
Dusky Thorn *(Ennomos fuscantaria)*
Elder Pearl Moth *(Anania coronata)*
Elephant Hawk-Moth *(Deilephila elpenor)*
Gold Triangle *(Hypsopygia costalis)*
Heart and Dart *(Agrotis exclamationis)*
Jersey Tiger *(Euplagia quadripunctaria)*
Lesser Broad-Bordered Yellow Underwing *(Noctua janthe)*
Light Brown Apple Moth *(Epiphyas postvittana)*
Mint moth *(Pyrausta aurata)*
Mother of Pearl *(Pleuroptya ruralis)*
Oak Processionary *(Thaumetopoea processionea)*
Rose Flounced Tabby *(Endotricha flammealis)*
Ruby Tiger *(Phragmatobia fuliginosa)*
Ruddy Streak *(Tachystola acroxantha)*
Scalloped Oak *(Crocallis elinguaria)*
Scarce Footman *(Eilema complana)*
Silver Y *(Autographa gamma)*
Small Magpie Moth *(Anania hortulata)*
Tree Lichen Beauty *(Cyrphia algae)*
Yellow Shell *(Camptogramma bilineata)*

A beetle I sometimes catch in my moth trap is the Sexton Beetle *(Nicrophorus* spp.*)* There are several Sexton beetle species which can be very difficult to tell apart, they are fairly large, with reddish/orange markings on their elytra and have large, clubbed antennae which helps them to locate dead and decaying animals. Sexton beetles are interesting in that they display parental care to their offspring which is uncommon within the insect world. Sexton beetles will drag dead animals below ground, which will become food for their offspring. Its not advised to handle Sexton beetles as they can secrete foul smelling odours.

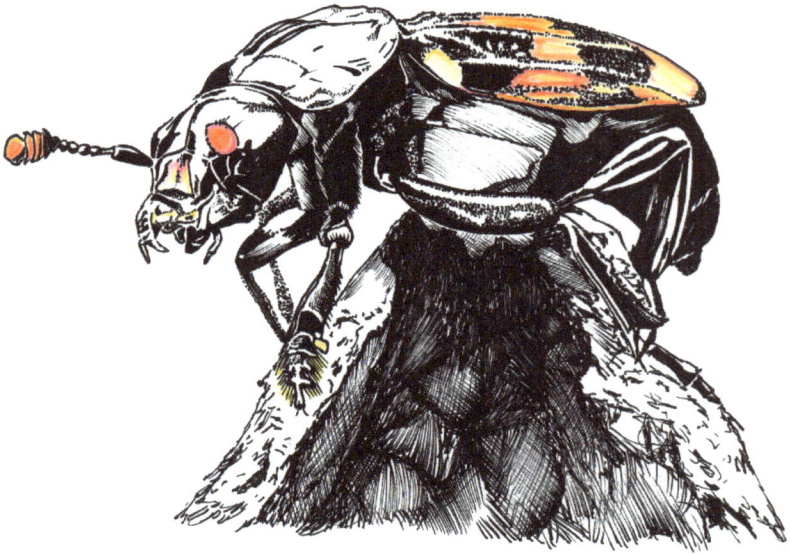

Clubbed antennae of Sexton Beetles often have an orange tip. Like many other beetles, this one was attracted to the light of my moth trap.

Continuing with another Coleopteran, the Rose Chafer Beetle *(Cetonia aurata)* is beautifully coloured with metallic reds and greens along its body with distinctive white marks on its elytra. The floral genus *Cosmos* did a good job in luring this beetle to the garden, although as their common name suggests, they will be attracted to a range of roses. As I watched this beetle clamber all over the flower, it was interesting to see the different colours and shapes that made up its exoskeleton. Its behaviour is interesting in that it seems to wander around on flower heads for a while before actually feeding, its can consume many parts of the flower including petals, pollen, and nectar. Being able to feed on different parts of the flower must help the beetle to maintain its rather chunky size, which can be between two to three centimetres.

The shiny iridescence of the Rose Chafers exoskeleton is beautiful to look at, with a range of colours on show.

The Lesser Stag Beetle *(Dorcus parallelipidedus)* is in the shadow of its larger more recognisable friend, the Stag Beetle *(Lucanus cervus)*. The Lesser Stag Beetle is also fearsome looking with a stout body and large mandibles. The only time I've seen this species is when its been attracted to my moth trap. They require dead wood for their larvae to feed on. As dead wood has an extremely low nutritional value, it can take a very long time for beetle larvae to grow sufficiently to pupate into adults, this is well documented with *L. cervus* which can spend up to five years as a larva. Its always good to have some logs lying around as many species require dead wood in which to live.

This male specimen was attracted to my moth trap. Males have a broader head with larger mandibles in comparison to females.

The next few species I'll mention are all Hymenopterans, first we will start with the Honeysuckle Sawfly *(Zaraea fasciata)*. The first time I saw this species, I thought it was some kind of strange bee or wasp. I always forget to consider Sawflies (sorry Sawfly lovers!) but that's because I don't come across Sawflies very often. It has a pretty, dark blue metallic sheen and distinctive black marks on the wings. At first it looks like it only has two wings as the forewings are large in comparison to the hindwings, but on closer inspection you'll clearly see it has four. Once spotted its quite difficult to take your eyes off it, I feel like there's something futuristic about the appearance of this Sawfly, perhaps its the colour combination and shape. Perhaps Android Sawfly would be a better name. I happened to notice this species feeding on nectar from our neighbours *Buddleia* alongside many bees and butterflies.

A common and constant visitor from the world of Hymenopterans is the Leafcutter Bee *(Megachile centuncularis)*. This bee will be seen frequenting many flowers within our garden. I have always found it difficult to photograph this particular species as they seem to move away every time I get close. They are distinctive with the way in which they collect and store pollen on the underside of their abdomen which contains many bristles. Evidence of their presence can be circular shaped hole in leaves which have been etched out by this species as they gather material to build their nests. These bees are solitary and will make use of bee hotels.

Leafcutter Bee collecting pollen, notice the hairs underneath the abdomen which aid in pollen collection.

The next wasp is a beautiful insect with an exoskeleton comprised of metallic blues, yellows and reds. The parasitic Ruby-Tailed Wasp *(Chrysis ignita agg)* was drawn to the Creeping Thistles around my pond and was found upon the wispy seed heads. Its a small wasp, around five millimetres long but that doesn't take away from the fact its beautiful, it just makes it an even greater find, like a tiny jewel amongst the foliage, the larvae of this species will feed on the larvae of other small insects.

A Ruby-tailed Wasp, perhaps scouring the thistle seed head for a suitable host.

Cerceris is a genus of parasitic wasps which are largely solitary. They will parasitise hosts which will then become food for their offspring. As the order Hymenoptera is extremely speciose it can be difficult to accurately identify species, especially as so many species appear to be identical, and then throw in some convincing dipteran mimics and it makes the whole process even more difficult. It just shows the need to inspect specimens closely to be able to distinguish and identify species. It should be remembered that many wasps are also important pollinators of plants as well as being predators.

A *Cerceris* spp. feeding on the nectar of thistle flower heads.

An important member of our garden is the Creeping Thistle *(Cirsium arvense)* and it appears to attract a massive range of invertebrates from ants to aphids to wasps to spiders to butterflies to moths, the list goes on. I would strongly recommend allowing at least a small group of these to grow in your garden, as they are heavily used by wildlife, including birds! Once the petals fall you're left with an extremely fluffy seed head. These seeds will be carried by the wind to a number of distant lands, perhaps Isleworth or Kew or Richmond, maybe our thistles will add to the flora of Osterley Park!

Creeping Thistles have many flowers at the apex of their stems.

Extremely soft seed heads begin to appear in July.

Creeping Thistle flower being utilised by a False Oil Beetle. These thistles will produce many flowers and is a useful addition to any garden.

Back in 2017 as I was helping my Dad clear parts of the garden which contained random items like breeze blocks and weights, I found a medium sized moth pupa hidden underneath a 10kg plate. The pupa was a deep red and because I had disturbed the area around it and there were some rather chunky spiders surrounding it, I decided I would take it and keep it safe in a tub. I had no idea whether it was still alive or dead and I was apprehensive about poking it just in case I caused some damage, so I just left it on my bedroom table for a number of weeks. Low and behold, there was emergence! To my surprise what emerged was not a lovely moth but in fact a large parasitic Ichneumonid wasp. As it had just emerged it was pristine and shiny, with long antennae and black and yellow markings, it seemed to be trying to understand its surroundings with its antennae analysing the immediate area. These type of chance encounters with nature can bring about a lot of surprises and peak curiosities. It also left me with the question, what species of moth was parasitised?

Often, Ichneumonid wasps will have bands on their antennae, in this case the bands are white but can be yellow and of different lengths.

Left:- The pupal casing from which the Ichneumonid emerged. Right:- The wasp probing its environment. Notice the pterostigma on the wing, the thin waist and the large reddish eyes.

Now for the Hymenopteran mimics that are actually Dipterans. I have mentioned hoverflies before but during this month even more hoverflies are visible in the garden. I know many people that dislike wasps and will not go anywhere near them. If you happen to like, or not mind wasps and bees, then its worth having a closer inspection of anything that looks remotely like either of them, I can almost guarantee that not all waspy/bee-looking flies will be exactly that. Mimics can be extremely convincing, and this disguise acts as a great mechanism in deterring predators from feeding upon them.

The Hoverfly *(Chrysotoxum arcuatum)* feeding on a thistle.
The large eyes and one pair of wings can distinguish this
species from wasps.

Butterflies are still abundant in our garden around this time of year with many basking on leaves or sipping nectar from flowers. Sometimes it can be difficult getting close to a butterfly, the Cabbage Whites *(Pieris spp.)* I find nearly impossible to get close to, so having a good zoom lens is very helpful when photographing them, on the other hand, one of my favourite butterflies is the Green-Veined White *(Pieris napi),* which I have been able to get close to on many occasions. The interesting thing about *P. napi* is that the spring generation can differ in appearance to the summer generations, this is noticeable in the appearance of the ventral side of the hindwings. Spring variants tend to contain a lot more of a yellowish tinge to their wings compared to those of the summer variants. A good way to recognise a Green-Veined White is to look at the underside of their wings as the dorsal side can look very similar to the Large White *(P. brassicae)* and the Small White *(P. rapae)*.

One of the many times I have been able to get close to a Green-Veined White. The antennae are intricately patterned black and white.

A difficult insect to spot is the Eared Leafhopper *(Ledra aurita)*. Although distinctive in appearance, it can easily blend into its environment. The distinctive characteristic of this species is mentioned in its common name relating to what look like large 'ears' protruding from behind the head of the insect. Its very difficult to spot in its natural habitat which tends to be a variety of trees, where it can be found on bark or amongst lichens. I have to thank my moth trap for introducing me to this insect as I imagine I would have very little chance of spotting one without it! Apparently this species can stridulate quite loudly but I haven't been able to hear it yet. Stridulation is the process by which an insect creates a sound by scraping highly adapted body parts against each other[28]. This is clearly audible in species such as Grasshoppers and Crickets, but many other species also stridulate. This can be a way of attracting potential mates during the breeding season, so keep those ears open for the Eared Leafhopper!

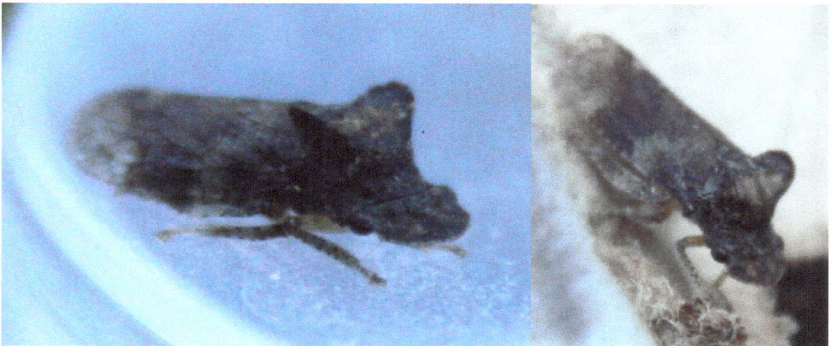

Just from these photos, its easy to understand why this species is called Eared Leafhopper,

The first time I noticed the nymph of the Common Darter *(Sympetrum striolatum)* I had no idea what it was, its chunky round body was like nothing I had seen before. Active during the night, it was easy to look at them moving around in the pond with the use of a torch. Maintaining a water source is essential for Odonata as well as many other organisms as their larvae are aquatic and require long periods of time to grow and undergo several moults before turning into an adult.

Common Darter Larvae in the shallow end of my pond amongst stones and algae.

Ponds continue to be busy during this time as various larvae are growing and birds are visiting. A distinctive aquatic larva is that of the Drone Fly, which has a name to fit its appearance, the Rat-Tailed Maggot. The larvae are found in waterbodies and have a long tail, like a rat, that acts as a breathing siphon. Knowing certain morphological features like this can be helpful in being able to narrow down the number of species it could be.

The siphon trailing behind the body of this larvae is just about visible.

105

Newt efts continue to grow bigger, and their gills begin to be absorbed as they get closer to becoming an adult. Newts require a few months within a pond to develop fully before being able to leave and live terrestrially.

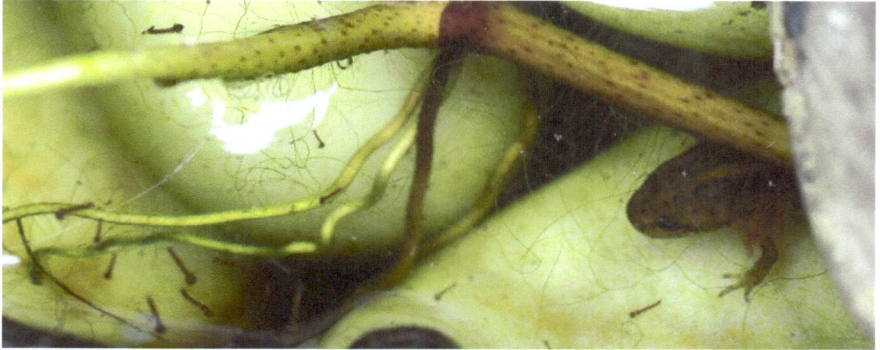

Newt eft with a number of larvae to feed from.

Swimming through the water, this Newt is almost ready to leave. Newts are great to watch as they grow through the spring and summer, changing drastically in their appearance from an egg to an adult.

With the abundance of insects, certain predators become more active. spider diversity increases in the summer, or at least in our garden it does. Going outside into the garden during the night with a torch can help you discover many different species as many invertebrates are active during the night (nocturnal). As I have mentioned before, different spider species hunt in different ways, some are active hunters, some are passive, some will spin a web and others will set traps. This difference in hunting techniques is clear from the various types of webs you will often see. Sometimes webs can be so thin that you may miss them altogether, and sometimes on sunny days you will see shimmering light being reflected off silk threads that seem to be never-ending strands flowing in the air.

The Eurasian Garden Spider is an orb weaver which is usually visible during the summer months, and they can prey upon a variety of insects, including bees, wasps, butterflies, wasps, and Shieldbugs. Their webs are the typical orb type that people most associate spiders with. This species is extremely quick on its web but if you've ever seen them on the ground their movement is slow and clumsy, this may be due to their large abdomen which I can imagine is difficult to carry around. During the day these spiders may be out of site, hiding on the underside of a leaf or within foliage where they lie in wait for a disturbance on their web. Vibrations from insects trying to escape the web draws the spiders attention through a silk strand that's connected to the 'hub' or centre part of the web. Sometimes you can lure them out if you tap the web with a stick, but not too hard otherwise you can damage the web! The web itself is made of various types of silk and is carefully constructed to allow spiders to move quickly across the web, trap prey, and be strong enough to withstand the elements, such as wind and rain. On occasion I have let my curiosity get the better of me and I have used muddy sticks to try and lure out spiders to see where their hiding place was, which has left behind little splodges of mud on the web, its interesting to see the 'cleaning' behaviour of spiders, they will remove any debris on their webs with great dexterity and care. Also, when prey items have been fed upon their empty carcass/shell will be disposed of. Eurasian Garden Spiders are known to perform autotomy (self-amputation) of their legs when they've been stung by prey such as bees or wasps but its not something I have ever witnessed. Its just another reminder that prey are not always helpless and that extreme measures can be taken in order to survive.

Garden Spider feeding on a Common Wasp.

Overall, I would say that July is the busiest month of the year in our garden in terms of species diversity and abundance, especially insects and spiders. During any time of day during July you're likely to find something of interest. I would recommend allowing a number of weeds to grow as their flowers can provide insects with valuable nectar sources which subsequently brings in many different predators that capture prey in extremely varied ways.

August

The month of August always seems to be quite humid with a mixture of weather patterns, rainy to sunny to stormy. The amount of daylight continues to decrease, and many annual and perennial flowers begin to lose their petals and break down. With this reduction in flowers there are less insects visiting although there is still a lot of activity occurring, with a continuation of numerous moths and butterflies fluttering around.

There appears to be a big change in bird activity in our garden from July to August. The number of bird species seems to decrease substantially from July to August, Great Tits, Blue Tits, Long-Tailed Tits, Robin and Goldfinches continue to visit the garden during this month with the odd visit by other species such as Blackbirds and House Sparrows. Still, I keep the birdfeeder filled so these visitors can continue to use it as they please. As berries can begin to be hugely abundant during this part of the year I imagine that many bird species would flock to those areas where they may also be able to feed on berries and insects. Plants which produce berries need animal vectors to disperse their seeds over greater distances so its not just the bird that benefits from feeding on berries, the plants do too!

Its not uncommon for Robins to continue breeding late into the summer if the conditions are favourable, these two fledglings were waiting for a meal from their parents.

Depending on the number of flowers in your garden, August is still a good time to see a range of butterflies and moths. The usual garden visitors in terms of butterflies continue to bask and use nectar sources, these include Cabbage Whites, Peacock, Holly Blue, Red Admiral, Gatekeeper and Meadow Brown *(Maniola jurtina)*. The migratory Painted Lady may also visit during this time.

Painted Lady nectaring from a *Buddleia*.

A Small White nectaring.

In terms of moths, species diversity begins to decrease compared to previous months but there are still many species to see. Setaceous Hebrew Character and Heart and Dart begin to reappear. Its common for several moth species to have two to three generations per year, and for many species they will require an overwintering period as pupae. Not all moths rest with their wings flat, some moth species rest with their wings upwards like butterflies. It can be easy to confuse these moths with butterflies, a good example of this is the beautiful Geometrid, the Early Thorn *(Selenia dentaria)*.

The Early thorn can be distinguished from a butterfly by looking at its antennae which are not clubbed as well as looking at the wing markings. The body is also quite thick and robust. Its also attracted to light, I should point out that I have never found a butterfly within my moth trap.

Moths to be found during August;
Box Moth *(Cydalima perspectalis)*
Brimstone Moth *(Opisthograptis luteolata)*
Broad-Bordered Yellow Underwing *(Noctua fimbriata)*
Early Thorn *(Selenia dentaria).*
Heart and Dart *(Agrotis exclamationis)*
Jersey Tiger *(Euplagia quadripunctaria)*
Lesser Broad-bordered Yellow Underwing *(Noctua janthe)*
Light Brown Apple Moth *(Epiphyas postvittana)*
Mother of Pearl *(Pleuroptya ruralis)*
Plume Moth *(Emmelina monodactyla)*
Ruby Tiger *(Phragmatobia fuliginosa)*
Ruddy Streak *(Tachystola acroxantha)*
Shuttle-Shaped Dart *(Agrotis puta)*

A Coleopteran that also appears to be attracted to the light of my moth trap is the Dor Beetle *(Geotrupes stercorarius)*. Large and bulky, this beetle is often found with mites attached to it. It trundles around the bottom of the moth trap slowly and if it finds itself on its back it can spend quite a lot of time trying to right itself. The exoskeleton of this beetle has a lovely iridescence and contains shades of blue, purple and green. Being coprophagous, this species feeds on dung and is a member of the Dung Beetle family.

A Dor Beetle plodding along the edge of my moth trap.

Dragonfly activity continues in August and several Dragonfly species may enter the garden, including the Common Darter. It always makes me happy to see Dragonflies, the diverse colours, large eyes and permanently outstretched wings are always nice to see. The stop-start, jerky motion of their flying as they probe the surrounding areas for a suitable place to bask, oviposit or hunt, makes them a joy to watch. If a Common Darter happens to be basking around a pond its likely that it will be defending that patch as they can be highly territorial, and so it may be possible to see the individual fairly frequently even if it does fly away for a short period.

A Common Darter perched upon a dry poppy seed head.

Bees are still abundant during this time of year and various species can be found visiting flowers. These include the Buff-Tailed Bumblebee and Red-Tailed Bumblebee. Sometimes it can be difficult to determine the sex of bees but in the case of the Red-Tailed Bumblebee it can be fairly easy, as males have long red hairs protruding from their hind tibia as well as a fluffy section of yellow hairs on their heads.

Left:- Female Red-Tailed Bumblebee lacking any yellow facial hairs or bristles on legs. Right:- Male with hairy legs and yellow tufts on its head.

Spider activity is still high in August and many different species can be seen in the garden. Two species which appear with regularity during this time of the year are the Missing-Sector Orb Weaver and the Stone Spider *(Drassodes lapidosus)*. The Missing-Sector Orb Weaver is one of my favourite spiders, probably due to how easy it is to identify and the fact that its web is distinctive. As the name suggests, it constructs an orb web but with a segment or quadrant missing from the web, it looks like an empty wedge. They can be found outside in well sheltered areas, the corners of windows or even snugly situated within the lid of a bird feeder. These spiders will often lay in wait for prey with its legs tucked in, reducing its visibility in terms of size. The front two legs of these spiders are longer in proportion to the other legs and they can move very quickly along their webs, I often find this species close to False Widows *(Staetoda spp.)*. The patterns found on the abdomen of this species are quite attractive with various lines and shapes, as is the case for many spider species. Despite being easily visible during this month this species can be found throughout the year.

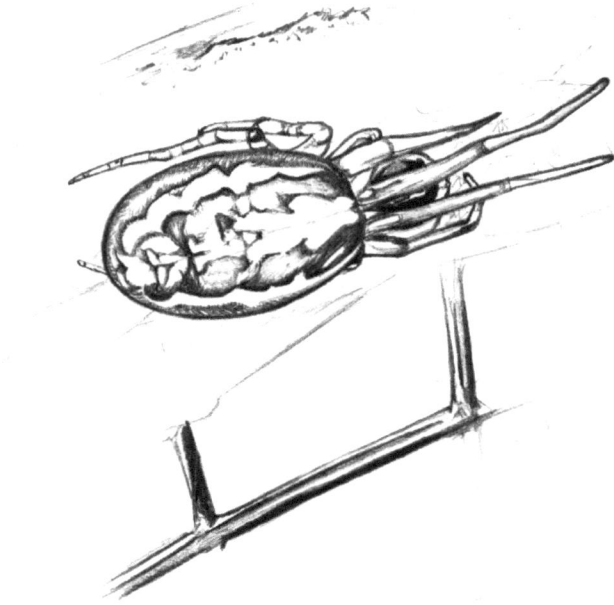

Drawing of a Missing-Sector Orb Weaver, long front pair of legs are typical of this species.

The Stone Spider on the other hand, is always outside in damp areas, under stones, gutters or on the inside rim of the lid of the water butt, which seems to a perfect habitat for this species. The appearance of these spiders is quite distinct, with a silky beige abdomen and protruding spinnerets. The chelicerae (fangs) of this species are also quite prominent and darker than the rest of the body. Often I'll find individuals of this species located quite close together within thick silken webs. I would say these spiders are medium size (approx. 1-1.5 inches) with females being bigger, as is usually the case. I have never witnessed this species hunting or feeding so I imagine its probably a nocturnal hunter as during the day they are nestled away within their webs. One interesting ability of this spider that I've been able to observe is the fact they can move on top of water without breaking the surface.

A Stone Spider wandering along the edge of a water butt. Notice the protruding spinnerets at the end of its abdomen.

August is great time for spotting bats, as hours of daylight continues to decrease as the year progresses, bats can emerge earlier than previous months which may make it easier and more suitable for you to try and spot them. Soprano and Common pipistrelles are the two species which I have been able to record in my garden.

Overall, August is a good month for being able to spot interesting species at any time of day. The main differences for me in the garden during this month is the fading of various flowers, although some do continue to flower until quite late into the year, and the drop in bird diversity. Insect abundance and diversity is still quite high but not as high as July. Some moth species seen earlier in the spring may also begin to be seen again during this period. Spiders are out and about and making the most of the insects that are left. Many spiders will also begin looking for potential mates around this time too.

A Red Admiral making the most of a Buddleia which can continue to flower throughout the summer and into early autumn.

Summer Summary

Summer is a time of peak activity in the garden. There are numerous birds, beetles, spiders, moths and butterflies as well as many other organisms. The garden is at its brightest during the summer as most plants are in bloom and there are many hidden gems waiting to be found, so all the senses will need to be utilised to spot them. My sense of smell is almost non-existent, and I wear glasses so my eyesight isn't the best, but nevertheless I have a lot of patience and can spend a long time trundling around in one area. Patience is the key to finding anything! Hearing also plays a big part when trying to understand the surroundings. Summer is the season when there are likely to be many sounds which are unfamiliar, whether they be bird calls, mammal calls or insect stridulations, by listening carefully to the sounds outside you may be able to pick out a species with confidence. I would personally say that insects take over during the summer, as this is when they are most abundant, particularly June and July, and will be found all over the garden as well as in and around ponds. Its a great time to really appreciate how important water bodies, plants and flowers are, in bringing wildlife into our gardens. Moth trapping during July is also when you're likely to see the most diversity in terms of species with a good chance of getting various insects of different orders. Conversely, by the end of August, summer visitors like Swifts have come and gone and insect abundance of various species begin to dwindle heading into the autumn.

The distinctive blue and red spots of a Gypsy Moth
(Lymantria dispar) caterpillar.

The Garden: Autumn (September, October, November)

Autumn, a time of transition, when plants and trees begin to fade, and many organisms prepare for the upcoming winter. Perhaps the most beautiful season of all, temperatures begin to drop slightly, and the leaves of the trees transform the surrounding landscape. When I look outside my bedroom window, in the distance I can see golden trails of leaves from various deciduous trees, some may even find their way into my garden. The changes from September to November are usually drastic although in recent years it has remained mild, and autumn seems to be somewhat delayed by a month or so. Fruit bearing trees and berries may be at their most abundant during this time which can be another attractant for a range of organisms.

September

September is a month where many bird species begin to reappear in our garden with regularity. Drops in insect numbers are likely to force many bird species, especially passerines, to return to gardens and utilise birdfeeders.

A couple of bird species that begin to reappear in our garden are the Coal Tit and the Dunnock. Both species will rummage around low-lying foliage in our garden and pick off insects and spiders, although Dunnocks spend more time around the base of our apple tree collecting fallen seeds from the birdfeeder. In the evening large groups of corvids can be seen flying over our garden, most likely returning to their roosts. It can be quite a challenge at times to distinguish corvid species when they're just one big mass, but the silverly eyes and calls will give away the Jackdaws! Carrion Crows tend to be bigger than Jackdaws and will also have a larger beak and a slightly different wing shape, not to mention a different call.

The temperature during this month remains warm enough for many bee species to remain active and continue to collect pollen and consume nectar from flowers. I usually see several solitary bee species, alongside Honeybees and various *Bombus* spp. feeding from the same shrubs, busy working away, they don't appear to take any notice of each other.

Various Bee species all foraging for nectar. Its always nice to see these creatures working away.

Many lepidopterans are still around during this period although not as many as the previous months. Butterfly numbers in the garden are significantly reduced by the time it gets to September, with the Red Admiral being the only species to consistently be seen during this month, possibly looking for a suitable spot to overwinter as well as making the most of any flowers that are still in bloom.

Red Admiral *(V. atalanta)*

The shortening of days means there is less time for many insects to remain active particularly if days are cold, temperatures during early morning and after sunset can be low at this time of year. September is usually when I have to start putting a jumper on when placing my moth trap outside in the evening. The moth trap still attracts new species to the garden and many Yellow Underwing species become abundant. These include the Large Yellow Underwing *(Noctua protuba)*, Lesser Yellow Underwing *(Noctua comes)*, Broad-Bordered Yellow Underwing *(Noctua fimbriata)* and Lesser Broad-Bordered Yellow Underwing *(Noctua janthe)*. As each of the common names suggest, the underwings are yellow and can be seen when the moths take flight. Very occasionally will the underwings be seen when resting. A lot of moths seem to be quite stubborn when it comes to showing off their underwings when resting, which is a shame as they can be extremely bright and colourful in comparison to forewings which can be a lot duller, although displaying underwings may make them stand out to predators.

N. protuba is quite variable in colour and as the moths age the colours and patterns can fade quite drastically.

N. fimbriata displays sexual dimorphism, where females are a buff colour (left) in comparison to darker males (right).

N. janthe is similar to *N. fimbriata* in the broadness of its thorax but its smaller in length and also less chunky. The colours of *N. janthe* is what makes it stand out, it has shades of purple, red, yellow and green. Its a pretty moth!

123

Now onto a very unique moth, which uses mimicry to avoid predation. The Chinese Character *(Cilix glaucata)* is a member of the family Depranidae, also known as Hook-tips, it has evolved a great way of disguising itself from predators, which is essentially to look like bird droppings. Funnily enough I think this moth is quite charming, the various colours consisting of blue, grey, pure white, black and tinges of orange, with a clear marking which resembles a Chinese character, makes this moth very distinctive. This species is attracted to light. The shape of this moth is also distinctive, it reminds me of a wide isosceles triangle but with curved edges.

Another lovely moth found during September is the Beautiful Hook-Tip *(Laspeyria flexula)*. The shape of this moth is accentuated by the wing tips which appear hooked, they make me think of 'Batarangs', a reference for Batman fans. The interesting aspect of this species is that the caterpillar feeds upon lichen.

Beautiful Hook Tip with its extremely distinctive shape.

The importance of lichen should be emphasised as without them many species would not be able to sustain themselves. A partnership between plant and fungi creates an abundance of structures that are often overlooked but lichens can be found almost anywhere and they can be extremely beautiful structures when viewed closely. If you've looked at old stone fence posts they are normally covered with a range of orange and yellows, all being lichen, creating microhabitats for other organisms.

The golden colour of certain lichen can cover branches of trees, providing a habitat for a host of invertebrates which are also fed upon by birds.

Moths to be found during September;
Beautiful Hook-Tip *(Laspeyria flexula)*
Box moth *(Cydalima perspectalis)*
Brimstone Moth *(Opisthograptis luteolata)*
Broad-bordered Yellow Underwing *(Noctua fimbriata)*
Centre-barred Sallow *(Atethmia centrago)*
Chinese Character *(Cilix glaucata)*
Cypress Pug *(Eupithecia phoeniceata)*
Large Yellow Underwing *(Noctua protuba)*
Lesser Broad-Bordered Yellow Underwing *(Noctua janthe)*
Lesser Yellow Underwing *(Noctua comes)*
Light Brown Apple Moth *(Epiphyas postvittana)*
Ruddy Streak *(Tachystola acroxantha)*
Setaceous Hebrew Character *(Xestia c-nigrum)*
Willow Beauty *(Peribatodes rhomboidaria)*
Yellow Shell *(Camptogramma bilineata)*

Syrphidae (Hoverflies) continue to hover about by the pond, lapping up nectar from any remaining flowers and basking in the sun on various plants.

Left to right: *E. tenax, Myothropa florea* and *Syrphus vitripennis*

Shieldbugs begin to pop up again, some basking on leaves on sunny days as well as feeding away on various shrubs and trees. You may find Shieldbugs at various instar stages. Its interesting to witness a hemimetabolous insect at various stages of its growth before becoming an adult as they can look extremely different at each stage.

Common Green Shieldbug Nmyph (left) and an adult (right).

A non-native species of leafhopper I was able to come across (once again due to my moth trap) is the beautifully mosaiced Japanese Leafhopper *(Orientus ishidae)*. This tiny leafhopper, around 5mm in length, has an intricate pattern etched into its forewings. This species is thought to have made it to these shores around 2011[29], mainly around the London area. Its possible that this Leafhopper could be a vector of various plant diseases and so will need to be monitored so that its effects can be understood.

Japanese Leafhopper with its intricately patterned wings.

Although not generally found in the garden, I feel like I should include the House Spider *(Tegenaria* spp.). Males often come out of hiding at this time of year from a corner in the house to find a female. They always seem to appear at night, kamikaze running across the floor when you least expect it. Many spiders cannot maintain long periods of running and these spiders tend to slow down after a few short bursts. This species does not cope well in cold conditions and is likely to die if placed outside, so its best to put them in a sheltered area like a garage or shed if you are intolerant of big spiders being in the house (I know many arachnophobes). These spiders are most active during the night. I once had the unfortunate experience (more unfortunate for the spider) of stepping on one in the darkness of the night as I was heading to the bathroom. It was terribly bad timing, and the crunch was audible. The chelicerae of this species are large and will easily pierce exoskeletons of various invertebrates including woodlice, flies, other spiders, and centipedes.

T. domestica one of the largest spiders you're likely to find at home.

Mating between spiders is highly ritualised and there are many different ways in which the initiation of mating can occur. In many cases the male is eaten after copulation and in other cases the male simply mates with the female and leaves. I was able to photograph a pair of mating Hammock Weavers *(Linyphia triangularis)* during October 2018.

Their webs look somewhat chaotic, and the spiders are usually found hanging upside down within them, waiting for prey to become entangled within their webs.

The spider on the right with light and dark markings being the female and the brown male on the left.

Overall, garden activity in September is still busy, and one of the better months to observe birds at feeding stations or ponds. Ripening of fruits such as apples and berries add another source of food for birds and insects. I feel September is the last month where insect activity is quite high before chilly nights return and sends insects into diapause or death. A number of flowers may continue to flower during this period, but many will have completely lost their petals and begun to shrivel. Its nice to feel those colder temperatures towards the end of the month again. September is a month-long sayonara to the summer and calmly transports us into the serenity of autumn.

October

By this time, cold nights are the norm, and it can begin to get harder to have the gusto to go outside and rummage around in the garden, but you can always put layers on! Insect numbers drop drastically during the month of October, this drop can actually be a good thing in terms of monitoring as you can focus on the characteristics and behaviours of just a few species. Being able to identify a species is a great skill but being able to understand the behaviour of a species is also hugely important, that is why time must be spent in observing organisms.

Many birds are visiting the garden at this time of year, although the Robins territorial behaviour becomes more apparent during this period, as I can witness it chasing off other birds which happen to be feeding from the birdfeeder.

A Robin keeping a close eye on the activity of the garden. We're not the only ones that observe the world with interest.

Great Tits and Blue Tits will consistently be around during the early part of the day, flying back and forth between trees and the feeder with a short stop at the pond.

Blue Tit perhaps waiting for the perfect moment to get to the birdfeeder, away from the prying eyes of the Robin.

By now a majority of butterflies are nowhere to be seen in the garden apart from the odd Red Admiral still hanging around, continuing to scope out sheltered areas to overwinter in. Only a handful of moth species seem to be attracted to the moth trap. The Yellow Underwings are still around in low numbers. I imagine their large size and large wings can help them fly during periods of harsher weather in comparison to smaller insects, although it probably takes them a little longer to warm up. Often in the mornings when checking on the moth trap I can see moths vibrating their wings to raise their body temperature enough to be able to fly.

The Light Brown Apple Moth is a non-native species originating from Australia. I regularly find this moth in low numbers throughout the year even during the coldest months, though I would say they are most abundant during this time. The apples on our tree are ripe and I imagine these moths enjoy them, although this species is typically polyphagous and can feed on a variety of plants.

Eurasian Garden Spiders are still waiting in the shadows connected to their web, waiting for the slightest triggers on their web, like ringing a bell for the next meal.

This Shieldbug happened to ring the bell and met its end at the fangs of this spider.

There can still be a lot of activity in ponds during this time, with Pond Snails, Damselfly nymphs, Lesser Water boatmen and other species going about their business. October is a good time to try and clear the pond of plants that have become overgrown and excess algae as its before the harsh winter has arrived and there are likely to be less organisms disturbed in comparison to earlier months. If you're taking plants out of the pond be sure to leave them by the side of the pond for a short while to allow any organisms to make their way back into the pond.

Spot the damselfly nymph, the Ramshorn Snail, Pond Snail and Lesser Water Boatmen.

Beside my pond I have a small log pile along with overgrown grass, I thought it would be a good place for insects to overwinter in and possibly act as a refuge for any amphibians like newts. I am not sure if any newts did use it but nevertheless its a good idea to have a log pile. What the logs did provide is a couple of fungal species, fruiting bodies of Crystal Brain Fungus and Sulphur Tuft reappear during this month.

A small group of Sulphur Tuft mushrooms pushing through the soil.

An additional fungus I have found during this month with some regularity is the Honey Fungus *(Armillaria* spp.*)* The fruiting bodies of this species are quite large, initially the cap is convex but as it matures it becomes flatter and slightly concave.

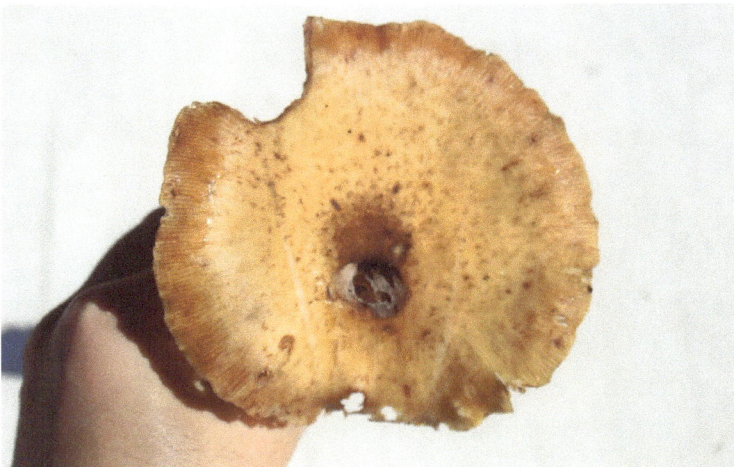

A fairly large *Armillaria* spp. This dry specimen was quite rubbery.

White spore print of *Armilaria* spp. shows up well against a darker background.

Armillaria spp. are saprobic and will break down dead wood, although it can also be described as parasitic as it can be found attached to living woody plants and trees, so this fungus is not always welcomed by gardeners, the rhizomes are black and have earned the name 'bootlaces' because of this. I often find woodlice scouring around within the cap of the fruiting body along with maggots of other insects. I enjoy finding fungi in the garden, one day the garden may be completely barren and devoid of any fungal fruiting bodies and the next day they can pop up and cover a small area, and then the day after that they can all be gone!

On to the controversial Grey Squirrel, some people will say 'its a pest , non-native and doesn't belong here' and others will say 'its fine they're fluffy and cute, let them be'. I think its quite nice to see the Grey

Squirrel appear in the garden, hopping about, running along fences, digging away, trying to feed from the bird feeder (but I stopped that). I would say I would prefer to see Red Squirrels; they had a tough break in the arrival of Grey Squirrels to these shores, hopefully the 'Reds' can maintain a foothold in the few pockets of the U.K where there are Pine forests, particularly in Scotland where populations are surviving[30]. There are a lot less Squirrels in our garden now compared to previous years, probably because of all the trees that have been cut down in the surrounding area and neighbouring gardens, which is a shame. The Grey Squirrel is in full caching mode around now, preparing for winter by burying food into the soil and flowerpots, these include acorns and berries, they seem to love our Cotoneaster berries.

A rather plump Squirrel nibbling away on birdseed.

October is a good month for finding fungi in our garden, another aspect of nature to look forward to as things begin to slow down. As the last flowers disappear, the garden is mainly awash with greens of foliage and browns of the soil and mud. Its a good idea to keep the birdfeeder topped up as many birds will quickly diminish the birdseed. October is also a great time of year to keep your ears alert to the various bird calls during the dawn chorus and throughout the day.

November

Finally, November. A month of cold weather and the beginning of short days. By now mornings are cold with frosts appearing and very few flowers if any, remain. The Robin is present for large parts of the day, keeping an eye on its territory and making it known to the birds in the surrounding area who's patch it is. Bright colours in the garden mainly consists of the birds that enter it, or maybe a flash of reddish, orange may wander through in the shape of a Fox. Cotoneaster provides a constant presence of red, and we've harvested a number of our apples but left some to naturally fall and provide a source of food for invertebrates, birds and mammals. By now my Dad will have started his annual 'tidying up' of the garden, removing any flowers that have wilted and general thinning of plants. By the time he's completed what he deems to be finished, the garden is tidy and feels like its ready to sleep for the winter.

As the garden is now devoid of flowers there appears to be hardly any insects at all. The cold weather certainly doesn't aid most insect species, and many insects will have begun a period of dormancy or diapause by now. Best thing to do if you do happen to find a chunky insect in a sheltered area is to leave it alone, its likely that its chosen that spot specifically.

Birds continue to flock to the feeder as much of the plants and trees in the surrounding environment wind down for the winter. Many birds may already be scouting for new areas to build a nest for the upcoming spring. Collared Doves and Woodpigeons are regularly sitting on the roof cooing away throughout the day. Robins are going full pelt headfirst into other passerines at the birdfeeder, their aggression is something to behold. The Tits and House Sparrows seem to get along fine though, sharing the birdfeeder at the same time. Coal Tits and Dunnocks will shuffle around underneath the birdfeeder picking off the odd seeds here and there, although when the coast is clear above, both of these species will sit on the birdfeeder and have their fill…and then the rats and Pigeons come and take their share too.

Great Tit and a House Sparrow sharing the birdseed.

For a while we have wondered if the rats were going to be a problem but over time we realised that the neighbourhood cats and Foxes were using their hunting instincts effectively. A bird species that always returns to the garden during November after months away, is the Chaffinch. Again, probably a lack of food sources and ease of access to garden birdfeeders was the cause of their return but either way, I am always happy to see a Chaffinch. A male Chaffinch brings some much-needed colour to the garden.

Male Chaffinch in all of its colourful glory, clearing up any seeds that are left under the birdfeeder.

A moth that is renowned for being active in cold conditions is the aptly named Winter Moth. Its quite a drab looking moth but its an amazing organism, being able to maintain movement and survive the harsh weather of winter months is no easy feat, especially for an insect. That's not all, ecologically, this moth species is hugely important for birds such as Great Tits and Blue Tits which will try to match their breeding season with that of Winter Moth caterpillars, for which the birds will feed their young[31]. Only males of Winter Moths can fly, the females are stumpy little moths which lack fully developed wings, but the females are capable of emitting pheromones which attracts males.

The Great Tit, a species that coincides its breeding season with the emergence of Winter Moths.

The Common Brown Rat is often looked down upon by those that class them as dirty or vermin, but rats are incredibly clever and also extremely clean animals. Its interesting to see how playful they can be when they're young and witnessing how they have quite a repetitive routine. By routine I mean they run the same paths every day to get from one place to the next. Its easy to see where rats might be going due to the 'lanes' or 'tracks' they create over time. In our garden they tend to be flattened lines of soil which run along the length of the fence. There were many generations of rats beneath our apple tree, I have an inkling that the rats may have helped the growth of the apple tree by aerating the soil underneath from where it was growing, I could be complexly wrong about that though, but there are always so many interactions occurring we can never disregard the ideas! Our apples have not become maggoty as so many do over time, maybe I'll give the rats the credit for that. Our garden is great for rats as they have shelter under the tree and then a few metres away they have a water source in the form of our pond. It does get a bit annoying when the young ones eat all the bird food though. Perhaps the rats could be credited with providing spaces for bees that build hives underground such as *B. terrestris*.

Rats are incredibly good at climbing, thankfully this rat was too heavy to take all the food from the feeder.

Back in November 2016 I decided I wanted to try and grow some trees from seed. The species I chose were Rowan *(Sorbus aucuparia)* and Hawthorn *(Crataegus monogyna)*. Both being native to Britain and not growing into huge trees like an Oak, I thought they would be suitable for our garden. Planting trees from seed requires a lot of patience but also requires a period of cold, or vernalisation to stimulate growth, hence why November is a good time to plant these seeds. I used a mixture of sand and John Innes compost for my tree seeds for good drainage. They faced south for lots of sunlight, and I kept them sheltered so when it rained heavily they wouldn't get waterlogged. They eventually began to grow several months later; one seed took its time and began to grow around 18 months later so patience is required! Both Hawthorn and Rowan trees are great for wildlife especially insects and birds, they both produce red berries which can also be used for making jams and jellies. I've tried making a jam out of hawthorn berries and its very nice! The Rowan jelly that I have made wasn't so nice, next time it'll be better. Hawthorns are likely to attract the Hawthorn Shield Bug *(Acanthosoma haemorrhoidale)* which has a colouring of red and green, much like the Hawthorn itself.

By late autumn, flowers have all but gone, the garden appears somewhat duller, senses focus on things further out from the garden, Robins singing from the tops of trees, crimson reds and oranges in the skies during sunsets, bright stars during extremely cold but clear nights. I often find myself in the garden on clear nights looking up to see Polaris (North Star). These are aspects of nature that should not be forgotten or disregarded and looking up at stars is one of them!

True residents of the garden, the Robins are always there.

Overall, wildlife activity is heavily reduced by the time it gets to November, with regular visitors and residents predominantly being birds and mammals. Ponds continue to be utilised by both. I find November to be a good time to begin reflecting upon the findings of year, as this can take a lot of time depending on how much data/ monitoring has been done. Identifying species can take a very long time and so its always best to begin early. You may be lucky enough to get migrating visitors to the garden during this month, but I haven't had that luxury yet, perhaps when the Hawthorn and Rowan trees are fully grown, they'll attract the likes of Redwings and Fieldfares.

Autumn Summary

The contrast and change in the appearance of the garden between September to November is drastic and thus has a huge impact on the species seen. Factors such as weather and climate and hours of daylight drive many of these changes. It'll be interesting to see how weather patterns continue to change in the future. Fungi thrive during this season and many species can be found in gardens. Autumn is also a great time to focus on bird activity and there is always the possibility of attracting migrating birds to the garden, perhaps a Hawfinch *(Coccothraustes coccothraustes)* will make its way here one day. If you have broadleaved trees in your garden then autumn is the time to pay attention to the colours of the leaves and witness how they change. Autumn is a beautiful season and even as plants and leaves begin to break down they can produce stunning colours. Late autumn is also a good time to plan what needs to be done in the garden as wildlife activity is low, this reduces the possibility of disturbing many species and if space allows, think about growing shrubs, thorny plants and trees. The relatively low number of species left in my garden by late autumn are all fascinating in their own way, but time needs to be taken to learn about their routines and to observe their behaviour. Despite all the changes occurring during this time, I find the garden to be at its most peaceful during autumn.

Garden Summary

I've gone on about how great gardens are at attracting wildlife and some of the species that can be seen throughout the year in Heston. Our gardens are ever changing habitats and from one month to the next, the species community changes and adapts as the state of the garden changes. Birds, amphibians, insects and many other organisms all come and go as they please, so its up to us to be alert enough to spot them. Considering how towns and cities are becoming more built up to accommodate human needs, its likely our gardens will become increasingly important as refuges for an endless number of species. The Natural History Museums' Wildlife Garden is a great example of how a relatively small space within one of the busiest areas of London can contain so many species (thousands of them!). Not only will our gardens attract species, but they are also likely to allow animals safe passage from one area to the next. Front gardens, back gardens, any patches of greenery are a haven for something. The great outdoors is not just about travelling to a protected patch that's been labelled as an Area of Outstanding Natural Beauty (AONB) or a Site of Special Scientific Interest (SSSI) located hundreds of miles away, the great

outdoors IS our gardens. Learning about nature in great depth can be achieved within just a few metres of our homes. I am hugely grateful for having a garden and I have tried to (and continue to) learn as much as I can about the species sharing this space. My love for nature has deepened through understanding what goes on in the garden. It has given me so much joy and exposed me to so many species that I would otherwise not have known existed. Think about what you may be missing by not paying attention to your gardens, and treasure them until the end of time!

Part Two: To the Fields!

The next part of this book, takes me further away from the garden and into the fields of Heston, located within 100 yards from our home. The space is expansive in relation to our garden, the grassland is bordered by thick shrubs, thin strips of woodland and hedgerows, all of which are specific habitats themselves, each containing numerous microhabitats suitable for an array of species. Its a place I have grown to love and probably my favourite place to be in, whatever the weather. I have spent a lot of time wandering the same paths, visiting the same trees, logs and patches of grassland just to see if I can spot anything new and to see old friends, those old friends being Kestrels, Stonechats, Starlings and Whitethroats, not to forget Chris and the Horses! The fields feel different to the garden, of course the fields are much bigger, but many of the species contained within the fields differ to the ones found in our garden. In the fields I must move differently, think differently and be alert in different ways compared to when I am in the garden. Wandering through land that's not my own I also have to be aware of other people and the way they interact with it. It appears littering and leaving rubbish behind is an increasingly common behavioural aspect of many people. The fields are surrounded by the works of man, the M4 running along one side, farmland on the other, a football training ground separated from the grasslands by only a thin wire fence, school fields, and housing estates, the fields are a little pocket of semi-natural, unkempt growth utilised by a man and his horses and the lucky few that realise the space is there. Its never busy, I went through one summer without ever seeing more than ten people. I wish for it remain this way forever so that the species there can thrive and continue to flourish, but I also want people to realise how special the place is.

This second part of the book will once again explain how species communities change over time from one month to the next, what to expect in terms of species and when they are visible. Everything is based on my own experiences and monitoring habits. I am sure there are many species that I haven't been able to spot yet but hopefully in time I'll be able to find them!

Key Items

Before venturing out its good to be prepared, I always think I'll only be out for an hour or two, but then I end up wandering around for four or five hours. Every time I go out to the fields, I have my rucksack with me, containing the following

- 1.5 litre bottle of water
- DSLR camera
- Sun Hat
- Binoculars
- Plastic bag (any shopping bag will do)
- Pen and pencil
- Notepad
- Whistle (you never know when you might need a whistle!)
- Tissues

Be mindful of the fact that early morning walks to fields can be wet because of the morning dew, its a simple thing to forget, well for me it is. Invest in good, solid walking/hiking boots and some wellies! Its also important to let someone know where you're going. Its ALWAYS important to have my DSLR with me because you never know when animals will appear and its the easiest way for me to record a sighting.

In the beginning I was initially unsure of the species I was looking at so having photographical evidence always helped me to track down the name of the species from online resources or reference books. Binoculars are helpful although I rarely use mine, probably due to the cheap zoom lens I have attached to my camera.

I never really plan when I am going to go to the field. Being so close to them I just go whenever I feel like it. Having a routine can be good if you're pressed for time but going at varied times will expose you to more species as different species appear at different times of the day. Being in an open space feels very different to the confinements of a garden. The ability to look out at an open expanse and spot objects from a distance is good for my eyes as its easy to become accustomed to being confined by surrounding houses, fences, and walls, although I am prone to looking up at the sky and the clouds. Another aspect of being in the fields is that its nice to be out of the comfort zone of the garden and trying to wade through thorny or spiky plants (i.e., bramble or stinging nettles) in order to get somewhere, its part of the adventure of exploring natural areas. Exposure to more aspects of life can only be a plus, that's my way of rationalising the scratches and abrasions I tend to return home with, although I will admit I would rather not get bitten by bugs and Mosquitoes. The 'Heston Fields' are a special place for me, a place where I can fully relax and not feel any stress or pressure, a place where I can learn and observe. I have seen many species and witnessed some amazing events taking place in those fields as well as experiencing some of my happiest moments. The fields have also been an important part of my academic career and have been key to my development in becoming an ecologist.

A bright sunny day in the fields with the horses and a range of trees, including Wild Pear and Elder.

Fields: Winter (December, January, February)

The fields during winter welcome a few migrating birds to the area. The grass is crispy in the mornings with a slight frost due to the coldness in the air, but the sun quickly softens and relaxes the grass, although a hard frost will make the ground very crunchy, which is quite nice to walk on. Large groups of birds can be found feeding on seeds in the grasslands and many corvids are seen in the trees keeping a lookout for any raptors that may be close by. Due to lots of grazing from the horses the grass is usually quite short during this time and wildflowers are nowhere to be seen. The hedgerows and trees of the woodland bear no leaves and muddy days are common. My wellies are good friends of mine during this period. Although it can become extremely cold and windy when walking through open grassland, the woods offer some much-needed shelter. Its amazing how much of a difference it makes being within woodland during a windy day, they serve as a very effective windbreak. Birds and fungi are the focus of this season, although during milder February days a number of insects may begin to make an appearance. Lack of food and insects will bring many birds to these areas and migrating species will make the most of any leftover seed heads and berries from Blackthorns *(Prunus spinosa)* and Hawthorns.

December

Cold! The fields are cold during this month as you'd expect, but its a good time to be outside. Something about the harshness of the weather during winter resonates with me, perhaps I am just as harsh. It could be that it makes me appreciate the strength and survival instincts of the species that I see during this time. Temperatures can drop below freezing and for many birds that can mean death. Many bird species will huddle together when it becomes very cold. I will admit I find it comfortable to be the only person in the fields during these days. Cold, wind and rain are all fine because my focus is elsewhere, I want to see wildlife. I would maintain that its best to wrap up during cold periods though. If it does happen to be raining I seldom see any birds, not in flight anyway. I have to venture into the woods to see birds perched in the canopies of branches above, waiting for the downpours to stop.

During the dry, sunny days of December, the few hours of daylight are enough to see a range of wildlife. A bird that I have come to love over the years is the Stonechat *(S. torquata)*. For me, Stonechats are the winter birds of Heston. Their common name relates to the sounds they make which can be described as stones hitting each other. They remain within these fields throughout the whole of winter and have all but gone by the time March comes. Possible to see throughout the day, these birds will often be found in tall grasses and shrubs. Moving in small groups across the fields. The male never seems to be far from the female and there is clear sexual dimorphism between the two in terms of their plumage. Males have a bright red breast with a dark charcoal head and dark wings, whereas the females have subtle shades of brown and peach.

Female Stonechat perched upon tall dry plant stems.

Male Stonechat standing atop of a dried umbellifer looking out at the surroundings.

Stonechats make lovely silhouettes during the setting sun as do many other birds.

Many passerines which are found within our garden are also found in these fields including: Wren, Blue Tit, Great Tit, Long-Tailed Tit, Dunnock, Goldfinch, House Sparrow and Robin. All of these species tend to remain within the trees, feeding on invertebrates as well as berries. Wrens and Dunnocks tend to stay close to thick vegetation and hop around from one area to the next.

Dunnocks can be confused with Wrens but once you've seen them enough they're easy to tell apart, look at the tails, plumage and beaks which are all different between the species, the difficulty comes when you see a small brown mass fly past at 100mph. That's when you'll have to rely on bird calls or knowledge of their habitat to distinguish which species it is, but never guess! Accurate identification is always key.

I find Wrens to be extremely difficult to photograph as they come across as extremely cautious and can quickly merge into the shrubbery that they call home. Acquiring a good photo of a Wren is a victory.

Just like the Wrens, I am rarely able to get close to Dunnocks but sometimes they allow me to get close enough to get a good photo. Its common to see passerines in winter at their feathery best. Trying to retain as much warmth as physically possible by fluffing their feathers.

Dunnock perched on a tree branch during a sunny cold wintry day.

Its nice to see colourful passerines during my walk in the fields during the winter as they add a fleeting stroke of colour to the surroundings as they fly past. Goldfinches are a great mix of colours and their chirpy song as they fly overhead is always welcome. They seem to bounce across the sky with short bursts of loopy flight. Goldfinch flight reminds me of skipping stones. Being in an open space allows me to appreciate the flight patterns of various bird species, its something that's difficult to witness within the garden as bird movement is usually broken up into short distances covering only a few metres. For as long as I can remember there has always been a good number of House Sparrows in this area, although funnily enough I have heard many people from around here say that they rarely ever see them which I find interesting. The House Sparrows come to these fields and tend to stay within the safety of brambles picking off any ripe berries or invertebrates that may be around.

A couple of House Sparrows laying claim to a patch of Bramble.

The Pied Wagtail *(Motacilla alba)* is a small, black and white bird that suddenly appears in winter. They follow the horses around as the horses disturb the ground underneath and expose invertebrates, which the Pied Wagtails happily pick off. The closest I have gotten to this species was at Heathrow Airport, food scraps left outside terminals are often picked up by these birds. I usually find them in the fields in small groups, where they proudly stick out their chests and run quickly across the grass. They move so quick its almost as if they're skating. Another fun behavioural trait of this species is to chase off much larger birds, I once saw a group of these birds harassing a Kestrel much to its annoyance, but the Wagtails were successful in sending the Kestrel on its way.

A Pied Wagtail ready and waiting to pick off invertebrates.

At this time, I often see small flocks of Blue Tits, Great Tits and Long-Tailed Tits flying together, moving from one tree to the next in search of food. A bird that's not been mentioned up until now is the Great Spotted Woodpecker *(Dendrocopos major),* its a distinctive bird in terms of its appearance and behaviour. The mix of hedgerows and mixed woodland with the odd solitary tree in the middle of the grassland as well as dead trees for which they can use as nest sites, makes the area a good habitat for this species. These Woodpeckers are extremely alert and will fly away at the slightest sound. With their black, white, and red plumage they are instantly recognisable. As they are often found high in the tree canopy, if seeing them is a problem then the sound of them pecking away on trees will give away its presence. Its impressive how acrobatic these birds are on the branches of trees and how they can manoeuvre themselves so quickly and effortlessly.

Greater Spotted Woodpecker displaying its acrobatic abilities on a branch.

Pheasants *(Phasianus colchicus)* are beautiful birds, the males are showy with all their various colours, intricate feather patterns and extremely long tailfeathers, whereas the females are smaller and a little more subtle with their range of colours. Quite robust birds, when disturbed, they run along the grassland into the depths of overgrown areas and tall grasses. The only issue I have with these Pheasants is that they always make me jump when I'm walking past. As they typically hide in the tall grass its easy to miss them, and they don't leave quietly or slowly, instead they make a screeching sound as they fly upwards and away, with the number of times its happened I feel like they're doing it on purpose. Pheasants are non-native and were brought here as gamebirds for hunting[32] but they have now become a common addition to a range of habitats across the U.K.

A beautiful Male Pheasant displaying a range of colours and extremely long tailfeathers.

A winter migrant that makes its way to these shores is the Redwing *(Turdus iliacus)*. A small thrush, the Redwing is easy to identify due to its red flanks which are clearly seen when they're flying and also when resting. As they make their way into these fields they feed on a variety of berries, making the most of the Hawthorns and Rosehips that are available as well as seeking out worms. I have never seen these birds in our garden although I imagine if suitable food was available to them they may visit. Maybe one day my Rowan and Hawthorns will attract them to our garden. Having birds that migrate to these areas during certain times of the year provides something to look forward to during each season, its also nice to have a species that consistently comes back each year. Redwings will typically be found in groups, amongst woodland areas and hedgerows, stripping plants of their berries. Redwings will also eat a range of invertebrates including earthworms which they pick off with ease as they rummage through leaf litter and muddy grasslands. Redwings are a lovely addition to those cold sunny December days when they're red flanks shine brightly in the sun.

A Redwing feeding on a worm and blending in nicely with the surrounding leaf litter.

The Mistle Thrush *(Turdus viscivorus)* is full of character, bold in its physical stance, standing upright and charging along the ground in search of invertebrates. This bird likes to perch on top of trees and fence posts as well as running along grasslands. Its another bird that doesn't visit the garden, I have only ever seen it perched upon a neighbours chimney once and heard them flying overhead with their rattle-like sounds but in the fields they pop up with regularity during the winter. In the beginning I wasn't sure if I was looking at a Song Thrush *(Turdus philomelos)* or a Mistle Thrush but the upright standing position of a Mistle Thrush along with its long, slender body and silvery wing feathers help to distinguish them. Early mornings and dusk are good times to see this species.

Seeing and hearing a Song Thrush always makes me happy, their famous singing always provides a lovely chorus for evening walks through the fields as the sun sets. I rarely see two together. When I walk through certain areas of the woods I find several empty snail shells and I think to myself, a Song Thrush has been here. This species will smash Snails against a solid object (e.g., a stone), known as an anvil to break the shells and feed on the soft body. Song Thrushes will often be found amongst hedgerows, they utilise the tall shrubs and dying Elm trees in the fields in Heston and sing until their hearts are content. Smaller and rounder than the Mistle Thrush, their breast spotting is also distinctive when compared together with the Mistle Thrush.

Next up are the birds of prey! I have always loved birds of prey, they're majestic, the way they soar in the skies, that menacing glare, yellow eyes (depending on the species) and fantastic hunting abilities. They are awesome to watch, but they also vary tremendously, there are falcons, hawks, owls, kites, eagles, all with distinctive features. I have not seen any eagles in these fields, but maybe one day it'll happen!

First up is the Common Buzzard *(Buteo buteo)*, this bird of prey is quite large, although slightly smaller than a Red Kite *(Milvus milvus)* and feeds on a range of animals including songbirds, rodents, carrion, insects, worms and even in some cases, other birds of prey such as owls[33]. Quite often I'll see Buzzards perched on fenceposts or high up in a tree looking over the terrain, looking for the next easy meal. There appears to be a fair amount of variation in the plumage of Buzzards, some appear to be a light brown whereas others are dark or have different patterns on their feathers, so sometimes I have to ask myself "Is that really a buzzard?". Its always fun to watch a Buzzard standing up straight in grasslands with its feathery legs looking like its wearing short fluffy trousers. Corvids seem to be temperamental about having Buzzards around, I have seen many corvids chase away Buzzards but conversely I have also seen Buzzards feeding and standing in close proximity to corvids. I imagine the corvids risk attacking when a Buzzard happens to be close to a nesting site.

Buzzard perched upon a lichen encrusted, concrete fence post.

The largest raptor to be found in these fields is probably the Red Kite, this beautiful bird of prey is large and has an impressive wingspan which can be seen as they effortlessly soar through the skies. Red Kites are common in Heston, the fields and farmland provide perfect feeding opportunities for these birds and are often seen circling these areas, up until they get chased away by Crows and Jackdaws. Red Kites had become extinct in both Scotland and England less than 150 years ago, so the progress made by conservation efforts for this species has been astonishing as they are now steadily increasing and are no longer considered endangered[34]. I for one am grateful that they can still be seen.

The forked tail of the Red Kite makes it one of the easier birds of prey to identify.

The next species is very special to me, its a bird that I have spent a lot of time observing over the years and have photographed more than any other species. The Eurasian Kestrel is a remarkable species in so many ways. Firstly, its iconic with its hovering ability and just by that alone it can be instantly recognised. Watching a Kestrel hunt is a treat, and these fields are a perfect habitat to witness that. It will find a vantage point in which to look over the grassland to target its prey, once spotted, it will hover above it and when its ready to go in for the kill, it will nosedive towards it and at the last second sink its talons into its prey. Once caught, the Kestrel will, most of the time, fly off to a nearby tree or fence post where it consumes its prey by tearing off strips of meat. Prey items usually consist of small mammals such as voles or shrews, but they will also eat worms and insects. Kestrels are a highly adaptable species, and this allows them to remain in these fields all year round and to hunt effectively during the day and with their excellent eyesight they can hunt well into dusk when light is significantly reduced.

This Kestrel was hunting in farmland, feeding on worms and invertebrates.

A bird I was originally surprised to see in the fields was the Grey Heron *(Ardea cinerea)*. I had become so accustomed to seeing this bird standing tall in shallow waters of lakes, rivers and other wetland areas, that to see it in a grassland was quite unexpected. Their hunting technique remains the same, standing still for long periods waiting for the right moment to launch a surprise attack on a small mammal or nestling. The fields can be a good alternative hunting ground for Grey Herons once lakes freeze over or if food becomes scarce in their primary foraging areas. Once the sun begins to set I often see this bird flying away towards what I imagine is its roosting site as it flies away in the same direction every time.

Grey Heron standing tall in the grassland, perhaps looking for small mammals.

With a lack of people around in these fields sometimes I get the odd glimpse of a Fox wandering through the grassland, I sometimes end up in a staring contest with them before they vanish into cover. Their coats in the sun are a lovely shade of orange, contrasted nicely against the dried grass and the dark trees in the background. With all the shrubs, tall grass and bramble in the area, these fields are a good place to call home for many Foxes.

A Fox within the cover of tall stems and grasses, returning to hedgerows.

Looking for fungi is always fun, some may pop up in the fields but most of the fungi I find are found within woodland areas. There is a good mix of trees within the woods, a mix of Oak, Birch, Maple, Holly, Hawthorn, Elm, Cherry, as well as others, make the mixed woodland a suitable habitat for many species of birds, insects, and fungi. Some fungi are host specific and will only be found on certain species of tree. A prime example to start us off is the Wrinkly Peach Fungus *(Rhodotus palmatus)*. This fungus is predominantly linked to Elm trees, due to the outbreak of Dutch Elm Disease, this xylophagous fungus has become quite common in Heston, as its been able to break down dead Elms that are abundant in the hedgerows of these fields. Droplets of a pinkish liquid can sometimes ooze from the stipe of the fungus, but all in all its quite an attractive mushroom. This fungus is often regarded as being rare as Elms continue to vanish across the country, reducing availability of suitable substrate from which to feed and grow. Its finding pockets of woods like the ones in Heston that make monitoring local areas so valuable.

Wrinkly Peach Fungus growing on a dead tree.

Collecting spore prints of fungi and analysing spores under a microscope is a good way of being able to identify many fungi and the process of creating a spore print is very easy. To collect a spore print, the cap of a fungus needs to be face down on paper, its best to spray the fungus with water before placing it onto the paper, then cover the fungus with a container. Its best to leave the fungus overnight to allow collection of spores. A number of fungi produce white spore prints and so for these fungi its best to use dark coloured paper.

The white spore print of *R. palmatus*. Its best to use dark coloured paper/card as a background.

Another xylophagous fungi found throughout winter is the Velvet Shank Mushroom *(Flammulina velutipes)*. An edible species which is popular in Japan, *F. velutipes* is a lovely mushroom to spot during the cold and grey days of December. They are typically found on dead birch trees as was the case in these woods. They protrude from along the trunk of the tree and are usually found in bunches. Similar to *R. palmatus* in being xylophagous they also have a similar spore print, which is also white. Even though Velvet Shank is edible I have not tried it yet, maybe at some point I'll find a good recipe for it.

The ladder-like formation of a clump of Velvet Shank mushrooms.

The Bay Polypore *(Polyporus durus)*, obtains a deep red colour as it matures which is complimented nicely against the creamy underside of the cap. I found this specimen (below) on a large decaying log along the woodland edge. Quite large, it also had a very leathery texture. Its important to appreciate the differences in physical structures and textures of fungi as this will help aid identification. This fungus was like a tough leathery sponge.

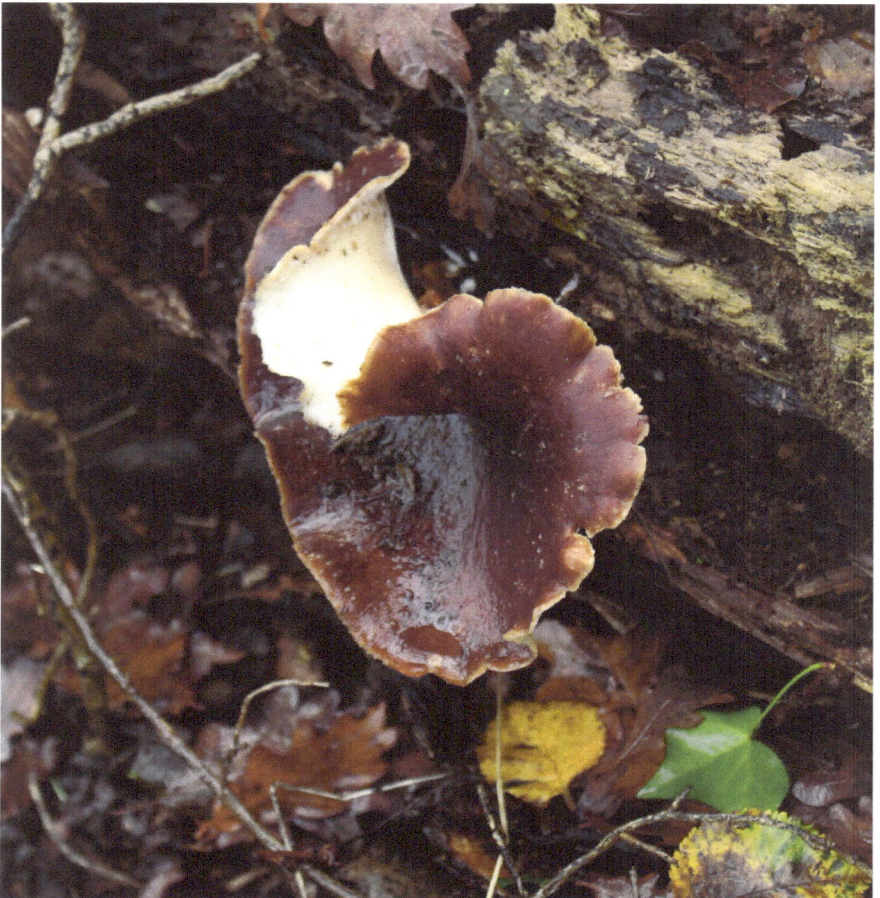

Tough and leathery, *P. durus* growing on a decaying tree log.

From a tough leathery sponge we move on to a brittle and delicate mushroom, the Conical Brittlestem *(Parasola conopilus)*, its colours can range from a cinnamon brown when fresh to a dull grey or beige colour when old and dry. The stipe of this fungus is hollow, and the spore print is an inky black. Handling this fungus without breaking it can be very tricky, as the name suggests they are extremely brittle so its best to hold them from the stipe. I usually find them in small clumps or groups around dead wood and logs underneath leaf litter.

Perhaps one of the prettiest fungi that I have found in terms of its structure is the Split Gill *(Schizophyllum commune)*. These fruiting bodies are typically found on dead wood, logs and branches.

This immature specimen displays its gills radiating from the centre. As the fungus matures and grows larger, it adopts a light brown, beige appearance.

A common winter fungus is The Yellow Brain Fungus *(Tremella mesenterica)*. *T. mesenterica* is a jelly fungus that I often find on the woodland floor breaking down small twigs and branches. Its brightness catches the eye despite its small size. Its another example of how varied fungal fruiting structures are.

This bright yellow blob of a fungus is one of the easier fungi to identify.

Identifying fungi is always a challenge, even with the help of reference guides. Spore analysis can be really helpful as fungal spores are distinctive in shape and size although this requires a microscope. Knowing the colour of spores can narrow down which family the fungus belongs to, which can save a lot of time. The shape and colour of many fungi can change dramatically within a short space of time, so if you do decide to conduct fungal forays always keep in mind the state of the fungi (i.e., young, or mature) as well as the substrate that its found on. Gill shape can also help with fungal identification as can smell and taste, many *Russula* spp. are known to be quite fiery/hot in taste. Most fungi will also appear at specific times of the year, predominantly during the autumn months, although this does seem to be changing due to climate change with species now fruiting earlier than previous decades and for longer periods, which means the fruiting season has extended[35]. It can be a messy business conducting forays but its well worth it just to see the diversity in colours and forms that you find. You never know, you may come across a species that is rare or perhaps even a species that is new to science! Fungal forays also add something new to walks that can otherwise get repetitive, there is always something to look out for.

For my Masters I decided to explore the link between fungi and insects, an interaction that I had never really considered before I entered the world of ecology. It involved me collecting naturally occurring fungi from the woods and fields of Heston and rearing insects from them. Fungi are important for many insects across many different orders. The fungal fruiting body provides food, shelter, and a site for reproduction. Many insects will oviposit their eggs into or onto the fungal fruiting body which then feed off various parts of the fungus, when they're ready to pupate many insects will leave the fungus and pupate within the soil[36]. Other insects may use the mushroom to pupate in. The number of fungal-insect interactions that occur throughout the year is amazing, and the year I spent reading and researching this topic led me down an extremely interesting path. A mushroom is essentially an ecosystem, hosting many different species, providing a hunting ground for predatory organisms such as parasitic wasps, spiders, earwigs and beetles to name a few. I could go on and on about this topic but instead I'll point out a couple of insects that I was able to rear that are active during this month.

Insects that were present as larvae in fungi collected in December ultimately emerged as adults during the months of January and February, reflecting the time needed for those larvae to become adults, there were also a couple of insect species that emerged as adults during the month of December. First up we have the amazingly adaptable *Megaselia rufipes*. Belonging to the insect family Phoridae (Scuttle Flies), this species has many different food sources, rotting fungi being one of them. *M. rufipes* appears to feed on decaying organic matter. I was able to rear these flies from an *Agaricus* spp. specimen.

The humpbacked appearance and wing venation of this genus helps to narrow down identification.

From the same fungus I was also able to rear a parasitic wasp (right) belonging to the Braconidae family, I will once again confirm that I find parasitic wasp identification extremely difficult. Finding this parasitoid suggested to me that the wasps used *M. rufipes* as a host, whether the parasitic wasp is host specific remains to be seen. Food webs relating to fungi and their associated insects is an interesting and important aspect of ecology to explore and hopefully I'll be able to find out more about this subject in the future.

Insects that were at egg or larval stages from fungi collected in December include *Tarnania fenestralis* (Fungi: *R. palmatus* and *F. velutipes*), *Trichocera* spp. (Fungus; *R. palmatus*), *Mycetophila* spp. (Fungus: *P. durus*), *Diapriidae* (Fungus: *P. conpilus*), *Exechia fusca* (Fungus: *Mycena inclinata*), *Allodia* spp. (Fungi: *Bolbitius* spp. and *Hygrocybe nivea*), *Bolitophila* spp. (Fungus: *Clitocybe* spp.) and *Copromyza equina* (Fungus: *Pleurotus* spp.).

December is a great time to go to the fields and woodlands, when everything seems to be quiet in the garden, the fields offer the opportunities to see many different species, whether its birds, mammals, insects, or fungi. The fields have great diversity in terms of bird species during this time and there is always a chance of spotting migrating species such as Redwings. Being a place that is seldom used by the public, there are more chances to see some of the more secretive species such as the Song Thrush. December is a time when the grasslands and woodland appear somewhat bare, and its interesting to witness the transition in growth and appearance of the area from winter to summer and vice versa. With regards to fungi, there are still many species fruiting during this period and the colours and variety of forms that these fungi display is more than enough of a reason to go out and explore these woodlands and fields.

Buzzards are always watching with keen eyes from somewhere.

January

January is usually very similar to December in terms of weather. The frosts and cold conditions may have killed off any chances of many fungi from fruiting, but some can still be found. Most bird species found in December will also be seen in January, but more species do seem to arrive from different areas during January. The fact that weather conditions can be bad during this time, and many birds are migrating it could mean there's a good chance of spotting species that are in mid migration and just happen to be passing through the area. As more area is lost due to development of land, areas of grassland and woodland will become more and more important as they become scarcer. The U.K. is an important stop off point for many birds that migrate large distances and so having suitable habitats to feed from will be hugely important to these species.

One of these migrating species is the Fieldfare *(Turdus pilaris)*. Fieldfares are large thrushes and can be seen picking off berries from Hawthorns. They usually appear in Heston around January for a couple of months before moving on. They form groups with other Fieldfares as well as Redwings. Fieldfares are beautifully marked and have the most displeased expression out of the thrushes, I imagine trying to stare down a group of Fieldfares and House Sparrows would be quite daunting. The dark patch around the eyes contrasts nicely with a yellow bill. Seeing Fieldfares and Redwings on the tops of hedgerows contrasted against a snowy background accentuates their colours and is something special to witness. Fieldfares are another bird that I have never seen visit our garden and I imagine a lack of berries available to them is a good reason for that.

A Fieldfare with distinctive dark patches around its eyes.

The Green Woodpecker *(Picus viridis)* is the largest of all three Woodpecker species found in the U.K. It can be difficult to spot these birds when they are standing in grassland due to their olive-green feathers but the red patch on their heads can give them away. They seem to be very cautious and fly away once they've spotted me. They fly somewhat close to the ground at times and can vanish from sight very quickly. They can be seen throughout the year, but I tend to see them more during this period and they are also common in Osterley Park which is near these fields. Green Woodpeckers feed on ants and there are many anthills in these grasslands, so I imagine these fields act as a giant buffet table for this species.

The colours of a Green Woodpecker strongly contrasting against a pale sky and the tree it perches on.

177

Another visitor to these fields is the Reed Bunting *(Emberiza schoeniclus)*, I tend to see this species throughout autumn and winter, I have never seen this species in my garden or any nearby parks. Its a pretty bird with lovely plumage. The males are distinct with darker parts on their head whereas the females have a more streaked pattern on their heads. They will form small groups and perch in trees as well as upon tall, dried stems of various plants. Their outer white tailfeathers are easy to spot when they are in flight which can help to narrow down identification. This species also has a habit of flicking its tail very quickly.

The Meadow Pipit *(Anthus pratensis)* is a pretty passerine which is predominantly found in upland areas but during the winter many will migrate to southern areas. When I first saw this bird I thought it may be a Reed Bunting but on closer inspection of photos, I saw that they were actually very different. The Meadow Pipits bill is longer than a Reed Buntings and the plumage is also different, although the tailfeathers are white for both species.

Looking at the claws of Meadow Pipits can also help to distinguish them from other similar looking birds as they have very long hind claws. Meadow pipits don't seem to be very shy; I came across one individual running along the grassland picking off insects, seemingly undaunted by my presence. Male Meadow pipits will fly high into the sky in a staggered way whilst chirping before flying back down again, like a Skylark *(Alauda arvensis)* although not staying in the sky for as long. I came across one man in the fields who told me there used to be many Skylarks in these fields a couple of decades ago but have since vanished.

Great Tit looking majestic in the sunlight, holding on to the stem of an Ash tree during one of those sunny but bitterly cold winter days. I love the colours of these birds.

The fences and fenceposts are readily used by most birds in these fields so its always worth scanning fences when out and about. Raptors such as Buzzards and Kestrels often use the fence posts along with Mistle Thrushes, the smaller passerines will sit along the fence and the Wrens or Dunnocks will tend to use the gaps within the metal wiring to perch and leap off from, to quickly immerse themselves into foliage. I imagine this type of fencing is a lot more practical for birds than solid wooden ones since all heights of the fence can be utilised.

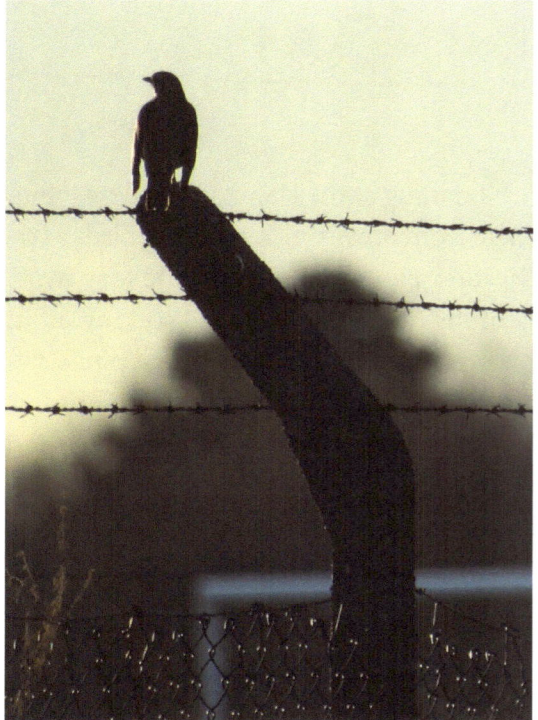

In terms of fungi, *R. palmatus, T. mesenterica* and *F. velutipes* are still present and their vibrant colours continue to brighten up the woods. As long as they are around insects will continue to utilise them. Winter Crane Flies (Trichoceridae) are adapted to being adults during winter and can survive freezing temperatures[37], an amazing feat for a creature so small and seemingly fragile. Other insects that are found as larvae within these fungi include *T. fenestralis* and *Bolitophila* spp.

A parasitic wasp species that emerged from a *P. conopilus* fungus
I collected in December and emerged as an adult in January.
A member of the family Diapriidae, this wasp was very small,
around 5mm in length, so its host must have also been very small.

Being able to emerge during a period of harsh weather suggests that this species is well adapted to dealing with cold temperatures. Notice the long antennae as well as the very thin petiole (waist) which is characteristic of many parasitic wasps. The long antennae may allow the wasp to locate hosts by detecting volatile organic compounds (VOC's) which are emitted by insects. Alternatively, the wasp may use fungal volatiles as cues to narrow down the search for suitable insect hosts. The world of chemical ecology is hugely complex but also amazingly interesting and insects are incredibly adapted to detecting VOC's[38].

January is a time for birdwatching in these fields. The weather can be at its harshest during January and shelter within the fields can be a haven for many migrating birds. Its a great month to see migrating species as their timings overlap with each other. Redwings, Fieldfares,

Stonechats, Meadow Pipits and Reed Buntings make themselves welcome in these fields and so its good to see them make the most of the food available to them. Buzzards, Kestrels and Red kites continue to hunt and soar over the skies and Foxes continue to wander out into the open for a short time. I cannot stress enough the importance of consistently visiting and monitoring an area, I have walked the same routes an endless number of times and each time I have had the feeling that I might see something new. It'll take a lifetime to understand what goes on in those fields and woods.

February

February, the last of the winter months. The weather can still be chilly, but the odd mild day is thrown in and days are longer than they were back in December, the increased amount of daylight can kickstart the growth of various plants such as the beautiful Snowdrop or the sunny Daffodil. A few different fungi pop up again continuing to display great diversity in shape and colour. February is the month that feels like those moments between being asleep and waking up and being aware that the day is about to start and soon there'll be lots of things to see and do, its the transitory period. The last moments of pure serenity, the dreaminess of winter comes to its end.

Migratory species are still hanging around in February but now they are preparing to leave, its the last time to see the Stonechats before they fly away. Its always a little sad to see the Stonechats leave, so brazen in their behaviour, standing atop of the fence posts and conquering the dried hogweed, gliding over the grassland, and chatting away throughout the winter. I get so used to their presence during wintertime that when they are not there, its noticeable. Oh well, at least I can look forward to their return (…I hope they return)! The Fieldfares, Reed Buntings, Meadow Pipits and Pied Wagtails have also decided that they've had their fill and vanish from the area. Grey Herons realise that the lakes and rivers are not frozen anymore and return to their primary feeding spots.

Stonechat perched on an umbellifer during a lazy afternoon.

Even though many bird species tend to leave the fields around this time, there is still an abundance of birdwatching to be done, many species remain all year round, in both the fields and woods, and soon enough the spring and summer migratory species will arrive. Starlings are ever present in these fields, flying from bramble to bramble then to the pear trees and then back to the bramble, they seem to have a good routine. I like to take photos of Starlings when they are flying in groups, because then I can look at all the different shapes each individual makes.

Small group of Starlings flying together.

The shapes of birds as they fly is a helpful way of identifying a species, especially amongst raptors, for example when looking at a Red kite what will usually give it away is the forked tail. A Buzzards' wings and body is quite broad in comparison and a Peregrine Falcon *(Falco peregrinus)* can be given away by its thin and angular wings, a bit like a cheese wedge. The Peregrine falcon is an awesome predator, reaching speeds of over 200mph when performing a stoop during hunting, its the fastest animal on the planet, and it just so happens to appear in Heston. Perched upon the tallest trees, I used to see this apex predator from a distance. I would enjoy walks as the sun was setting and seeing the statuesque peregrine perched on its chosen tree. Peregrines will slam into their prey with force, penetrating their talons into their prey before delivering a life-severing bite to the back of the neck. Peregrines will pluck the feathers from their prey before tearing into them. I have found many pigeon feathers (a staple of peregrine diet) and parakeet feathers along the woodland edge which may have been the work of a Peregrine although you can never rule out a Sparrowhawk *(Accipiter nisus)*. Peregrines make a range of calls and I have one recollection of where I felt as if the Peregrine was warning me, even though I was about 100 metres away. I happened to be on one of my many walks along the woodland edge when I saw the peregrine

and so I stopped and began to photograph it, and it began making this harsh screeching sound and flying in circles around a specific spot before returning to the spot it was originally. Wings and tailfeathers fanned out. I watched it for a few minutes, and I couldn't really understand its behaviour, it wasn't hunting. The next thing I knew, I saw the peregrine flying in my direction, and it flew straight over my head. I've wondered many times whether it realised that I had stopped and noticed it, I think it did, perhaps I was deemed a threat, maybe it was like me and didn't want to be seen and just wanted to get on with life in peace. Even so, it was a memorable moment for me. Thankfully I was lucky to get a photo of it as it flew over. A special moment that I'll continue to cherish!

Another raptor that I am extremely fond of is the Little Owl (*Athena noctua*). This lovely little raptor has tremendous character and was on my list of animals to see for a long time before I finally found it. Little Owls were introduced to the U.K. a couple of hundred years ago and have prospered around farmland and open woodland[39], which is where I see them most. Picking off voles as well as an array of insects, these owls are perfectly adapted to these surroundings. On the odd occasions of finding Little Owl pellets, they have been packed with the iridescent exoskeletons of Dor Beetles and bones of voles. The stomach acid of an owl is not strong enough to dissolve or break down bones so owl pellets will usually contain skeletal remains that are still intact. The Little Owl pellets themselves are shaped like capsules and around 4cm in length.

Shiny iridescent remains of a Dor Beetle and undigested fur.

Field Vole Skull partially intact, found within a Little Owl Pellet. Pellets provide valuable information into the diets of birds and what organisms may be abundant in an area.

Little owls are predominantly crepuscular (most active during dawn and dusk) and will sit on fence posts or low-lying branches keeping a look out for any potential prey. They cover short distances whilst flying low to the ground. Alarm calls of these owls are like a cackle, so it can be helpful to listen out for these cackles when its dark outside. The resident Little Owls in this area have been here for many years, I've been told by local farmers that many generations of Little Owls have lived within a certain part of the area and so its always nice to see them. Usually located around a couple of extremely old and large oak trees, on sunny days they can be seen basking in the sun. I have many fond memories of searching for the Little owls, I would go to the fields at dawn to see if I could spot them, which I did, but not up close, I wanted to see them from just a few metres away, I would go again at night, when the sun would be setting, but by the time I could notice them it was dark and so I would be watching their tubby little frames as silhouettes. Typically, I ended up seeing a Little Owl during the day perched in a tree just gazing out into the fields and then at me and then back to the fields before vanishing into the tree, almost as if it was saying, "you've seen enough" and off it went.

A Little Owl camouflaged within a tree behind lots of foliage.

I have happened to come across a number of fungi during February, each with a distinctive look. First up is a member of the genus *Geastrum*, also known as an Earthstar. Earthstars have a unique form which contain a globular sac (endoperidium) centrally positioned with protruding arms (exoperidium) radiating from underneath. I found a number of Earthstars on very rotten wood, located next to a bunch of Elm trees and what looked like a very old, rotting bed mattress, you find all sorts of things when rummaging around in hedgerows and shrubbery. Its been the only place so far I have been able to find any type of Earthstar around these areas, so I am glad that these fields and woods continue to reveal more of itself to me.

An Earthstar fungus with its leg-like projections underneath the cap.

Alongside the Earthstars was another type of Puffball fungus, this time it was from the genus *Lycoperdon*, although it was an old specimen and difficult to accurately identify down to species level. What I love about both fungi is the way in which their spores are released. A slight tap of the endoperidium causes a puff of spores to emerge. Wind or rain may initiate the release of spores, but either way, its an ingenious method of spore dispersal. It can be difficult spotting fungi when they are past their prime as many degrade quickly and look very different from fresh or young specimens. As fungal fruiting bodies break down they seem to blend into the environment and so in order to find fungi I feel its best to scour an area carefully and slowly.

A group of *Lycoperdon* puffballs growing upon a heavily decayed log.

The next fungal species which I found with some regularity during winter is from the genus *Tubaria*. The fruiting body of this fungus is a cinnamon brown/orange colour, and the spore print it produces is also a cinnamon brown. A small mushroom that I usually find around clumps of rotting logs and leaf litter, they stick out from the ground like little buttons and add a nice sprinkling of colour to the landscape when found in a group. As a saprobic fungus it breaks down dead wood. I was able to rear several insect species from this fungus making it likely to be an important fungus in the survival of mycophagous insects during the winter period.

Several Fungus gnat species begin to emerge as adults during February. Fungus gnats embody a hugely diverse array of insects, belonging to many different families. Mycetophilidae are typically characterised by humped backs and long thin legs, these fungus gnats are closely associated with fungi and their larvae are often found within fruiting bodies[40]. Its likely that the fungus gnats which emerge during this period are well adapted to cold conditions which may allow them to outcompete other species which cannot survive in cold conditions.

T. fenestralis is a large fungus gnat with forewings that have a yellowish tinge, along with quite thick antennae in comparison to other fungus gnats.

T. fenestralis emerged from *F. velutipes* and *R. palmatus*.

Allodia spp. emerged from *Bolbitius* spp. and *Hygrocybe nivea*, each of these fungi are common in grassland areas.

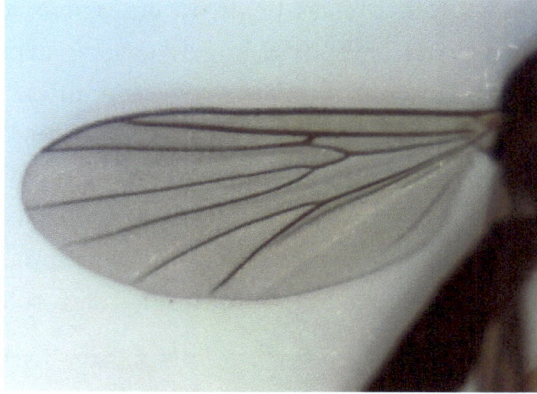

Fungus gnats can be quite variable in their colours between and within species depending on sex, age and condition of the specimen.

Trichocera spp. emerged from *R. palmatus* and *Panaeolus acuminatus.* Members of this genus have incredibly long legs.

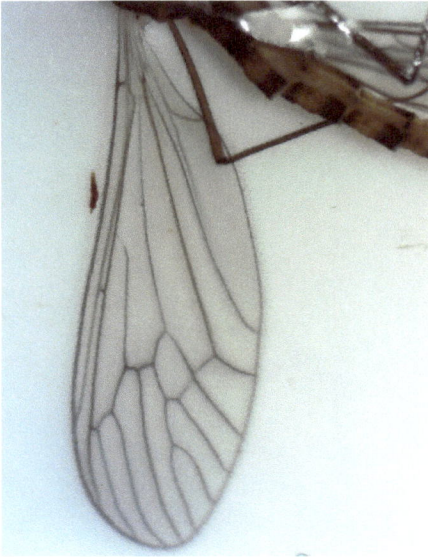

The wings of *Trichocera* spp. are very distinctive and have many veins.

Mycetophila spp. emerged from *P. durus.*

Copromyza equina emerged from *Pleurotus* spp.

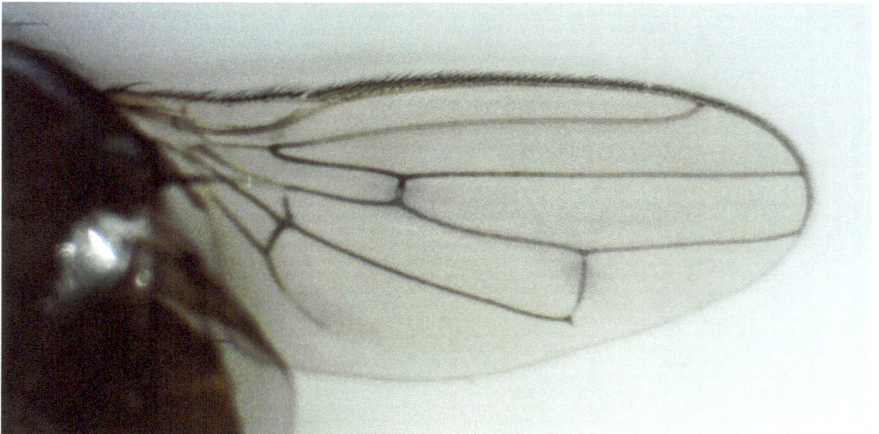

Wing venation of *C. equina.* Wing venation is not always accurate for identifying species as many different species have very similar, if not the same wing venation. Therefore, its best to analyse the entire specimen.

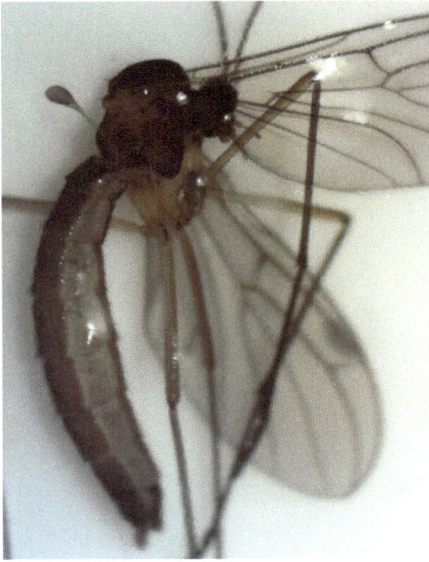

What I found to be amazing was the emergence of several *Bolitophila* spp. individuals from a single small *Collybia* specimen collected five months earlier in October. The larvae had survived the winter and subsequently emerged in February. The ability to survive throughout that time in a stage of dormancy is quite remarkable and I wonder how they can achieve such a feat outside, when there are likely to be several predators lurking above and below ground. *Bolitophila* spp. emerged from *L. nuda, Collybia* spp. and *Clitocybe phyllophila,* this genus can be easily distinguished by the black markings (also called pterostigma) on the wings and general wing patterning although to narrow it down to species, examination of genitalia is required.

Pterostigma visible at the end of the subcostal vein of the wing.

One of the earliest flowers to bloom in the year, if not THE earliest, is the Snowdrop *(Galanthus spp.)*. These delicate white flowers appear just a few inches from the ground, and for me, symbolise the forthcoming spring. Its always a nice flower to spot after months of winter wandering through the grasslands and woods.

A small clump of Snowdrops blooming together. I love the way the flowers face downwards.

I love walking through the fields as the sun begins to set, the skies can really be appreciated when you happen to be in an open space. It sometimes seems like even the birds will take note of the sky and just casually sit on top of the trees or fence posts and relax for a few moments. The lone trees stand, perfectly silhouetted against deep reds and oranges in the sky, small groups of birds will fly past and a Robin or a Song thrush may be singing its way into the night. Those surroundings are special and the more they can be experienced the better.

A perfect sunset illuminating the sky with various colours and exposing endless shapes.

Overall, activity in February within the fields begins to pick up despite several bird species leaving the area, fungi begin to appear, and signs of spring are showing, with a peppering of Snowdrops. Its an interesting time of year to explore in the fields as you can see and feel the transition between seasons.

A Kestrel perched upon a tree silhouetted against the sky during a February evening.

Fields: Winter Summary

In contrast to the garden there are many more birds to see in these fields during winter, so when things become quiet in the garden these fields are the perfect place to go to see wildlife in all of its glory. The mix of trees and food sources for birds attracts the attention of migrating species and so you may be lucky and see some rare species. Going to the fields during winter confirms that life is continuous throughout the year, although places may seem to be quiet, there are many things to see and observe. By observing both the garden and fields I could see that they both harbour very different species communities, of course there is overlap, especially with the smaller passerines, but there's just no way I would find a peregrine or a Little Owl or a Stonechat in my garden and yet just a couple of hundred yards away, they are there. Its a strong reminder that although gardens are extremely important, grasslands and woodlands must also be maintained and cherished. Perhaps this Squirrel is ready to emerge for spring...

Fields: Spring
(March, April, May)

Spring in the fields is a wonderful time. The grass is a little bit thicker and taller, shrubs and plants are beginning to grow again, buds of various trees are emerging, butterflies start to appear and a canvas of numerous shades of green begin to take over. Usually, the weather also starts to become slightly warmer but cold days are not uncommon during this time of year. I tend to wear my coat up until April. Walking in an open grassland can be deceivingly cold when the wind is blowing. By the time its May, a couple of spring and summer migrants have flown in, adding to the many existing sounds that can already be heard.

March

There is a surge of growth during March, the fields and hedgerows look brighter with a light spraying of green as leaves start to emerge from trees and shrubs begin to grow. The horses continue to graze, keeping patches of grassland trim and the odd butterfly appears fluttering about in the sun, or casually resting on some leaves. Warm days will also bring out other insects such as bees and hoverflies. Red-tailed bumblebees and Buff-tailed bumblebees will begin to show themselves after waking from the winter period.

In terms of birds, March probably contains the least species, I imagine many birds are preparing for the breeding season or looking for a mate, or perhaps nest building, but the fields are not devoid of birds. It could also just be me missing species as I've wandered around. One bird species that can arrive in late March is the unassuming Chiffchaff. You're likely to hear it before you see it as its a small olive-green bird that can easily be hidden within foliage. The Chiffchaff is famous for its song which is distinctive. Its a unique sound which contrasts to the chorus of sounds in the fields and is a sign that spring has arrived.

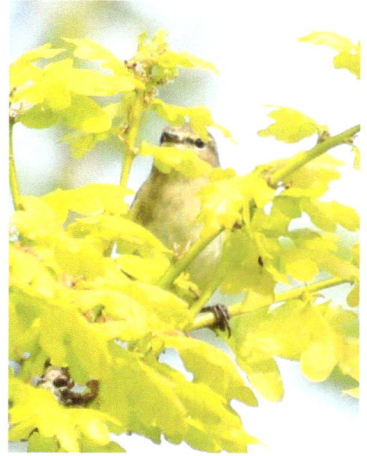

From a tiny bird in the chiffchaff to a large bird in the Red kite. Red kites are busy scouring the area for easy meals, such as carrion, or worms in the grassland. On warm sunny days you can really appreciate the beautiful feathers of the Red Kite and the shapes it makes as it soars in the sky.

The Red Kites' large wingspan on full display as it soars across the grassland creating an array of shapes and angles.

March is the final time for me to see Redwings as they return to their original areas which can be scattered across Europe.

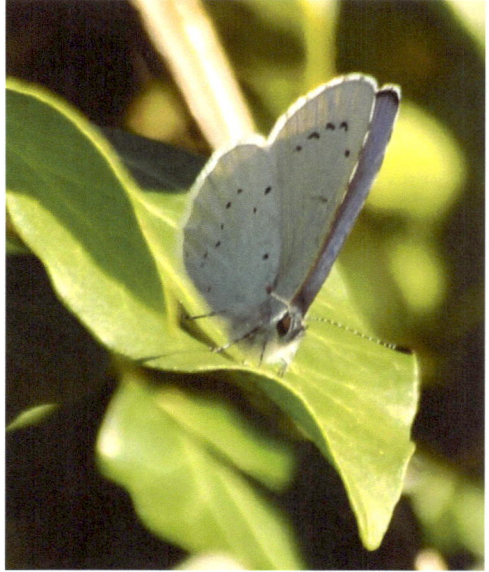

The Holly Blue appears in the fields before it does in our garden and is one of the earliest butterflies to appear in the year. I found this specimen basking on Ivy in mid-March. The light blue on the ventral side of the wings contrasts nicely to the darker, richer blue of the dorsal side of the wings. They can be difficult to spot as they are quite small and can shine a silvery blue in the sunlight. They will often be flying in and around hedgerows.

The Small Tortoiseshell *(Aglais urticae)* is a common butterfly. With regards to its wing patterning, the front edges are like shortened tiger stripes. The undersides of the wings are very dull in comparison to the dorsal side, but this can help them hide in plain sight from predators. Caterpillars of this species feed on Stinging Nettles *(Urtica dioica)*, and there are many stinging nettles to be found within these fields, particularly along hedgerows and where farmland meets the woodland edge.

These two happened to be mating when I found them, the sun was out and it was quite warm, perfect conditions! The smaller individual is the male, as is the case with many butterflies which display sexual dimorphism.

To the last of the butterflies that I see during March, the Comma. Similar to the Holly Blue in terms of time of emergence, this species also appears earlier in the fields than it does in our garden. Interestingly, the Comma seems to be an important species in terms of monitoring the effects of climate change upon insects. It appears this species has been able to alter its foodplant host preference, which has subsequently allowed it to expand its range[41]. Being polyphagous (able to feed on various plants) this species has a choice in which plant to consume. This is extremely beneficial, as climate change causes plants to expand or contract in their ranges, Comma's can adapt and track the movement of suitable host plants.

The Comma will often bask on leaves of trees and shrubs, in both hedgerows and woodland areas.

I have managed to find a couple of fungi during March but overall, it appears as though March isn't a great time to find fungi in these fields or woods. Very few insects also emerged from fungi that I had collected from previous months, which suggests to me that mycophagous insects would avoid being adults during this period due to the lack of fungi available.

Glistening Ink-Cap *(Coprinus micaceous)*

From time to time, I would come across this black cat, perhaps it was trying to find its way back to Kiki (for all those Ghibli lovers, im one of them), its very cautious but doesn't look out of place when I see it, casually wandering through the grass or sitting upon a log on a fallen tree, I wonder whether it feeds on birds or small mammals or both.

The man of the fields, I had seen him park his vehicle on our road an endless number of times, as I was growing up as a kid on my way to school, I always wondered what his role in the fields was. Turns out he feeds the horses and he's done it for many decades, I wonder how the grasslands and farmlands have changed throughout his lifetime? He told me of a story once, of an Adder *(Vipera berus)* biting one of his horses. I have never seen an Adder but perhaps decades ago there were Adders about, I know there are some in Hounslow Heath, its not unfathomable that snakes may have been in these areas. I would like to see an Adder. I helped him a few times to feed the horses, its a bit like going back in time with the horse and cart. The foals are inquisitive, checking what I've got in any bags that I am carrying and they love biting at my coat hood and sleeves, but they're harmless.

The males can be aggressive at times and its quite intimidating when a horse appears agitated, always respect an animals' space! I love the sound of horses running on the grass, that rhythmic sound of horseshoes against the ground. People passing through, feed them apples and carrots. The foals will often hide in the hedgerows and woodland edge but never far away from their mother. Engaging with people that have been around in the area for a long time is invaluable, they have knowledge of aspects we're unable to understand because we haven't had the same experiences or been around at the same time. Communication is key for passing on information. Go and talk to these people! People are nature and make a place just as much as any other organism within it.

I'm sure the decades of carrying out this routine has kept him fit and strong.

The greenery of the fields and woods is beginning to wake up in March, and during warmer days its time to take notice of the insects that are emerging, bees and butterflies will be buzzing and fluttering about. Listen out for the sound of Chiffchaffs because that means its spring! Kestrels, Buzzards and Red kites continue to be majestic and soar in the skies. With grassland being exposed to sunlight for the whole day, changes in vegetation can be rapid and drastic and therefore March is the perfect time to appreciate the transition from winter to spring.

April

Vegetation is a lot thicker and dense by the time its April, more insects continue to appear as days get warmer and more foliage is available for larvae to feed on. Birds are abundant and summer migrants are arriving, colours of newly bloomed flowers are beginning to dot the grasslands, like the making of a Seurat painting. Its a good time to start expanding knowledge about wildflowers as identifying plants and flowers can be a little overwhelming at times, and at this time, the number of flowers isn't at its maximum. Its also the perfect time to start getting used to being in foliage as you'll often find yourself trying to photograph birds that are hiding within shrubbery.

During one of my walks through the fields I once happened to witness an occurrence of kleptoparasitism. This is when an animal steals the food of another animal and is quite a common occurrence, its common in the human world too but its usually referred to as stealing. The incident took place just a few metres away from me and transpired between two Red Kites. One individual happened to grab a piece of carrion from the ground and perched upon one of the pear trees before another Red Kite swooped in towards the perched individual, they locked claws for a second before both flying away. I later realised the object they were fighting over was in fact part of a Magpie. Its often the case that an animal will expend the least amount of energy in order to carry out a task, stealing from another is often a lot easier than endlessly searching for food.

Partial Magpie remains that the Red Kites were competing over.

Two Red Kites displaying kleptoparasatism.

Another thing that struck me during this episode was the size of the Red Kites, they are big birds, the wingspan alone is massive, so I can only imagine how big the largest raptors are. Being surrounded by so many smaller passerines it can be difficult to appreciate the sheer size of bigger birds, especially as its a rare occurrence being able to be close to them.

Red Kites heading into battle against each other.

A common visitor to the U.K. at this time of year, is the Whitethroat *(Corruca communis)*. After arriving from their long-distance migration from the Sahel in Africa, their breeding season begins, and they can be seen carrying long blades of dried grass and small sticks in their beaks. The song of a Whitethroat is very distinctive and along with Blackcaps and Chiffchaffs, they make the sound of spring and summer in these fields. They will commonly feed on insects as well as berries when they become available. Whitethroats are common in these fields and they always arrive in good numbers.

Another bird that arrives in these fields during April is the Blackcap. Blackcaps in these fields are likely to be migrants as they tend to stay for the spring and summer before vanishing from these fields, perhaps they migrate to Osterley Park or other local places for the winter. The song of the Blackcap is very melodic and full of life, different to the raspy sounds of the Whitethroat. A shy bird, the Blackcap often hides within the hedgerows and shrubs making it extremely difficult to photograph. If you want to photograph Blackcaps in these woods then you'll have to be prepared to find yourself in amongst a lot of foliage as well as having sharp ears and eyes. They seem to avoid spending time in the grassland and cling to the hedgerows and woods, where they can pick off unsuspecting insects. Blackthorns and Hawthorns are their favourite hideouts.

Next up is the Linnet *(Linara cannabina)*, this pretty little bird is a species that has been struggling, its declined fairly rapidly over the last few decades across various areas and continues to do so[42], so when I realised these small slender birds were Linnets I was quite surprised to find them hanging around in a group feeding on seed heads. They can be variable in appearance depending on the time of year, age as well as their sex. Males are brightly coloured, with a rosy tuft on their head as well as a red breast, the females lack these red features. They remained in these grasslands for a couple of weeks before heading off to another spot. I wonder if I will see them again.

A pair of Linnets basking in the sun of the grasslands.

Chiffchaffs continue to flit about in the trees, dashing in and out, sometimes perching on higher parts of the trees, often around the Elms and young Oaks, they seem to prefer the hedgerows.

Butterflies! One of my favourite organisms, more butterflies begin to appear during April. The increase in vegetation and rising temperatures bring out overwintering Peacocks, some of the 'Whites' begin to appear along with Speckled Woods, basking in the sunny glades of the woodlands. Hedgerows are a great place for finding butterflies. Hedgerows often contain shrubs and smaller to medium sized trees which harbour an abundance of nectar rich flowers, a prime example being Hawthorns and Blackthorns. Blackthorns by this time are abundant with flowers, they are easy to tell apart from Hawthorns as they flower before they leaf whereas Hawthorns flower after leaf growth. The flowers are also slightly different although both are a creamy white. Its important to remember to look at every height of the hedgerow and not just focus on a particular section because butterflies can be found across all heights, from the ground to above the tree canopy, some species will even remain in the canopy a majority of the time, such as the previously mentioned White-Letter Hairstreak. The White butterflies are among the easiest to spot as they are large and often fly along hedgerows. Their flight patterns are erratic, and I would describe their flight as a looping zigzag.

A butterfly that is often associated with sunny spring days is the Orange-Tip *(Anthocaris cardamines)*. I really like the colours and wing patterning of this species, the underside of the wings are patterned with green markings, helping them to blend into the foliage when they are basking. I find this species flying alongside hedgerows most of the time, flying to Blackthorns and Hawthorns and visiting wildflowers. The males are easily recognisable with orange tips on their forewings whereas the females lack any orange pigmentation. I'm still searching for that clear, close-up photo!

Green-Veined Whites appear a lot earlier in the fields than they do within our garden. This species can be found across all habitats within these fields. Once landed on a chosen leaf or flower they can remain still for quite a while, so I always enjoy photographing this butterfly, where I can really appreciate its beauty and markings.

Its always nice to see a butterfly fluttering in the brightness of the sun.

Farmland is also a good place for some butterflies, and they can be drawn to the flowers of various crops. I will often see Peacock butterflies in high numbers flying amongst crops in farmland. Within the woodlands a species that begins to appear is the Speckled wood, its pigmentation can range from orange to a dark brown, dotted with creamy eyespots it can be extremely difficult to spot when still, hidden amongst dry foliage and dead leaves. Open glades within forest or woodland are a favourite place for this species as they fiercely defend their sunny territories. Males will guard their territory by chasing away other butterflies before returning to their basking spot[43]. If you do happen to disturb a Speckled Wood it can be a good idea to stop moving for a short period as the butterfly is likely to return to its original spot.

Speckled Wood displaying its distinctive wings whilst basking in the heat of the sun.

The blooming of wildflowers can bring out Hoverflies such as this male *Syrphus ribesii*. As adults, they'll be fulfilling their role as pollinators whilst their larvae will be munching away on aphids. Its a good ally of plants!

The Seven-Spot Ladybird *(C. septempunctata)* is another friend of many plants, as their larvae feed on various species of aphids. The field is host to many of these Ladybirds during this month and can be found basking in the sun on the growing leaves of Hogweed. At this time of year many Ladybirds will be mating and reproducing, in time for the massive increase in plant growth that occurs over the summer, making the most of the increase in aphid abundance.

The Large Red Damselfly also appears much earlier in the fields than it does in our garden. This one happened to claim a nice sunny spot. I distinctly remember finding this Damselfly because I had been thinking to myself, "its about this time that they emerge!" I hadn't seen one for months and I remember specifically going outside to the fields just to find one. When I did actually find it, I thought that some species can be really predictable in their emergence patterns.

Bee flies will be hovering from one flower to the next using its long proboscis to reach the nectar it craves.

A Bee fly feeding from a Red Dead-Nettle *(Lamium purpureum)*

As I walk through the fields and look at the Horses they're often surrounded by several birds, all feeding away. Its always great to see a range of species sharing a space together, seemingly unfazed by each other.

A group of Starlings feeding alongside one of the many horses found in these fields.

The number of passerines continue to increase as spring and summer migrants begin to enter these fields and the plants continue to branch out and grow at a rapid pace. Early emerging insects are making the most of the nectar sources that are available as wildflowers bloom, and the fluttering of butterflies starts to become a common sight, whether you're walking through grassland, alongside hedgerows, woodland edges or the woodlands. I must admit that during all my walks and wanderings during April, I rarely find any fungi, although it is weather dependent to an extent, but on the whole it seems April isn't the best month to start fungal forays, but you never know what you'll find and so it is important to continue to look for things, great qualities for an ecologist are patience and persistence! In spite of the lack of fungi, there are more than enough organisms to focus on in these fields and woods to make April a fantastic month to be out and about!

A Song Thrush keeping an eye out for intruders, quietly going about its business.

May

Entering the last month of spring, May follows the pattern of intense growth, longer days and increasing temperatures. Wildflowers carpet the grassland with a bright sunny yellow. My almost non-existent sense of smell stops me from enjoying the various floral scents of these areas but I'm sure they're lovely! The foals in the fields begin to vanish behind tall Hogweeds and whilst the ground is painted with the colour of wildflowers, there is a white haze at head level from the white umbellifers of Hogweed. As they all move together with the light breeze on warmer days, its really quite beautiful to watch.

Now's a good time to focus your attention upon the variety of flowers and plants that are in these areas. Its impossible to escape the tall plants and thick grasses as they begin to envelope you. Paths through the grassland are kept somewhat flat by the horses as well as people (like me) that walk through them, but its also great fun to bundle through the unkempt areas, just be mindful that some birds will use the tall grasses and shrubs to hide in or may even be nesting in. Whitethroats are often perched quite low in shrubs. Some of the wildflowers that are in bloom at this time include Birds foot trefoil *(Lotus corniculatus)* Dandelions, Hogweed *(Heracleum sphondylium)*, Ribwort Plantain *(Plantago lanceolata)*, Knapweed *(Centaurea* spp.*)*, Ragwort *(Jacobaea vulgaris)*, White Clover *(Trifolium repens)*, Creeping Buttercup *(Ranunculus repens)* and Mugwort *(Artemisia vulgaris)*. Each of these plants are beautiful in their own way but more importantly they are important foodplants for many insects and may also be consumed by birds. If I had to pick a favourite flower out of this group it would have to be Knapweed or Ribwort Plantain, the colour and shape of Knapweed is pretty, but the shape and structure of Ribwort Plantain is so distinctive. It should be recognised that constant grazing in patches by the horses aids the growth of wildflowers as it stops tall grasses from outcompeting them for sunlight and nutrients.

I find botany extremely difficult, and I have a lot of admiration for people that are able to identify a whole range of plants when so many look so similar. What I can identify is that the grasslands contain a diverse mix of plants and wildflowers and is definitely a great place to start polishing those botany skills.

Butterfly diversity increases in the grasslands and woodland edges during May, additions include the Common Blue *(Polyammatus icarus)*, Meadow Brown and Red Admiral whereas the Brimstones begin to leave the area.

Brimstone nectaring from the wildflower Common Vetch *(Vicia sativa).*

This butterfly can easily be mistaken for a leaf with its green/yellow appearance.

Males of the Common Blue have various shades of blue on the dorsal side whereas the females have browner wings, the underwings of both sexes are dotted with spots and lines. Males of this species are territorial and can be seen patrolling their chosen area. Similar to Speckled woods, Common blues often return to a favoured spot in grasslands.

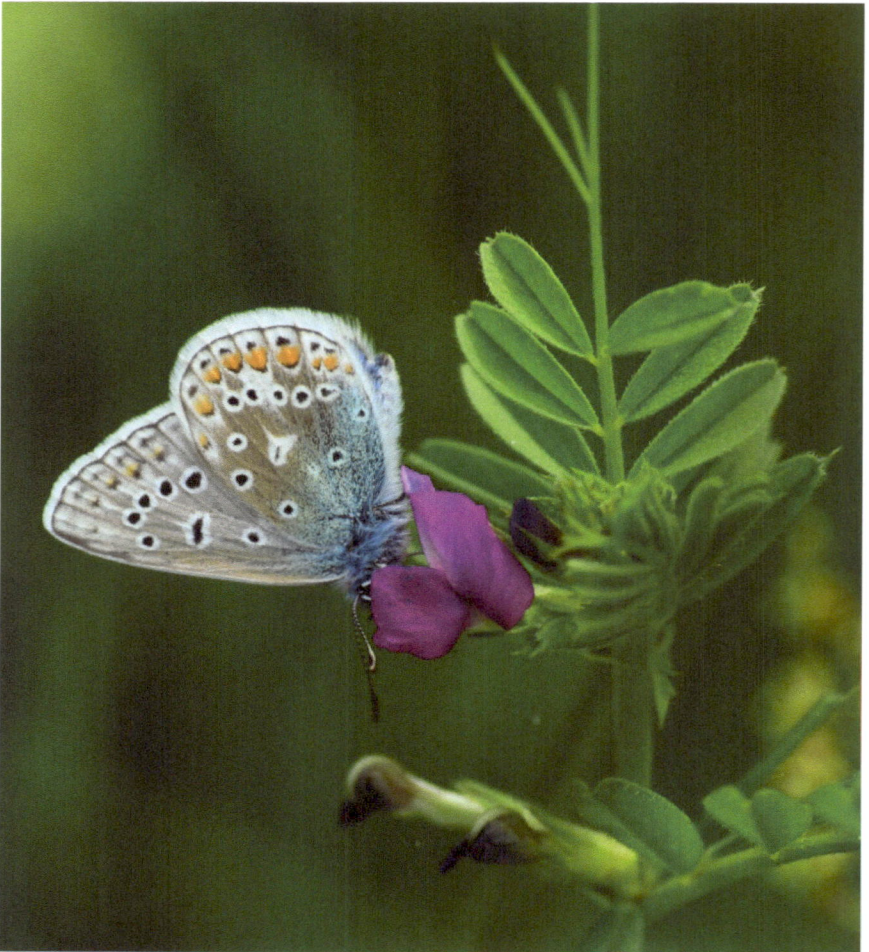

A Common Blue feeding upon Common Vetch.

I often see Common blues resting on the tops of Ribwort Plantain flower heads. In this area, Common blues are not hugely abundant in comparison to many other butterfly species.

Another very common and abundant species is the Meadow Brown. This species seems to thrive in grasslands as they feed on the nectar of wildflowers. A medium sized butterfly they shine a lovely orange in the sun with a number of wing variations in terms of eye spots. Males will chase after the females and bask in the sunlight.

Meadow Brown *(M. jurtina)* displaying its eye spot.

Red Admirals increase in numbers as they migrate to the U.K. from various countries in Europe and Africa and they can be seen flying along woodland edges and the sunny glades of the woods. There is one spot in the woods that remains sunny throughout the day, and I always end up seeing Red Admirals there, basking on the leaves of trees or a pair chasing each other. Butterflies numbers are not at their peak just yet but there is a steady increase throughout the month of May.

The last insect I'll mention for this month is St. Marks Fly *(Bibo marci)*. This species is known to appear around the end of April (St Mark's Day is the 25th), so its no surprise to see them in May. I like the appearance of this fly, all black, it looks like it could be the Neo of the insect world. I tend to see them clinging onto stems and blades of grass along woodland edges, but they can be found almost anywhere. They are important pollinators of various flowers and can be extremely abundant, so I imagine they are important food sources for a number of birds.

A male St. Marks Fly resting on a blade of grass, its large eyes clearly visible.

The thickness of vegetation around hedgerows makes it a perfect place for Foxes. By May, the grass is quite tall, and Foxes can be seen wandering through the grassland, perhaps looking for prey to ambush.

Tall grass concealing the Fox from the sight of potential prey.

The Fox was perhaps looking for a pheasant, like this one I happened to come across. Usually, Pheasants are creeping up on me but this time roles were reversed, I was able to get close to this individual without it flying away. It was a little strange to see this large bird so well concealed in the grass. I have become accustomed to hearing it screeching loudly as it flies away. Being so close to it I was able to admire its plumage. The feathers of Pheasants are amongst the most beautiful of all.

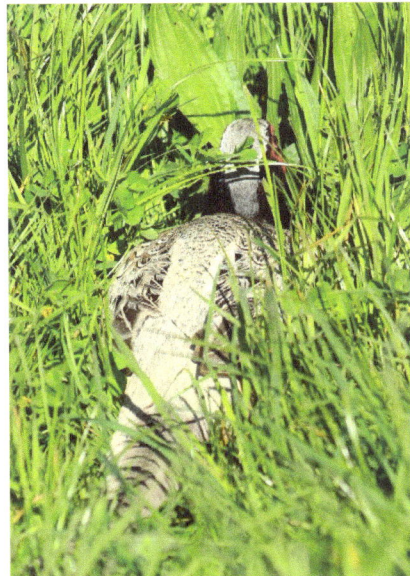

The way the grasslands change from flat open lands to overgrown dense areas of grass and shrubs changes the feel of the area. I for one enjoy the wild feeling of the overgrown grass and tall Hogweeds, having to push through the grasses and forging my own paths through areas whilst at the same time finding numerous numbers of species, although you do have to take care not to scare any of the horses, I don't fancy being kicked by a horse.

Umbellifers cover the grasslands providing shelter/food for many organisms.

May is typically the last time I see Linnets in these fields. They can be difficult to spot, especially when in amongst the flowers as they feed on various insects, seeds and flower heads.

A Linnet feeding amongst many wildflowers in the grassland. When standing just a few metres away it can be difficult to spot these birds.

Whitethroats continue to be busy during May, building nests, breeding and feeding their young all happens around this time. Wrens do the same as they scour the area for caterpillars to feed their chicks.

A Wren picking off caterpillars from surrounding plants.

Male and female House Sparrows can be seen carrying out their courtship behaviours as the male jumps and wags its tailfeathers to attract the female.

Swifts arrive in the fields and they soar the skies as well as slaloming around the tree canopies at break-neck speed. They'll be busy picking insects from the air. I wonder how much food is up there. Its easy to forget that there's a lot of life in areas above us and below us that we are unable to see but there is actually a mind-boggling amount of activity occurring.

As I walk back home from afternoon or evening walks from the field I always keep a lookout for a Kestrel, you never know when its serious face will pop up. Sure enough I'll see it keeping a look out over the fields in the tops of the trees. Sometimes nicely hidden amongst the leaves or standing exposed on a fencepost or hovering as silhouettes during sunsets. Either way, its a perfect way to end a walk.

After a barren few months in terms of fungi, fungi begin to reappear, perhaps ready to fruit after absorbing sufficient nutrients and resources from organic matter and precipitation along with increased temperatures, the perfect cocktail of conditions to initiate fungal fruiting[44]. Species that I usually see around this time include the Jelly Ear Fungus *(Auricularia auricula-judae)*, *Psathyrella* spp. and St. George's Mushroom *(Calocybe gambosa)*.

The Jelly Ear Fungus is an odd fungus. It has a rubbery texture and looks like an ear protruding from the branches and trunks of dead trees. Regarded as edible, they are meant to be good for absorbing flavours and can be used in soups. I've not tried them yet but maybe one day! Despite their strange jelly-like texture they are not free from insect attack, and I have been able to rear *Bradysia* spp. from this fungus. The fruiting bodies can be dried and stored for a very long time. Soaking them in water will allow them to revert to their original squishy texture.

Its been suggested that the Jelly Ear Fungus has responded to climate change by increasing the number of hosts it can utilise[45]. If this is the case then it shows great adaptability in a relatively short time and perhaps other wood-decomposing fungi are capable of doing the same. With the high amount of dead wood in the woodland, this fungus is easy to find.

Whilst trying to rear an insect from a *A. auricula-judae* specimen, I saw that the fungus was breaking down and turning into liquid, as so many fungi do over time. I decided to collect the liquid as it decomposed and look at it under the microscope. I was able to find that there was another community of organisms within this liquid which included a range of protists as well as nematodes. Nematodes are also commonly referred to as Roundworms, and they are utilised by many plant enthusiasts as they can act as pest control. They are parasitic worms which infect a range of organisms which usually like to munch their way through various plants. Nematodes were likely to be the cause of the death of the maggots that were within the fungus I had collected. This was interesting to me as I have always thought of nematodes being soil organisms, and the fungal specimen I had collected was a good few feet above the ground. How did the nematodes get up there? I found being able to witness the fast movements and bustling of a range of organisms within a drop of liquid quite amazing.

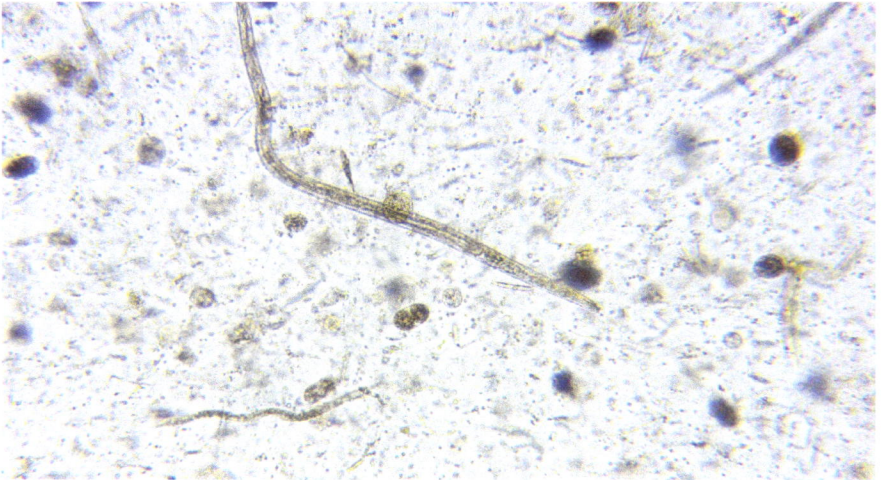

Nematodes move in a wriggling (sinusoidal) motion, smaller globular shapes are protists which were whizzing around.

St. George's Mushroom, is typically found during spring and can be visible as early as March. In the fields I have only ever managed to find it during May. A large mushroom, I have managed to rear over 100 insects from a single fruiting body consisting of 9 insect species, including a couple of parasitoids, this fungus is a great example of how important fungal fruiting bodies are to a number of insect species. It can be assumed that the insects that emerge from fungi are likely to make up a fair share of the diets of many birds and their chicks, especially during this time when many birds are likely to be breeding.

The specimens I found were amongst the Ash trees which I found interesting as I had previously struggled to find fungi amongst these trees. Starting off as a clean, creamy white fungus as it matures it appears to take on a pink or peachy colour, it also has quite a strong odour which can help with identification. The spore print of this fungus is white.

A very wet St. George's Mushroom located within grasses along the woodland edge.

This *Psathyrella* spp. was found in a grassy patch within the woodland but its likely to have been decomposing dead wood from beneath the ground as this species is typically saprobic. The whitish stem breaks easily. The spore print for this species is brown which is common of *Psathyrella* species.

Fungus gnats that emerge during May include *Allodia* spp., *Mycetophila fungorum* and *Pseudexechia* spp. Their wing patterning all being distinctive and help identify the genus, but it gets difficult trying to identify many fungus gnats to exact species. As mentioned previously examination of male genitalia is required. Many Mycetophilids can go from an egg to adult within 10 days as they develop extremely rapidly, its likely that increased temperature decreases the amount of time it takes for these insects to grow into adults[46].

A male *Pseudexechia* specimen, various parts of the body can be used to identify a species, including the wing venation, genitalia, leg structure, number of setae/bristles/hairs on legs, number of antennal segments, colour, patterning of tergites, feeding apparatus, size of specimen, timing of emergence of specimen, and in some cases the substrate the specimen used to feed from, as many organisms can be monophagous (only feed on a specific substrate).

The fields have completely changed from the winter months by the time its May. Tall grass covers much of the grassland, with several animals taking advantage of the extra cover. You can hear birds chirping in the undergrowth and the rustling of small mammals running through the mini jungle of various grasses and shrubs. Flowers are everywhere and this attracts various birds and insects. The fields are literally buzzing with life as you become encompassed by a natural symphony of sounds. The glades of the woodland become warmer and brighter, and butterflies continue to patrol these areas. Many of the woodland paths have become overgrown and it can be difficult to manoeuvre through the thick vegetation which also happens to be made up of thorny and prickly plants such as Hawthorns, Stinging nettles and bramble. I don't mind the battles through vegetation, I always end up with scrapes and cuts trundling through these areas but its all part of exploring!

Run! Explore! Be like this Fox!

Fields: Spring Summary

Spring is a great time of year to visit the fields, its not too hot and many plants haven't grown huge until mid to late May, so walking through the area isn't too difficult or taxing. The wildflowers add an abundance of colour, and you can easily forget that your right next to the M4. The trees which are full of foliage by May, act as a sound barrier and shields the fields and woods from the sounds of cars and lorries. Spring is a perfect time for birdwatching and trying to hone bird identification skills, learning the calls of different species becomes easier with regular walks through these areas. Listen out for the Whitethroats, Chiffchaffs and Song Thrushes! Keep binoculars close by as the Linnets may visit again for a short period.

The importance of monitoring areas like these cannot be underestimated, much of the citizen science that is collected by various charities and organisations rely on the efforts of amateur naturalists. Being able to spot species can help map out the ranges of various species and give an idea of how well a species is doing in terms of distribution and abundance. As spring is a vital month for many organisms its extremely important to take note of what is happening in our surroundings. With the apparent effects of climate change and the fact that spring is a time when many species are emerging, migrating and emigrating, there are many things to record and take note of. Events that should be monitored closely during spring are insect emergence times, bud burst of trees and earliest arrival of spring and summer migrants. Its also a good time for noting when winter migrants begin to leave. Spring will get you prepared for the summer months as species diversity continues to increase. By the time its the end of spring, I always like to reflect on the previous few months just so I can take note of the changes that have occurred and make sense of how quickly these areas can transform.

Fields: Summer
(June, July, August)

Summer is a time for spending many hours outdoors from morning well into the night. Activity is at its peak, just like in our gardens, the grasslands, hedgerows and woodlands are brimming with life, from below the ground to the tops of the trees and into the sky, organisms occupy each of these spaces. An important aspect to consider during summer, is the fact that its a busy time in terms of people going to parks and natural areas, people are quick to flock to the parks and Osterley Park is no exception, on a warm sunny day there are many people relaxing in the sun. As beautiful as Osterley Park is, I'll stick to the quiet fields. They remain quiet all year round, the odd person walking their dog or someone going for a stroll can be seen but most of the time its a place where the area is left to its nature filled brilliant best. Who knows how long the serenity of this area will last, and who knows whether this pocket of grassland and woodland will be able thrive for many more years? Osterley Park is a great place to go for birdwatching and I do recommend visiting there throughout the year, especially around the lake area as many ducks and geese may flock there, but all too often the business of the area can make it difficult to spot a lot of species. Bird species in the fields is at its maximum diversity over the summer, the abundance of insects and caterpillars makes the fields a prosperous place for birds with chicks. The summer is still capable of throwing in the odd surprise too so its best to stay as alert as ever!

June

Temperatures are consistently quite high by the time it gets to June and the odd heatwave in recent times have caused temperatures to soar well into the 30's, so, for me, this means wearing a big sun hat and spending as much time in the shade as possible, as well as always keeping my trusty bottle of water with me. Wildflowers continue to bloom, and sightings of insects continues to increase. Lepidoptera continue to increase in terms of abundance and diversity and specific species can be seen in specific habitats. June is a great month for butterflies, they are everywhere. Walking through the grassland, its impossible not to disturb the Meadow Browns that are resting upon the grasses or wildflowers. There isn't any real change in terms of bird diversity, although many more chicks of various species can be heard during this time including Robins, Tits and Whitethroats.

Butterfly species that appear during this month include the Large Skipper *(Ochlodes sylvanus)*, Small Skipper *(Thymelicus sylvestris)*, Essex Skipper *(Thymelicus lineola)*, Ringlet *(Aphantopus hyperantus)*, Brown Argus *(Aricia gestis)*, Painted Lady *(Vanessa cardui)*, Marbled White *(Melanargia galathea)*, Small Heath *(Coenonympha pamphilus)*, White-Letter Hairstreak, Purple Hairstreak *(Neozephyrus quercus)* and Small Copper *(Lycaena phlaeas)*.

Many caterpillars may be seen throughout the summer, here was a batch of Peacock caterpillars I found chomping away on Stinging nettles. They appear to be well defended with their spines which may allow them to fend off predators.

The Painted Lady is famous for its long-distance migrations from various parts of the Middle east, Asia and Africa, all the way to the U.K. which is amazing considering their size, and the weather conditions they are likely to face on such a long journey.

Painted Lady resting on Bramble with unripe berries beside it.

Large and angular in shape, these elegant butterflies are always nice to see, I generally see them feeding from a range of wildflowers, especially Bramble. Its easy to think that butterflies are fragile, but they are extremely tough and resilient, you would have to be to make that journey! The wing patterns are made up of scales which are shed over time or fall off due to collisions or impacts. The membrane that makes up the wing itself is extremely flexible, if you've ever tried to hold a butterfly in your hand as a kid you'll will know that they can fly out of the smallest gaps, although I don't recommend doing that now. Strong flyers, Painted Lady's can be disturbed easily and will fly away with speed, they can be seen racing across the grassland or along hedgerows.

The Marbled White is a beautiful butterfly with intricate black and white wing patterns, I have only ever seen a handful of these butterflies within these fields, always in grassland. Frequenting an area of Knapweeds and Thistles, they make use of the abundance of wildflowers.

The Ringlet first appears during June, it can be seen flying in a bobbling fashion, predominantly along woodland edges. From a distance it can be confused with the Meadow Brown, but the wing spotting is different, and Ringlets are typically brown all over. The name Ringlet comes from the creamy white rings that border the spots on their wings. Ringlets and Meadow Browns are both active during the colder, cloudier, and even slightly rainy days and are the most likely butterfly species to be seen on such days.

A perfect Ringlet with a slight hint of purple to its wings.

The Small Heath is a medium sized butterfly which on first glance looks quite similar to a Meadow Brown but inspection of the wing spotting makes for easy identification. These butterflies have unfortunately declined quite rapidly within the last few decades although they are still widespread. Much like the Marbled White, I have only ever found a handful of individuals in the fields. I have found this species amongst short grasses but also tall grasses of which they use as foodplants.

Onto the smaller butterflies, Skippers are small yellow butterflies which are located mainly along hedgerows and woodland edges, with few being found within the grassland and none in the woodland. They're typically found basking in the sun or feeding on flowers such as Knapweeds and Ribwort Plantains. Three Skippers found in these fields are the Large Skipper, Small Skipper and Essex Skipper. Skippers are distinctive in the way their wings are positioned when resting but narrowing down the Skippers to species level can be a little difficult, especially when trying to determine Small Skippers from Essex Skippers, where the tips of the antennae need to be examined, being small butterflies, this can be hard to do! Especially as they tend to fly away when you approach them. Size differences between species are not drastic, male Large Skippers have a chequered pattern to their wings which aids identification along with an angled mid-line on the forewing. Often males will be seen chasing the plainer females.

Male Large Skipper with clear markings on its wings.

Small Skippers and Essex Skippers are often found around the same habitat as Large Skippers, exhibiting the same behaviours. Subtle differences between Small Skippers and Essex Skippers are in the antennae, Small Skippers have yellow tips to their antennae whereas Essex Skippers have black tips to theirs. The mid-line on Essex Skippers wings run along the same angle as their wing edge, whereas Small Skippers mid-line is similar to a Large Skippers'. Essex Skippers also tend to appear earlier in the year in comparison to Small Skippers.

Left:- Small Skipper with yellow tipped antennae. Right:- Essex Skipper with black tipped antennae.

Another habitat that is often overlooked is the canopy of trees. This is where the Hairstreaks dominate. Staying clear from all the hustle and bustle of lower areas. White-Letter Hairstreaks and Purple Hairstreaks are both visible by the time it gets to June. Both species are host specific, with Elm being the preferred host for White-Letter Hairstreaks and Oak for Purple Hairstreaks. The best chance of spotting these species is during clear sunny days, although time of day does make a difference. White-Letter Hairstreaks appear to be most active during mornings, up until early afternoon whereas Purple Hairstreaks tend to be highly active during the late afternoon to early evening, I have seen many flying around as late as 7pm. White-Letter Hairstreaks are often basking on the tops of Elms with their wings folded upwards, I have never seen the top side of their wings, the Elm suckers in these fields are not very tall and so there is a higher chance of seeing an individual in comparison to Purple Hairstreaks, but I have seen many White-Letter Hairstreaks flying around the tops of Ash trees and young oaks too. Purple Hairstreaks look somewhat silvery in the sunlight as they float around the tops of mature Oak trees, the underside of their wings is silver whereas the dorsal side is purple. You may be lucky and find them coming down to ground level where they will bask in the sun for short periods before flying back up towards the canopy.

A Purple Hairstreak resting upon an Oak Leaf during a hot summers day.

The Small Copper is a lovely little butterfly, bold and bright, its never in these fields in very high numbers but its always nice to spot one. They'll often be found close to the ground, feeding on wildflowers in grasslands and woodland edges. The males of Small Coppers are similar to male Common Blues and Speckled Woods in that they are territorial and are prone to chasing off intruders that enter their space.

The smallest butterfly in these fields is the Brown Argus. Always flying around the tops of grasses, they can be difficult to spot due to their size and erratic flight. They also appear quite silvery in the sunlight. Confusingly, this butterfly is technically a member of the 'Blues' family of butterflies. It is somewhat similar to Common Blues but its size and wing spotting can differentiate the two species. On the dorsal side of the wings a small dot or line can be seen in the middle of the wing with orange dots on the wing edges.

The first real ecological project that I undertook looked at the diversity and abundance of butterflies within these fields and woodlands. Three months of constant surveying left me with results displaying the preferences for habitats of several butterfly species. I also looked at wing spotting of Meadow Browns and Ringlets which are both extremely variable.

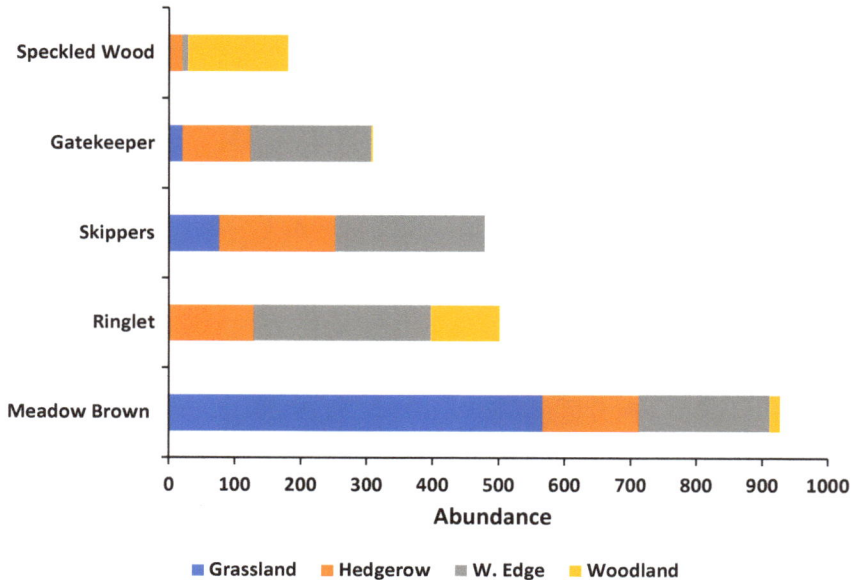

Grassland ■ **Hedgerow** ■ **W. Edge** ■ **Woodland**

This graph indicates the abundance of butterflies counted in each habitat between late June 2019 – August 2019. It should be noted that Skippers includes all three species (Large, Small and Essex).

The fact that different species seemed to prefer one type of habitat over the other signifies the importance of maintaining a range of habitats. In those few months of sampling, I was able to identify 25 species, nearly 50% of all species found in the U.K. These small pockets of grassland and woodland are so important for maintaining these species, especially as connectivity of suitable areas may be limited. The caterpillars of Lepidoptera are also likely to host a range of predators and are important for their survival, especially birds.

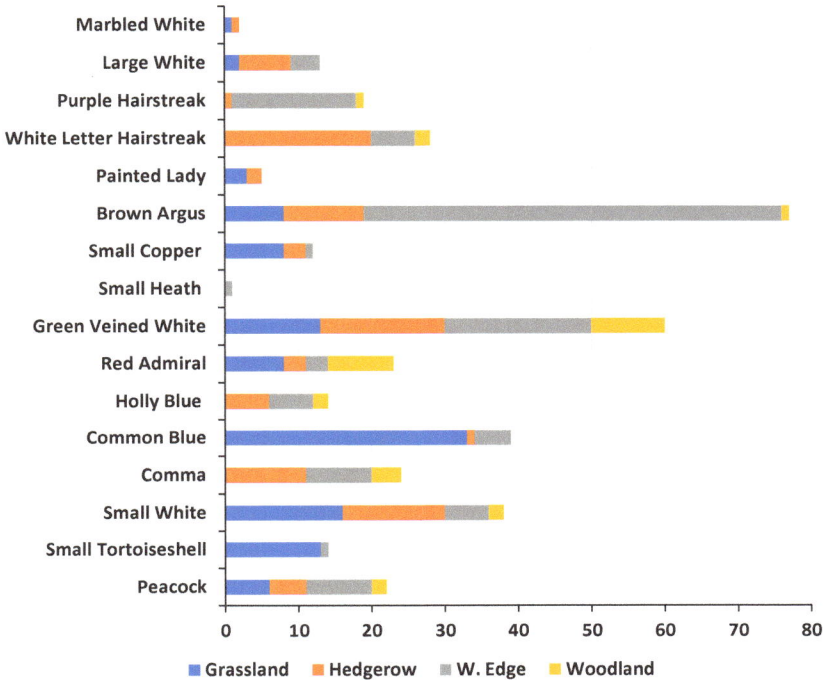

| Species | Grassland | Hedgerow | W. Edge | Woodland |

These were species that were found in low numbers but still display important information about habitat preferences.

Sticking with Lepidoptera, during June, day flying moths also become more common in the grasslands. These species include Burnet Companion *(Euclidia glyphica)*, Cinnabar, Silver-Y and Yarrow Plume *(Gillmeria pallidactyla)*. Burnet Companion is a pretty moth, with yellow underwings and a range of brown-orangey shades on the forewings. I often find this moth close to the ground clinging onto grasses. With so many butterflies around its a nice change to see a day flying moth.

Cinnabars have the luxury of being unpalatable to many predators, their unpalatability displayed through their bright red markings. Its a great contrast to the lush green environment of the grasses and the various colours of wildflowers that surround them. As there are a number of Ragworts available they are quick to lay eggs on their host plant.

The Silver-Y moth is extremely distinctive due to its wing patterning; it flies by day and also at night and I often find it feeding on nectar from a range of wildflowers. The Yarrow Plume is a plume moth which has a light orange colouration. It becomes active during the evening where it can be found amongst swards of short grasses and Yarrow, as the name suggests. I love the physical structure of this moth, its incredibly distinctive.

June is a time when Dragonflies begin to move into the grasslands to pick off unsuspecting insects. I was surprised with how many Dragonflies can be found in grasslands as I had always originally associated them with water bodies. The Emperor Dragonfly *(Anax imperator)* is a beautiful species, with a bright green and blue exoskeleton and a large wingspan, its one of the biggest and bulkiest Dragonflies found in the U.K. This species reacts to movement extremely quickly and so my movements in trying to get close made this species a difficult one to photograph. I see them around the tall grasses and umbellifers, but they will also shoot off into the canopies of smaller trees and hedgerows in search of prey.

An awesome predator, with its wings outstretched, the Emperor Dragonfly. Its large eyes help to spot potential prey and powerful wing muscles allow the Dragonfly to fly at speed in any direction.

The Black-Tailed Skimmer *(Orthetrum cancellatum)* is not as large as the Emperor Dragonfly but its just as captivating.

Females are yellow with black stripes running across the length of their body.

Males are blue with black tips to their abdomen, once perched, individuals can remain there for quite a while which helps with capturing good clear photographs. The black lines running along the sides of the females can help with identification. The abundance and increase of insects in the grasslands during the summer makes these areas perfect hunting grounds for Dragonflies. It should be remembered that the larvae of dragonflies can spend years as an aquatic nymph and so seeing an adult is always uplifting. Prey items of this species consist of a range of insects including butterflies, moths and grasshoppers and so these grasslands are a perfect area for finding these stunning predatory insects.

Male Black-Tailed Skimmer

Female Black-Tailed Skimmer

Soldier Beetles will be found on plants such as bramble and grasses and will feed on a range of soft bodied invertebrates including aphids. An ally of plants, these beetles are predatory during both immature and adult stages. Their abdomen extends beyond their wings and the pronotum contains a black triangular mark which can aid identification.

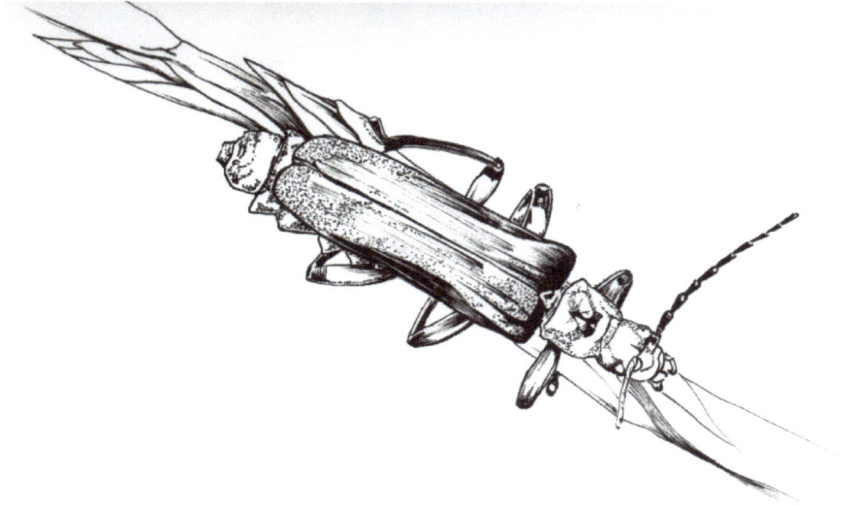

Pen drawing of a Soldier Beetle walking along a blade of grass.

The Dock Bug (*Coreus marginatus*) is a member of the order Hemiptera. Similar in shape to other Shieldbugs it has two small projections between its antennae which are unique to this species. This species is known to feed on a range of berries as well as foliage of plants. The high number of brambles is likely to provide a good source of food for this species, alongside the odd dock that is found in the grasslands.

The Two-Banded Wasp Hoverfly *(Chrysotoxum bicinctum)* is another example of a hoverfly using mimicry to protect itself from predators. The striking black and yellow colours resemble that of a Wasp and so this species tends to be avoided. Despite its Wasp-like appearance they are in fact harmless and will fly from flower to flower feeding on nectar as well as playing an important role in pollination.

Hoverflies are always worth a closer inspection!

This Crab Spider *(Xysticus cristatus)* was found climbing the stem of a plant perhaps looking for a suitable place to lie in wait to ambush an insect unawares. These spiders can prey upon insect species that are much larger than itself such as butterflies, moths, bees, and wasps.

Much of the bird activity is the same as it was in May, you can hear and see lots of birds and the odd chick appears from the shrubs and hedgerows. No doubt the birds are continuing to take advantage of all the insects and caterpillars that are available to them. The intense heat may also cause many birds to remain hidden in the safety of the shade too. It may be the last time to see and hear the Chiffchaffs in this area before they move on to other areas. Red Kites, Kestrels and Buzzards continue to roam above.

For this individual it appears that the Starlings didn't take too kindly to the Buzzards' presence. I agree with the Buzzards decision to avoid this mob.

Dusk sets the scene for the emergence of bats. Two species that are common in these fields and woodlands are the Common Pipistrelle and Soprano Pipistrelle. Often flying at head height following paths and channels created by the tall grasses and shrubs, these bats can be seen quite clearly, especially during cloudy nights when their black silhouettes become more prominent. They will be picking off insects, spiders and moths that are active during this time. I have had the experience of having a bat flying into my face so be careful!

A bat detector can help narrow down the location of bats but its not completely necessary, alertness, a basic knowledge of bat behaviour and emergence times and good eyes will do!

Fungi continue to appear during June and so do the fungus gnats that rely on them. Old and rotten *C. gambosa* are at their end and have turned a dull yellowish-brown colour. *Rusulla* species may appear at this time as well as the ectomycorrhizal *Laccaria* spp. By forming symbioses with host plants, the summer can be a productive time for such species as their host plants can increase their photosynthetic activity, thus providing more nutrients for the fungal mycelium, which in turn initiates fruiting body formation, although it should be highlighted that sufficient nutrients for fruiting body production may have been acquired from previous months or even years[47].

Small group of *Laccaria* spp. mushrooms.

Laccaria spp. are interesting as they can appear in different colours depending on the conditions of the environment, wet specimens may appear extremely orange whereas once they have lost their moisture they become a lighter beige or brown colour. Fungi that change colour due to loss or absorption of moisture are described as being hygrophanous.

Here is a Horse Mushroom *(Agaricus arvensis)* that I happened to come across during one of my many walks across the grassland in June. Its one of the few wild mushrooms that I have eaten. If you are going to forage on wild fungi be sure to soak the fungi in water multiple times as they can be full of insect larvae and other invertebrates, the water will flush many of the larvae out of the mushroom. After studying fungal and insect interactions in quite some depth, I've realised its probably best to let the insects consume the fungi. Cutting fungi is a useful technique when trying to identify species, many *Agaricus* mushrooms look similar to various toxic and potentially dangerous fungi. The Yellow Stainer *(Agaricus xanthodermus)* is a toxic fungus that can cause gastric issues, its name comes from the fact that if the stem is cut, it will quickly turn a bright yellow colour which edible agarics do not do. Checking gill colour is also useful for identification. The Horse Mushroom is typically characterised by the 'cogwheel' appearance of the veil, which is easy to see whilst it is still attached to the cap and stem. The veil hides the brown gills of this mushroom.

Large Horse Mushroom that was lovely pan fried in butter!

Many species of fungus gnats can take up to four weeks to emerge from their fungal hosts, many of the insects that emerge in June are in fact from mushrooms collected in May. Insects that I have managed to rear in June include the Mycetophilidae species, *Allodia, Pseudexechia, Mycetophila* and *Exechia*. Other insect species reared include parasitoids from the families of Braconidae and Diapriidae. The common Helemoyzid *Suillia variegata* also becomes abundant at this time of year along with the extremely common *Drosophila* spp. *C. gambosa* hosted many of these insect species.

Drosophila specimen with its distinctive wing venation and red eyes.

During June, each habitat is at its peak, trees are lush, grasses are at their maximum height and a range of wildflowers are in full bloom. The fields are a paradise hidden away from the business of main roads and the noise of cars and buses. Instead, those sounds are replaced with birdsong, screeches from raptors, stridulations from crickets and grasshoppers and the thudding sounds of horses running across the land. Insects become my focus during June, they're inescapable. Everywhere you look there are insects, and its great. So much diversity and variety, endless forms, and shapes. Entomology is an amazing subject, and a lifetime would not be enough to explore even one percent of it. I encourage everyone to try and learn even a little bit about insects and their importance, not just bees and butterflies but the fungus gnats and parasitoids that are understudied and overlooked. June is definitely a time to take an interest in butterflies due to their abundance and diversity and acts as a nice contrast to moth trapping in the garden. The woodlands, woodland edges, hedgerows and grassland all offer something different to what is in our garden. The appearance of some species (particularly insects) are likely to be found a lot earlier in the fields in comparison to our gardens such as the Painted Lady and various Dragonfly species and some species may not turn up in our garden at all, such as Burnet Companions or Purple Hairstreaks, although what can be attracted to the garden in terms of insect species is highly dependent on the plant diversity, short kept grass will not harbour the same butterfly diversity as tall grass does in grassland areas, conversely, a number of species which find their way into our garden will not be found in the fields. From morning to night these fields are teeming with activity and when burning hot days turn into cool evenings, walking through the fields is something to be treasured.

July

Heat intensity can often be at its peak during July. This has implications for the exposed grasses, wildflowers and south facing trees which are subjected to sunlight for most of the day. Insect diversity remains high and there are even a couple of newcomers to the area during this time. New species continue to appear with regards to birds and also invertebrates such as spiders. Wildflowers continue to bloom although many species are now beginning to wilt from heat stress and are replaced by later flowering species. Many of these later flowering species occur along the woodland edge, this specific habitat becomes a haven for a range of invertebrates.

Butterflies are at their peak in terms of species diversity and overall abundance during July. A species that begins to make an appearance is the Gatekeeper *(Maniola tithonus)*. This species can be mistaken for a Meadow Brown, but closer inspection of its wing spotting sets them apart, as Gatekeepers typically have two white dots within the black eyespot of its wings. I find this species flying amongst the wildflowers which cover the length of the woodland edge. This species is found at least a month earlier in the fields than it is in our garden, this may suggest that some butterfly species venture into gardens once their primary areas have become exhausted of nectar resources, for which our gardens can compensate for.

Gatekeepers typically have two white dots on their black eyespot.

Another addition to the day flying moths that can be seen in these fields is the Six-Spot Burnet *(Zygaena filipendulae)*. This species host plant is abundant in these grasslands, Birds Foot Trefoil, which it utilises by sequestering chemical defence compounds which helps it to deter potential predators[48]. As an adult this moth is easy to spot due to its vibrant red spots and metallic bluey-green sheen as it flies from flower to flower. This species isn't attracted to light and so I only ever see it in the fields. Its underwings are bright red and is heavily contrasted by the green and yellow backgrounds of the plants it rests upon.

Six-Spot Burnet Moth feeding on the nectar of a Red Clover.

A somewhat strange looking insect is the Scorpion Fly *(Panorpa communis)*. So called due to the males claspers which look similar to a scorpions stinger (also known as the telson). This insect looks like a combination of insects stuck together and has particularly long feeding apparatus which they use to feed on a range of materials including nectar, pollen and dead invertebrates. Scorpion flies are important pollinators of flowers. Although not obvious straight away, these flies have two sets of wings and are part of the Order Mecoptera. The wings have a mosaic of clear segments or cells due to the numerous veins they contain. This fly is often found along the woodland edge in search of food and potential mates.

The False Oil Beetle *(Oedemera nobilis)* is yet another insect that is highly distinctive due to its swollen hind femora, this only occurs in males. They have a green metallic sheen and a thin body. This species will often be found feeding on a range of flowers.

A male False Oil beetle on a Bindweed flower *(Convolvulus* spp.).

More Shieldbugs! The next Shieldbug to see in these fields is the Hairy Shieldbug *(Dolycoris baccarum)*. The exoskeleton of this species seems to sparkle with gold flecks. The antennae and connexivum (the flanks of the abdomen which look like stripes or barcodes) are black and yellow. Small hairs can be seen protruding from its legs and body, hence its common name. I have found this species feeding on blackberries. There are many species of Shieldbugs to be seen in our gardens and the fields, its well worth looking for them as they are hugely variable in terms of colour, size and shape.

There are hundreds of species of spider to be found within the U.K., many of which look similar and it can be hard to distinguish certain species. A spider that is easily identifiable within these grasslands during July, is the large-bodied Wasp Spider *(Agriope bruennichi)*, so called due to the yellow and black bands along its abdomen, perhaps as a form of mimicry to protect it from potential predators. This spider is thought to have recently arrived in the U.K. As spiderlings, individuals can be carried great distances by the wind. Perhaps that's how it arrived at these shores although it could have also hitched a ride on some imported goods. It can be safely assumed that the importation and exportation of goods, to and from the U.K., will result in many more non-native species introductions. I first found this species whilst wading through tall grasses and happened to see its web stretched across several grass stems. Its web is highly distinctive due to the ladder-like structure in the centre of its web called a 'stabilimentum'. I wonder whether this structure acts as a beacon for potential mates or perhaps it helps in luring insects to its web. What I found interesting about this species is that in such an open area, this spider remained within the same web for many weeks. I found it fascinating that I could return to the same spot of grassland and always see it there. Disturbing the spider would cause it to jump from its web into the undergrowth of the grass.

Female Wasp Spider feeding on a captured prey item.

One species that I never really considered seeing in these fields was the Common Cuckoo *(Cuculus canorus)*. Whenever I saw them in documentaries I would see them close to wet habitats like marshes where they could parasitise the nests of Warblers, but they do in fact have a range of possible hosts in a range of habitats. When I first saw the Cuckoo, I thought it may have been a Kestrel or a Sparrowhawk, due to the shape of its wings and slender body. Normally you would be aware of a Cuckoo first from its sound, which is perhaps what its most famous for, but I didn't hear it. All I saw was a low flying bird glide quickly across the grassland from one tree to another. I was unable to get a good close-up photo of it but was able to identify it from the photos I was able to obtain. Its tailfeathers providing me with clear identification. Cuckoos are summer visitors to the U.K. and so I imagine this was an adult ready to make its journey away from these shores.

The tailfeathers, wing positioning and shape make it possible to identify this as a Cuckoo, if only I was able to get a clearer photo!

The fact that there are many Cinnabar caterpillars in these fields may be alluring to Cuckoos as they are able to feed on them. It could also be that Cuckoos may have been passing through the area at that moment which, once again, highlights the importance of maintaining and monitoring these habitats that can act as suitable stop off areas for a range of migrating species. Its important to remember that Heston is a built-up residential area with several busy main roads running through it, including the A30 and M4.

The unmistakable Cinnabar Moth caterpillar, chomping its way through Ragworts across the grasslands.

I have spoken to many people that have a negative opinion of Ragwort due to the debilitating affect it has on animals that happen to consume it, but they do have positive impacts too. Ragwort can support many insects as well as providing nectar for important pollinators, this in turn attracts a range of predators from birds to spiders. The amount of Ragwort in these fields is not high and the horses ignore them.

A Barn Owl flying across the farmland into woodland.

Barn Owls *(Tyto alba)* are beautiful birds and amongst my favourite of all species. They're quite mythical to me in some ways, a species I would always hear about in stories or when I was small, I would see them characterised in children's cartoons. Owls for me, in general, are like hidden treasures of woodlands, they seem to appear when you least expect them to and then vanish just as quickly. For people that live in the countryside or rural areas where they are surrounded by woodland or farmland, seeing owls may be a common sight, but for me and the people that live around here, that's certainly not the case.

The first time I came across a Barn Owl was during July, and there was no chance for me to hear it, especially not when its flying, as its feathers are adapted for gliding and silent flight[49], I just saw a white object soar across the farmland from one part of woodland to another, before being hounded by a couple of Magpies, those corvids! I was surprised with how wide the Barn Owls' wingspan was. I imagine the crops that were growing at the time provided a perfect hunting habitat for the Barn Owl as it could use its excellent hearing to pinpoint the location of small mammals scurrying across the land.

These Magpies chased after the Barn Owl (bottom left) which retreated to the other side of the farmers field.

Swifts don't seem to stay for too long in the area, by the end of July they have all but vanished from these fields. Whitethroats are still abundant during this month as well as the ever-present Starlings. Juvenile Starlings can be seen perched on the trees. It amazes me how different juvenile birds look to adults and Starlings are no exception. Juvenile Starlings are quite plain, their plumage various shades of brown with no distinctive spotting or flecks. They have iridescence to look forward to! Despite the abundance of activity within the grassland its still a good idea to venture through the woodlands. Blackcaps can be found hopping from branch to branch within thick foliage of the Hawthorns, trying their best to avoid my camera.

A fungus I have come across within the woodlands during July is the Shaggy Parasol *(Chlorophyllum rhacodes)*. This saprobic fungus can grow large and can be found in groups or singly. The spore print of this fungus is a creamy white which matches its white gills. Young specimens are initially convex but as they age and mature the cap eventually flattens out. The Shaggy Parasol has shaggy scales on the cap, and as far as fungal identification is concerned, this is one of the easier species to identify.

Large mature specimens of *C. rhacodes* within the woodlands. Edges of the mushrooms show evidence of feeding from animals, perhaps Rabbits or Squirrels.

Several insect species emerge from fungi during July, these include, *M. rufipes, D. melanogaster, Muscina* spp., *Tricimba* spp., *Spelobia* spp.,

Diapriidae and *M. fungorum*. Some of these species tend to inhabit the same fungus at the same time, for example a *Russula* spp. that I had collected back in June had four different insect species emerge in July, each of them emerging on different days, which is interesting as it suggests that different insect species have different growth rates and may indicate a successional aspect to insect communities associated with fungal fruiting bodies.

Although many wildflowers are still abundant, it becomes noticeable that flowers are beginning to wilt, and many are preparing to disperse their seeds. During hot summers with little precipitation, this is even more noticeable as plants are placed under extreme heat stress. Many grasses are turning various shades of brown, and the lush green colour of the grasslands begins to dissipate. Most of the thistles have, by now, lost their purple flowers and the seed heads are all that remain, ready to be carried away by the wind. These seed heads are extremely soft and fluffy. Walking through the grasslands my clothes become a magnet for a range of plant seeds. Brambles begin to display the work of pollinators as their fruits begin to grow, small clumps of unripe berries begin to appear like small green globules.

July is a brilliant month to go out wandering, there is still tons of diversity, but there is a change in the environment, by the time it gets to the end of the month, much of the grassland has become dry. Wildflowers are beginning to wilt but there are still flowers available for insects, especially along the woodland edges. Whitethroats and Blackcaps continue to chirp and sing. There are many fledglings around and they can be heard within the shrubbery of hedgerows, grasslands, and woodland. The grasslands are full of butterflies, mostly Meadow Browns. Walking through the grasses causes butterflies to rise and then slowly settle, just a few metres away. With the abundance of butterflies, July is a perfect time to take note of the differences between habitats, and how there are clear preferences for some species. The transition from Meadow Brown filled grasslands to Ringlet dominated woodland edges to woodlands claimed by Speckled Woods is clear but can be easily missed if you're not paying attention. There is also the aspect of height, Skippers, Meadow Browns, Ringlets, Commas and Gatekeepers can all be consistently found below head height, whereas the Hairstreaks are usually way above head height, amongst the tops of trees. Its important to look everywhere, and July is the perfect month for exploring every aspect of these areas. The farmland next to these fields also offer opportunities to see wildlife as crops grow.

August

August is a time of change; a majority of migrating summer visitors have left by now and butterfly abundance begins to drastically decrease, although there are still butterfly species to be seen. The fruits of trees and shrubs begin to appear, and by the end of August, there are a few signs of autumn approaching. The days continue to be warm with long hours of daylight, and a number of plants are still in bloom so there is still a diverse range of invertebrates to be found.

After making these fields their home for the summer, Whitethroats begin to disappear from the area. Once I no longer hear the tweeting of Whitethroats it means the summer will be ending soon. The sound of summer is leaving!

One of the final times of the year to witness these lovely birds in these grasslands.

A smaller cousin of the Whitethroat is the Lesser Whitethroat *(Sylvia curruca)*, this pretty bird is very secretive and will flit amongst the trees and hedgerows. Its head is darker than the Whitethroat and also has black legs whereas a Whitethroat has yellow/orange legs. The Lesser Whitethroat is also a summer migrant so its likely they may arrive in these fields at the same time, although I only happened to see it during this month. Its breast is a clean white as opposed to the buff colour of the Whitethroat.

Lesser Whitethroat perched on a young tree within the hedgerows.

Goldfinches appear alongside juveniles which have yet to acquire their red facial markings.

An unassuming Shieldbug that appears as an adult during August, is the Bishop's Mitre Shieldbug *(Aelia acuminata)*. This hemipteran will be found on grasses where its shape, and beige and brown striped body makes it easily identifiable. The long pronotum of this species is quite distinctive and extends quite far in comparison to other Shieldbugs. The tops of grasses and wildflowers are great places to look for insects as they attract a vast array of organisms, some looking for nectar, others looking for seeds, and others looking for prey.

Dragonflies are still active as temperatures remain high. I found this individual resting upon a dried plant stem, notice the brilliant copper colour of the stem.

August in these fields is relaxed, there are still lots of species to be seen but it doesn't have that same erratic and bustling feel as July. At least half of the butterfly species from July have now stopped appearing and for the species that remain, its only the odd small group or individual that you'll find fluttering around. Freshly eclosed Painted Lady's may be spotted as they can have up to three generations in a productive year.

The rich colours of the wings of a newly emerged adult butterfly contrasts brilliantly against a background of ageing grasses.

Male Common Blues continue to sit and wait for females to pass by, putting on a display of their vibrant bluey-purple wings. I love to see how the colours can appear to change depending on the angle of sunlight hitting them, the iridescence is beautiful.

Brown Argus butterflies continue to shimmer along the woodland edges, skipping along, from one seed head to another, looking for a suitable place to rest undisturbed.

A Brown Argus resting upon a grass seed head. With its brown wings, its easy to see how it can be missed when walking through the area,

A second generation of Holly Blues may occur during August. It took me a while to realise this specimen was in fact a Holly Blue, with the sun shining upon this individual, the colour of the wings appeared brown but on closer inspection and analysis of the wings I realised it was in fact a Holly Blue. I have often found Holly Blues close to, or on Ivy plants, which is an important foodplant for their larvae.

August is usually the last month that I'll see many butterfly species including Painted Lady, Common Blue, Holly Blue, Green-Veined White, Brown Argus, Small Copper, Meadow Brown, Gatekeeper and the Cabbage Whites. During 2019, I was trying to find out how the butterfly community of the fields changed between the months of July and August and the changes I found were quite drastic.

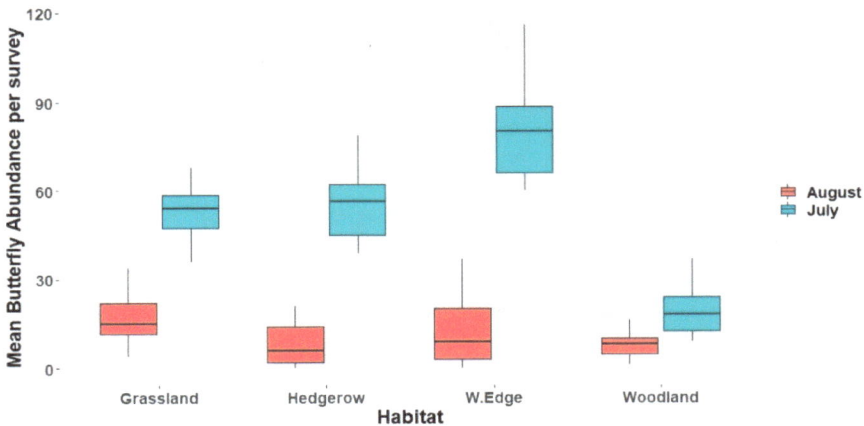

Butterfly abundance is higher in every habitat during July in comparison to August.

Being able to collect ecological data like this in local areas is really important and its the perfect way to understand and explore an aspect of ecology that interests me. Over time you can make plans of when to try and find things as you gain more knowledge and collect more data. If its done for long enough you may even find important patterns such as earlier emergence times or organisms that are present for longer than usual, perhaps owing to climate change or a change in habitat. Catching butterflies and carrying out butterfly surveys during the summer of 2019 was easily one of my happiest moments, and it also exposed me to a number of species that I had never seen before. By collecting observational data, I was also able to learn about the importance of various analyses and statistical methods in ecology which is a necessary part of becoming an ecologist.

The Wasp Spider continued to be successful in the grassland during August, catching a range of invertebrates including bees and grasshoppers.

A Grasshopper will make a good meal for the Wasp Spider.

The yellow and black striped markings of this specimen make it easily identifiable as a female, including its large size, males are brown and less striking as well as much smaller than the female.

A Wasp Spider on its web which clearly displays the ladder-like structure, the stabilimentum.

A couple of *C. rhacodes* mushrooms that I had collected from the woodland during July produced a range of insect species during August, all differing in size and shape, these included *D. melanogaster, M. rufipes,* Leiodidae, *Fannia* spp., Diapriidae, *S. variegata, Spelobia* spp., and *Leiomyza* spp. (Asteiidae). Leiodidae are known as Round Fungus Beetles, they are tiny brown beetles which feed on fungal tissue, they're very hard to spot due to their small size and tend to display crepuscular activity. They also seem to prefer older decayed fungal specimens to fresh ones, perhaps they are also able to graze upon fungicolous fungi which can be found parasitising a host fungus, this would be an example of mycoparasitism[50].

Fanniidae is a Dipteran family which has a relatively low number of species (less than 300) in comparison to other insect families. These small black flies can be difficult to identify without in-depth physical and morphological analysis, such as looking at wing venation, genitalia and bristles along the body and legs. These flies are generally associated with rotting matter such as carrion or decaying plants. As mushrooms begin to rot they can produce foul smelling odours which attracts plenty of insects towards them[51].

The Rosebay Willowherb *(Chamerion angustifolium)* is a tall, bright perennial that flowers around this time every year in the fields. The bright pink colour of its flowers as well as its distinctive physical structure makes this plant stand out clearly from the grasses that its surrounded by, especially as by this time much of the grassland has become a canvas of beiges and browns. Many of the flowers within the grasslands and woodland edges are quite small and are best appreciated up close, but the Rosebay Willowherb is a nice contrast to them, as it can be easily admired from a distance as a wavy pink haze. Individual plants can release thousands of seeds, which are dispersed by the wind, and new plants can also appear through the growth of rhizomes, this can cause the Rosebay Willowherb to colonise areas at a rapid rate. The flowers themselves are useful for a range of insects and important pollinators such as bees and hoverflies, it is also an important foodplant for the beautiful Elephant Hawk-Moth *(D. elpenor)*, which perhaps explains the colouration for the adult moth itself, as adults may be able to camouflage perfectly within a group of Rosebay Willowherbs. Males are brightly coloured in comparison to females and their brightness could be a way of attracting females.

A wall of Rosebay Willowherb is a nice addition of colour to the grasslands during a month where colours are starting to fade.

By this time, many plants have become dry specimens and are now ready to disperse their seeds which are ready to catch the wind and fly to new areas. The fluffy tufts of a Sow Thistle *(Sonchus arvensis)* contains thousands of seeds which are adapted for wind dispersal.

Even in its final stage the Sow Thistle retains its beauty, with its velvety seed head contrasting brilliantly against its tough darkened stems.

At this point of the year, many berries are beginning to emerge from various trees and shrubs. One of my favourite trees is the Rowan, berries appear on this tree in large clumps, the berries themselves are a bright red/orange which contrast strongly against the trees' serrated lush green leaves. These berries will provide food for many different birds over the course of autumn and winter, particularly Thrushes. There aren't many Rowan trees in the area or even within these fields and so its nice to see when a mature Rowan is displaying its colourful berries.

The Blackthorn is a shrub that also produces berries at this time, these are traditionally known as sloes which people use to make sloe gin. These large plump berries are similar in appearance to plums but are a lot tangier when eaten raw. Thrushes will feed on these berries but the plant itself is important for an array of insects, especially Lepidoptera. I am still waiting to possibly spot a Brown Hairstreak *(Thecla betulae)* or maybe even a Black Hairstreak *(Satyrium pruni)* from one of the many Blackthorns that fill the hedgerows within these fields. The fact that fruits and seeds begin to appear with regularity by the end of August lets me know that autumn is knocking on the door.

August sets the scene for autumn; it takes down the flowers and prepares a feast for birds with an array of berries and fruits. Whitethroats bid their farewells and the sound of summer is gone. Second and third generations of butterflies breathe new life into the grasslands and woodland edges with a burst of renewed colour, but these are to be enjoyed for a short time only before they vanish again. Fluffy seed heads cover the grasslands, but Yarrow continues to bloom. Species that I am unfamiliar with continue to pop up and seed heads of grasses continue to be utilised by birds and insects. In my experience, more species tend to leave these fields in the month of August in comparison to any other month, and so its an important time to take note of how the species community changes from the beginning of the month to the end of the month. There is a lot to be experienced during August!

Fields: Summer Summary

Summer in the fields is packed with wildlife, from the ground up to the skies, there are organisms to be found. There is also a great deal of contrast between the beginning of summer, with its lush greens and colourful fields and woodland edges, to the more subtle shades of faded flowers, feathery seed heads and grasses at the end of summer. Productivity is at its highest during summer in terms of growth, it reaches its peak between mid-June and mid-July. The brambles and nettles are overgrown within the woodlands and grasses are as tall as they'll become. July is the month for butterflies and can be seen everywhere you go. Bird species which are summer migrants enjoy the warmth of the sun and feast upon an abundance of caterpillars and insects, the result of which can be seen when fledglings of various species begin to emerge. Summer is the best time to see species that you're probably not so familiar with, especially when it comes to insects. Insects from a number of Orders can be found with relative ease and the diversity in form, shape, and colour within each group can be observed. Many species that I have found in the fields during the summer are species that I have never seen in my garden and probably never will, for instance, I don't think a Cuckoo will be visiting my garden any time soon! Summers in the fields have provided me with some of my happiest times and biggest moments of wonder. There is something for everyone to enjoy during this season, the birds, wildflowers, trees, tall grasses, butterflies, moths, dragonflies, beetles, foxes, fungi, no matter what aspect of ecology or nature you may be interested in, its likely to be present in this area during the summer (with the exception of amphibians or reptiles, although you may get lucky!).

A Small White *(P. rapae)* nectaring from a Ragwort.

Fields: Autumn (September, October, November)

The first thing that springs to mind when I think of autumn is colour, oddly enough. The falling of leaves and changes of the colours of the trees is something I strongly associate with autumn, but that's probably more akin to late autumn, early autumn still retains some heat from the summer, the days are still fairly long, and a good amount of wildlife is still on display. Autumn has a similar feel to spring for me, its relaxed, but where spring months are a like a calm before the storm, autumn feels like an evening stroll in the park after a busy day. Everything begins to slowly wind down in the autumn, days get a little cooler and some species seem to vanish from sight overnight. As you get further into autumn the real residents of the area begin to take centre stage and it can be a great time to observe certain species with regularity, with that being said, there are also autumn/winter migrants that begin to return, looking to make the most of the berries and fruits that the trees and shrubs have to offer.

September

September days are usually comfortable, the burning heat of the summer has passed, and everything has become less intense. A few remaining wildflowers along the woodland edge and grassland continue to bloom and show their defiance against the changing weather and slightly shorter days in comparison to the previous months. These continue to be utilised by butterflies, moths and beetles.

Butterfly species that remain in these fields during September include the hardy Red Admiral and Speckled Wood. There are not many individuals of either of these species but there tends to be a steady stream of a few individuals throughout the year.

I continued to find the friendly neighbourhood Wasp Spider during September, still in the same spot I had found it two months earlier. Its been suggested that this species has been spreading further north over the last couple of decades, perhaps due to climate change and favourable weather conditions such as longer summers and mild winters, which may reduce the risk of death[52]. September was the last time I saw this spider; I wonder if it survived the year or was predated.

As insect diversity has drastically dropped by now, my focus shifts back towards birds. The Kestrels remain within these fields throughout the year, its a perfect area to be a hunting ground, with a mix of suitable prey available to them as well as many corvid nests that they can make use of when nesting. I'll never get bored of watching Kestrels, perched upon the tops of trees, where they should always be.

Kestrel framed by tree foliage.

Reed Buntings (below) return and make use of the seeds of various plants that have now become available, they'll often be found in small groups on top of the dried Hogweeds. They tend to stick to areas with lots of tall grasses and shrubs in which they can hide in at the first sign of danger, they can also be seen perched upon the fencing from time to time.

Meadow Pipits also return to these fields, they appear sporadically at various times of the year, never staying for too long. Often perched on fenceposts or lone trees within the grasslands in all their rotund glory. They'll make the most of what is left in terms of invertebrates, picking off spiders and intercepting insects such as moths.

A bird species that I have had the privilege of seeing a couple of times is the Spotted Flycatcher *(Muscicapa striata)*. This species has reduced in numbers drastically within the last few decades and so it was a real surprise to see this species during one of my many walks through the grasslands. The Spotted Flycatcher is actually a spring/summer migrant and leaves these shores around this time to return to Africa. Its quite plain in its appearance, no showy colours or patterns but its simplicity is part of its charm. I had seen a couple of these birds perched upon a fence. The feeding habit of this species is distinctive in that it sits and waits for passing insects and quickly picks them off before returning to their original spot. Their timing and speed are impressive! I hope I get to see this species again. These fields provide me with endless evidence of why areas like this need to be protected, and that if suitable areas for species are made and maintained, its only a matter of time before they are utilised and inhabited by various species.

A Spotted Flycatcher waiting to grab passing insects.

Towards the end of the month, Stonechats will return, where they'll likely end up staying for the duration of autumn and winter. I am always happy to welcome these birds back to this area. The fences and dried Hogweeds become great places for birds to perch. The dense thickness of the shrubs and grasses also helps to attract these birds to the area. The Stonechats provide the grasslands with a stone-based soundtrack through the autumn and winter whilst they are here.

Insects continued to appear from my *C. rhacodes* specimen in September, these were *Fannia* spp. and *Leiomyza* spp. (Asteiidae). Asteiidae are extremely small flies (between 1-3mm in length) and the *Leiomyza* spp. I was able to rear were the last of the insects to appear from its fungal host. What was interesting to me was that no Mycetophilidae were reared from *C. rhacodes*, although perhaps they had emerged before I had collected the fungal specimen which was when it had already matured, as Mycetophilids typically do not require a lot of time to develop from egg to adult. I was able to rear over 200 insect individuals from one *C. rhacodes* mushroom which reinforced my thoughts that fungi are extremely important for insects. The more I learn about fungi the more I realise how important they are for the environment.

Leiomyza spp. collected from a *C. rhacodes*, these flies are very small.

The Common Mallow *(Malva sylvestris)* possesses a vibrant purple flower which continues to flower throughout September. Its flowers are an important source of nectar for any moths, bees and butterflies that remain. They are scattered around the grasslands in small groups and a pretty flower to look out for.

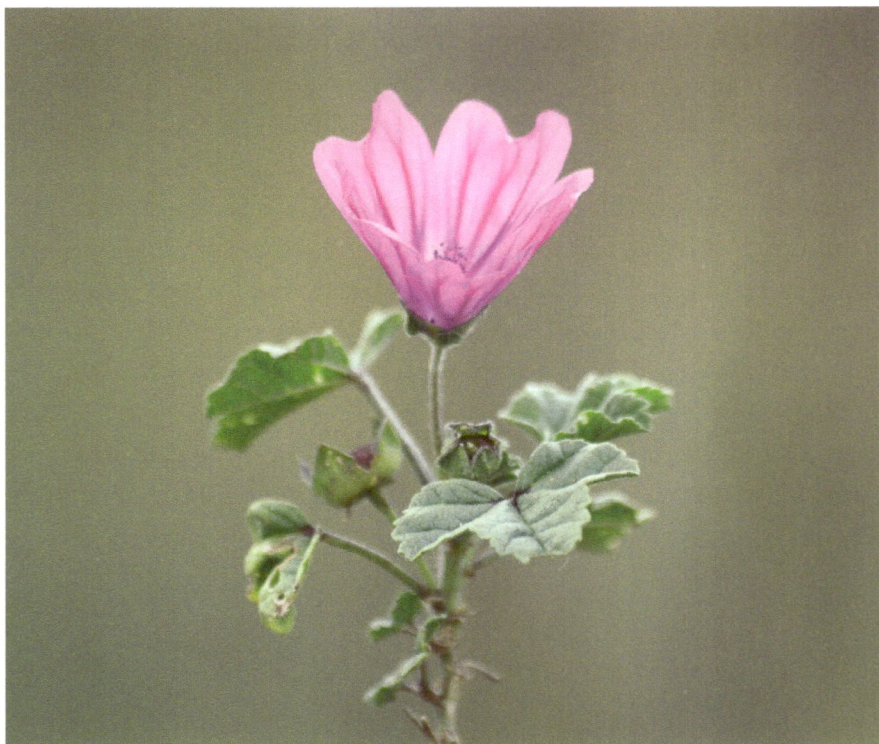

Much of the colour that was present throughout the summer has now vanished by the end of September as most plants have become withered, dry relics of their former selves, although there are still the odd flecks of colour dotted around the grasslands with flowering Yarrow, Mallow and Rosebay Willowherbs. Grasses have been grazed by the horses which maintains large patches of short grassland. Hawthorn berries dot the hedgerows and the greens of leaves on trees are starting to fade in spots. A slight chill begins to cut through the evening air. Autumn has arrived.

October

As we head into the latter part of the year, the days turn colder, and autumn is definitely in full swing by now. Day length continues to shorten, and the fields and woodlands start to feel a little barren, but the stillness of the fields does make it easier for the eyes to catch movements of passing birds or running Foxes. Its time to start accepting wet weather and embrace the muddy grasslands and trodden paths within the woodlands. The abundance of seed heads and berries continue to attract a range of birds to the hedgerows and can set up encounters with several uncommon species.

Only two species of butterfly are left in the fields during this time, the Red Admiral and Speckled Wood. Its the last time to see Speckled Woods, they have had a long season and by October its time for them to bid their farewells, the odd Red Admiral will continue to fly, perhaps looking for a suitable spot to overwinter without perishing.

This battle-hardened individual displays its battered wings.

October has always been a great month for birdwatching. Garden passerines are flying amongst many of the trees and shrubs, picking off berries, insects and spiders. Birds of prey are circling the skies as well as perching on top of trees, groups of Starlings and corvids are making the most of the available food, and migrating birds continue to pass through these fields. One of these migrating birds is the Whinchat *(Saxicola rubetra)*. A pretty looking bird, its predominantly a summer visitor in upland areas so I was extremely surprised to spot one in these Greater London grasslands. The white strip above its eye, also known as the 'supercilium', aids with identification as does the plumage, with its black and white tailfeathers and buff breast. Similar to a Robin in size it perches on top of dried hogweeds and branches of hedgerows.

I suspect this individual was passing through, a joy to see, nonetheless.

There's a lot of chatting going on in these fields with Whinchats and Stonechats about. Stonechat abundance increases steadily through October, as more and more pairs begin to appear. These birds are active throughout the day from morning to evening and can be spotted making rounds all over the grassland, flying from one clump of tall grass to another.

Another member of the Chat family that I was surprised to see is the Black Redstart *(Phoenicurus ochruros)*. I found a pair of these birds flying close to the ground, their red tailfeathers and black charcoal plumage makes them easily recognisable. I only ever saw this species once, from where I found them the M4 is probably about 50 metres away. When I first saw these birds I had no idea of what species they were, thankfully I had my camera on hand.

Two Black Redstarts (one is blurry on the bottom right); the other exposes its red tailfeathers as it begins to fly, illuminated by the sun.

Autumn is a great month for observing Kestrels in these fields. Some of my favourite moments in life have been watching Kestrels hunt, trying to understand their behaviours and patterns. The height of grasses is lower during October compared to preceding months and so provides less cover for a range of small mammals, many of which are prey for Kestrels. The times I have been able to get closest to Kestrels is when they're hunting. The shapes they make as they fly are great to record, the angles, the fanning of their tailfeathers for stability, wing position, its all perfect.

The head remains still as a Kestrel hovers above potential prey.

The result of a successful hunt, a Kestrel remains alert to its surroundings as it looks for a safe spot to consume its prey. The gaze of any raptor is always intense.

Planes often fly over these fields as Heston is under the London Heathrow Airport flight path, I was able to capture this shot at the perfect time, the rigid form of the plane contrasting against the beautiful, silhouetted form of a hovering Kestrel in full hunting mode.

I'll happily take thousands of photographs just to achieve one like this. The Kestrel will forever be my favourite animal.

October is a fantastic time for fungal forays. Autumn is the season for fungal fruiting for many different species and they can be found in each habitat, particularly the woodlands. Many fungi will be ready to disperse their spores at this time and so they produce mushrooms to do so.

The full range of colours and forms of fungi are on full display during October. The fruiting bodies of many species can appear and vanish within a very short time, so its best to visit the fields as regularly as possible to give you the best chance of finding various species.

This delicate mushroom, *Parasola plicatilis,* is the perfect example of a saprobic fungus that can vanish within a day of fruiting. It appears in areas of short wet grass; I tend to find it in small groups scattered around the grassland. As they mature the cap turns upwards and the gills tend to shrivel. The ochre-coloured centre of the cap contrasts nicely to the rest of the cap.

The Stubble Rosegill *(Volvopluteus gloiocephalus)* is another grassland fungus, this saprobic fungus is quite large and can be dotted across the grassland, when fresh and moist, the conical caps of this fungus are very shiny as well as being largely grey but whiter towards the edge of the cap. The caps can also be very sticky when wet. The crowded gills are white but can range from cream to pink depending on its age. The base of the stem will have a volva, which is similar to many *Amanita* spp.

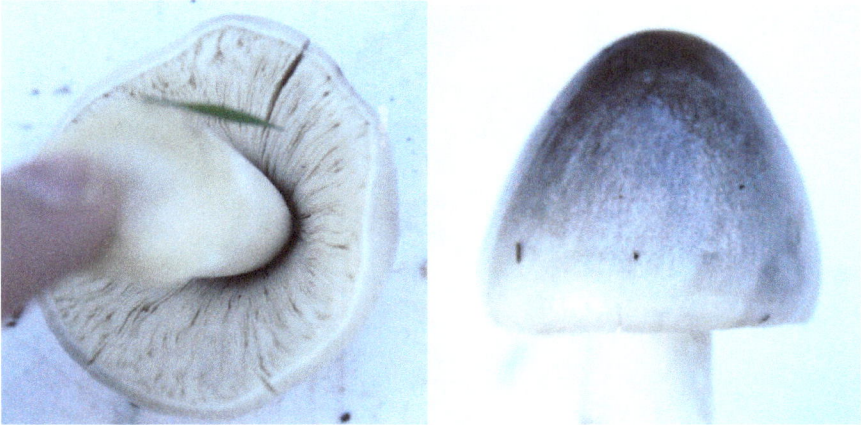

Left:- Underside of the cap displaying crowded white gills.
Right:- grey shiny cap, whitening towards the edge.

Good places to look for fungi within the woodland, are around the bases of trees, particularly Oak and Birch, although there doesn't seem to be many fungi in the Ash woodland. Areas of deadwood and where trees have fallen can be productive, as well as damp patches which have lots of leaf and needle litter.

This saprobic Mealy Funnel *(Clitocybe vibecina)* was found amongst leaf litter and is quite distinctive with its grey appearance and strong rancid smell.

Rotting wood and dead logs can be laden with fungi, this *Auricularia mesenterica* specimen is extremely common and was found on a decaying log of a fallen Elm Tree. The texture of this fungus is tough and rubbery. This fungus will break down stumps and logs.

Left:- The underside of *A. mesenterica* specimens. Right:- The topside of this fungus is typically hairy.

The woodland edge, which runs alongside the farmland is also a great area for finding a range of fungi. Sticks on the ground from fallen tree branches also provide a suitable substrate for many of the smaller saprobic fungi, as do mosses on the woodland floor, but you will need keen eyesight to spot these. Fungi that can be found around this time in these woods include *C. rhacodes*, *Lactarius* spp., *Auricularia* spp., *Collybia* spp., *Mycena* spp., *Psathyrella* spp., *Bolbitius* spp., and various *Agaricus* spp.

There is tremendous diversity and variability in the forms and colours of fungi.

With a plethora of fungi fruiting at this time, its a good time to collect a few specimens and examine their spore prints. Its a fun and interesting way of sharpening identification skills as well as providing a visually satisfying print. The spores themselves can be seen through a microscope although a magnification of 400x or higher is required.

Spore print of *P. conopilus*, the splitting of the stem caused the star effect.

October is a time for birds and fungi. Wandering through these fields I find myself spending more time looking at the ground and up at the sky then I do at everything else in between. October has exposed me to a range of birds I haven't seen anywhere else, Whinchats and Black Redstarts, birds I thought I would have had to travel to a reserve or a nature park to go and see. I keep the Kestrels company whenever

I can, spending hours watching them fly across the grasslands. Fun filled fungal forays in the woods is a must. The fruiting of mushrooms is a beautiful aspect of decomposition. Mycology is an area of ecology that is sure to be full of new discoveries and an area I wish to further my knowledge in. The days continue to get shorter and chillier and only larger bodied insects tend to be visible such as the odd bee or butterfly. Its time to start wearing a coat and paying attention to the trees as their leaves continue to change colour and drop to the floor.

A Crow on a lichen encrusted fencepost, perhaps waiting for the winter.

November

November brings more cold and damp weather, but now its cold most of the time, irrespective of time of day. Clear days filled with bright blue skies are the coldest. In terms of species to be found, November is very much a continuation of October, birds and fungi dominate the surroundings but with autumn in its final stage, the woodlands become colourful, various shades of red, orange, yellow and green are dotted across many of the deciduous trees, as they prepare for their winter dormancy by shedding their leaves. No more flowers are left and grasses are predominantly shorter than they are tall.

With many trees shedding their leaves it can be a lot easier to spot birds that are perched on the branches. Groups of Starlings can be found perched together basking in the midday sun, corvids will rush to the tops of taller, mature trees to stare out at the land before them, within the group of corvids you may sometimes come across a couple of Buzzards that for once are being ignored and left to sit in peace.

During early November the trees are awash with yellows, coppers, reds and browns.

The fields and woodlands feel increasingly bare as the tree canopies become more translucent, rather than an opaque mass of green that previous seasons have. The area isn't as sheltered as it feels during the spring and summer. Through gaps in hedgerows, I can see the M4, through the gaps in the woodland I can suddenly see farmland, and in the far distance I can spot the golden roof of a Gurdwara in Southall. The changes in landscape between seasons are so drastic, there are so many processes happening it is impossible to perceive it all. Being able to see so far, it helps with being able to spot birds as the number of hiding places for many species is reduced.

Some species don't require any cover, they'll perch out in the open, this is true of the Buzzards, bigger than most other species around here and armed with talons and a sharp beak, they can afford to stand out to an extent. Red Kites and Kestrels appear to know better and are a little more careful in their movements. On occasion a Sparrowhawk will appear, flying across the sky before vanishing towards Osterley Park. While battles between corvids and birds of prey are occurring, other species are becoming settled in the fields. The Stonechats are ready to spend the winter in these fields as are the Pied Wagtails. On occasion the Reed Buntings will hang around with Stonechats, flying through the dried shrubs together.

Mistle Thrushes return in search of food, they seem to be fond of fenceposts, constantly gazing out at the terrain, with their partners never far away.

A Mistle Thrush's mottled appearance blends in well with the fencepost.

Pheasants pop up in the fields once again, I found this male near some barrels, it soon ran into the cover of the shrubs. Pheasants add a lovely bit of colour to these muddy green November fields. I love the long tailfeathers of this species.

There are many fungi to be found during November. Before I began learning about fungi I naively thought that all mushrooms were either white, brown, or like those classic red and white ones, that I now know is *Amanita muscaria*, but fungi appear in a multitude of colours and its amazing how vibrant and rich some colours are.

R. *palmatus* is a perfect example of a colourful fungi, it begins to appear around this time amongst the hedgerows constituting of dead Elms, their peach colour living up to its common name.

One of the few fungi that I found within the Ash woodland is the saprobic *Stropharia caerulea*. It has a bluey-green appearance with flecks of ochre. The cap was around an inch wide and was found amongst leaf litter next to the base of an Ash tree.

The shiny bluey/green appearance of *S. caerulea.*

A very bright fungus often found in grasslands, is *Bolbitius titubans*. It has a bright lemon-yellow appearance, standing just a couple of inches from the ground, this fungus will not remain for long and can vanish within a day, so spotting one can be difficult!

Left:- Underside of *B. titubans*. Right:- Bright lemon-yellow cap of *B. titubans*.

If you're someone who likes to forage, then a mushroom that is commonly eaten is the Field Mushroom *(Agaricus campestris)*. This fungus has appeared a few times in these fields but its not massively abundant here. I wouldn't recommend eating *Agaricus* spp. as they are often inhabited with maggots, unless you don't mind the extra bit of protein! Flies can detect fungi extremely quickly and will subsequently oviposit their eggs into the mushroom.

Another colourful edible fungus that I often find in groups during this time is the sought-after Wood Blewit *(L. nuda)*. Saprobic on leaf litter, their thick purple stem and gills can be quite vivid, although finding this fungus amongst a range of leaf litter in woodland can be quite difficult, as the caps can be various shades of brown, grey and purple, which helps them to blend into the mosaic of leaves. This fungus should be cooked as once again it can be infested with maggots. What is quite common when breaking a mushroom from its mycelium, is that the larvae within the mushroom tend to emerge, the insect larvae within mushrooms require the fungus to be connected to the mycelium. Perhaps this is down to the nutrients and water that fungi are able to absorb, that sustains the larvae as they feed[53].

Lilac gills of the cap, attached to the wide lilac stipe of the edible Wood Blewit.

As autumn is filled with fungi its no surprise that there's an abundance of fungus gnats utilising these mushrooms. Mycetophilidae, the truly mycophagous insects that primarily use mushrooms as food, are abundant during this time and various species can be found emerging from a range of different fungi. Many of the larger bodied saprophagous insects that were abundant during the summer months are now nowhere to be seen and are perhaps overwintering in a state of diapause.

Mycetophilids that emerge in November include, *Allodia* spp., *E. fusca, M. fungorum, M. ruficolis, Leia bimaculata, P. trivittata, P. trisignata*, and *Allodiopsis rustica*. Other insects reared were *Bradysia ocellaris, M. rufipes*, Proctotrupidae (Parasitic wasp) and a Chironomid (Non-biting midge). Chironomids are usually associated with wet/damp places and their larvae are often aquatic, as fungi can be up to 90% water, they may be suitable places for Chironomid larvae.

Out of all the Mycetophilids that I have been able to rear, *E. fusca* (left) appears to be the most adaptable in terms of fungal host, they have emerged from a range of different fungi which is interesting as the larvae must be adapted to a range of chemical compounds in order to feed on such a range of different fungi.

As the days are now much shorter with sunsets occurring during early evening, I'll often find myself walking around these fields during dusk. Sunsets in the fields make for beautiful viewing, just before the skies darken they glow for a short while with various shades of pink, red, and orange which seem to transition into shades of blue. Various cloud formations during sunsets can be just as beautiful. Witnessing those moments ease my mind and give me a happiness that I could only ever obtain from observing the environment.

Fields: Autumn Summary

Autumn is a time to go for long relaxed walks in the fields. Birds and fungi take over during this time and there are lots of species to find and learn about. Admittedly colder and wetter than the previous seasons, the weather doesn't pose a problem as there are many things to keep your mind and senses occupied. Its a great time to witness the coming and going of many birds, as summer migrants are replaced by winter migrants and its also the best time to see how important the shrubs and trees are for many bird species as they feed on seeds and berries of various plants. Leaf litter provides many fungi with much needed nutrients and substrates on which to feed and grow on. The woodland floor becomes speckled with a range of fungal fruiting bodies ranging in size and colour. Nothing hones your visual searching skills like carrying out fungal forays, if your sense of smell is acute enough you may even be able to smell certain fungi before seeing them. Overall, every season is distinctive, and autumn is no exception, no other season will provide such a diverse array or abundance of fungi within these fields, and with that comes a range of associated insects. If you're interested in foraging, autumn is usually the time to do it with the range of berries available as well as certain edible mushrooms, although do be careful! By the end of autumn most of the leaves have fallen from the trees and everything quietens down, ready for the winter, and so we have come full circle.

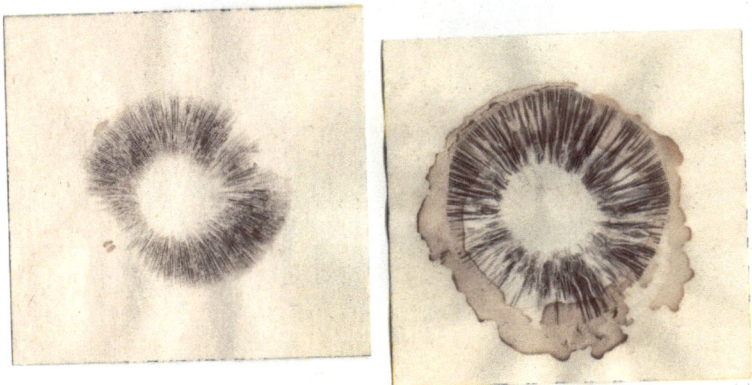

Spore prints of *Agaricus* specimens.

Feathers

I decided to write a little about collecting feathers, because they can occur in the fields with regularity throughout the year and feathers are beautiful. I rarely found feathers in my garden, and it was never something that occurred to me as something to look out for, but over time I would find feathers on the floor, usually there would be a trail of feathers, which would mean that something had been successfully targeted by a predator. Parts of a bird would be at one end of the trail, usually within tall grass or a sheltered area. Perhaps a Fox had been successful with a hunt. Birds replace their feathers regularly as they can become damaged, weakened or loose, and so birds will go through numerous moults during their lifetime, this ensures that their feathers can remain in tip-top shape for flying. I would often find single feathers of various species and the colours and shapes of all the different feathers fascinated me (and still do).

Its hard to grasp the size of certain birds such as birds of prey because its difficult to get close to them, finding a tailfeather of a Red Kite gave me an insight into how large these birds are. Red Kite tailfeathers are a cinnamon colour, and around 30cm in length. Collecting feathers can provide important information in relation to understanding the size of birds, especially if you have photos of the birds to cross-reference with.

Another feather I was able to collect was that of a Barn Owl, their feathers are beautifully patterned, coloured with white and orange and a number of dark spots or streaks running through them.

I love the vibrancy of colours and intricate patterns of certain feathers, another one of my favourite feathers belong to that of a Jay *(Garrulus glandarius)*. The alula of the Jay are electric blue and black (left) which contrast against the peachy colour of the rest of its plumage.

Other bird species have iridescent feathers such as Starlings and Magpies. Magpie feathers display this perfectly and can appear to shine with a range of colours.

There are a number of ways to identify the presence of a bird in a habitat, and feathers are one way of doing that. Collecting feathers has sharpened my identification skills and led me to discovering a variety of patterns, sizes, shapes and colours that bird feathers have.

A number of Pheasant feathers displaying the diversity of colours, shapes and patterns that one species can have.

Fields Summary

The fields are a special place, there is so much to explore, I hope I've been able to get across the diversity of life that is in this area, from the grasslands to the hedgerows to the woodlands. Each season provides a bounty of wildlife to observe. Much of the ecological knowledge I have gained has been from my walks in these areas. Its a space that allows me to think about things freely whilst also helping me to engage with the environment. I hope that others will treasure this area in the same way that I do, but part of me also wants it to remain hidden and left as it is. There is no guarantee that these fields will remain as they are for another 100 years, perhaps surrounding areas will encroach into these fields, if so its a great shame, but by documenting what is there, this book will create a reference guide and a time stamp for future readers that gives them an understanding of the rich species community of this area. Talking to farmers and the people that have lived here for many decades, the Lapwings, Yellowhammers, Skylarks and Swallows that were once abundant in the fields and farmland are no longer there. Its paramount that species data across all taxa continues to be collected and monitored, and if possible these areas must be maintained.

Technology and Equipment

There are many positives that come from advancements in technology, for example large amounts of information can be shared or captured through the internet or various computer programs, we're able to carry lots of information in the shape of portable drives or USB's and we can take thousands of photos with digital cameras and view them straight away, unlike the old SLR cameras where getting a film developed and delivered can take up to a week (and is now ridiculously expensive). Drones are likely to help with monitoring of a range of habitats and species and will help to uncover information about areas that are difficult to physically get to. Microscopes with powerful magnifications are readily available and affordable. For the statistics lovers out there, various computer packages can make analysis of large amounts of data extremely easy, the free program R Studio being proof of that. These are just a few examples but there are many more. Over the next couple of pages, I'll give my thoughts on technologies and equipment that I believe to be helpful in exploring ecology.

DSLR Camera

By this point, you will have realised I enjoy taking photographs, (even if many of them turn out blurry). Photography has helped massively in my ability to spot organisms and is the perfect way to document my sightings. Its a useful tool which can make identification of species easier as you can always zoom in and identify physical features clearly, and in the artistic sense it can help hone skills such as use of composition and help with understanding the importance of light, lines, tone and colour. A macro lens and a zoom lens are all I need to photograph everything I find in the fields and garden. Most of the time I'll have my camera on hand just in case something appears out of nowhere which is so often the case.

Its a good idea to play around with various settings on the camera, exposure times and shutter speeds. I tend to keep auto focus switched off as focusing manually is a lot easier and quicker for me, auto focus can sometimes take a couple of seconds to adjust, which is too long when trying to capture a flying bird or insect. The added luxury of having a DSLR is the ability to take videos as well. Its a good idea to have an SD card with lots of storage, at least 32 gigabytes. Saving images as RAW files will provide the best photo quality but will come at the cost of being a large file, often above 20mb per photo, hence why I say its best to have an SD card with a large storage capacity. The RAW files can always be edited and compressed into JPEG's on the computer if you want to save space, JPEG's will be much smaller in size but will ultimately be lower quality.

DSLR's can be quite heavy so you might want to purchase a strap for the camera which will allow you to carry it around your neck. Look after your camera! Always keep the lens cap on when not in use. It'll protect the lens and stop it from getting marked, this can be a problem if you're wandering around hedges, thorny plants and spikey grasses. I have a habit of having to change lenses whilst in the field so practice how to quickly change lenses as you have no control of how an organism will move or react, or how long it will remain in one place, so you need to be quick! I also recommend having a tripod for low light conditions, its almost impossible keeping a camera steady freehand, when trying to photograph subjects in low light. I found this out when I was trying to photograph Little Owls in the fields and all of my photos turned out to be blurry simply because the owls were emerging at dusk, and I couldn't keep the camera steady when the shutter speeds were low. Low shutter speeds allow more light to be captured by the camera, producing brighter photos and so are suitable for low light conditions, whereas during bright sunny days higher shutter speeds are better. Shutter speed is incredibly important as it can cause photos to either be underexposed (too dark) or overexposed (too bright, and grainy) depending on the light conditions. Phones can be great for macro photography and attachments for phone cameras can be purchased, so it may not be necessary to buy a DSLR camera, although you may find it difficult to photograph organisms from a long distance with a phone camera.

Wildlife Camera Trap

Another useful gadget is the Wildlife Camera Trap. These are often being used by ecologists when trying to capture images of various animals in remote places or places that are difficult to physically monitor for long periods of time. They are typically quite robust as they are meant for outdoor use. They usually come equipped with a strap that allows you to tie them to posts or trees, but they can also be mounted on a tripod. Again, tripods are extremely useful!

A Blackcap having a quick drink in the pond.

I use my camera trap for monitoring the garden throughout the day and night to see what activities are taking place, if you have a pond then its a great place to set up a camera trap as various animals will stop by for a drink, I have managed to capture footage of many different birds visiting our pond for a quick drink, to bathe and to feed on aquatic insect larvae. Its very possible that some birds will only visit the garden to use the pond and not the birdfeeder, so for areas that are out of your line of sight from inside the house (in my case its the pond), camera traps are a great asset. They are also great if you want to capture the moments when a chick finally fledges from a bird box, as its extremely difficult if not impossible to know exactly when the chicks will fledge, so having the camera on hand is a good way to settle any nerves about whether the chicks made it or not.

Another good part of the garden to focus on is the bird feeder. I left my camera trap facing the bird feeder for a while to see how different bird species interact and most of the time it captured a territorial Robin terrorising most of the other birds. An important thing to remember when using a camera trap is that they can be very sensitive to movement and you're likely to find that many videos or photos captured are due to a gust of wind moving a tall piece of grass or a branch moving and won't show any activity. I have spent many hours deleting 'empty' videos. The sensitivity of the sensor can be adjusted through the settings on many camera traps, so you'll just need to tinker around until you have a suitable setting. Once again, SD cards will be required to save any videos or photos taken. Camera traps typically require 8 double A batteries.

2018/12/11 11:31:48

Often times, dates, and temperatures will be displayed when photos were taken and so valuable insight into the environmental conditions at the time of recording can be noted, this may help to uncover certain patterns or trends for various species. Overall, a camera trap is definitely worth having to help you acquire knowledge about your garden that you may otherwise struggle to obtain.

Robinson Moth Trap

Moth trapping is something I would recommend to anyone that has an interest in nature. Moths are beautiful creatures, the wing patterning, colours, shapes, sizes amongst other characteristics are extremely varied within Lepidoptera. Moth trapping can also provide a sense of routine as it can be done once every two days if you have a garden, the idea behind missing a day is that you reduce the chance of capturing the same individuals repeatedly. I always find it quite relaxing setting up the moth trap at dusk, its a comfortable time to be outside. If you're able to place a moth trap within a wooded area I imagine the findings there would be amazing, but you will have to place a lot of trust in the people of the area as you never know what can happen, you would also need a portable power source.

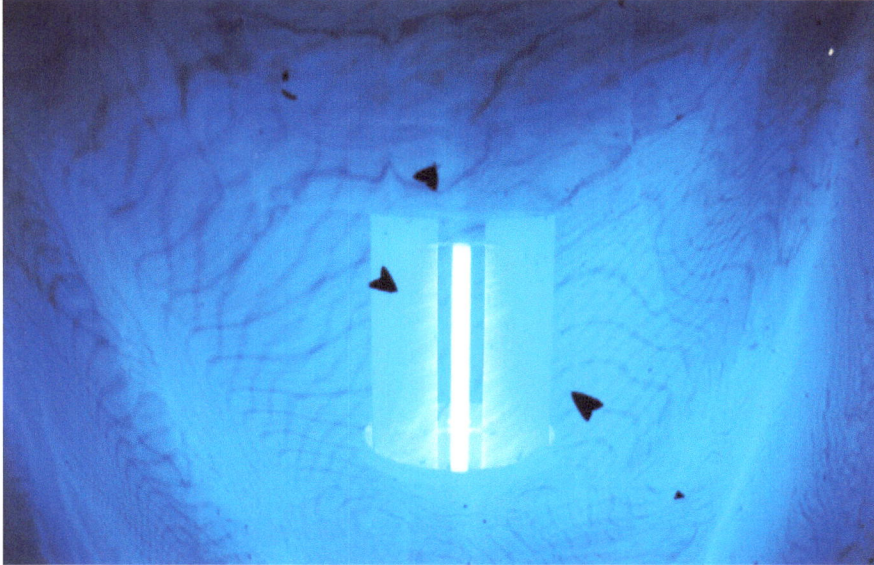

My Robinson Trap lighting up a net curtain in the middle of the night.

An effective trick in luring more insects to your garden is with the use of a net curtain, many species will not go into the moth trap itself but will hang around on plants or walls close to the light source. The net curtain absorbs light extremely effectively and I have been able to look closely at moths as they rest upon it.

Robinson traps are very robust, I have had no issues with regards to wear and tear or damage. Lining the trap with egg boxes will provide places for the moths to sit and rest once they enter the trap. Access to a plug socket is required to power the trap. Traditionally, MV (Mercury Vapour) bulbs were used for moth traps as they are extremely bright and can attract many moths, but these are being phased out for more efficient and safer actinic bulbs, MV bulbs are susceptible to shattering. MV bulbs can still be purchased but just be mindful that they can be extremely bright (brighter than actinic bulbs) so be considerate to your neighbours and let them know if you're going to use a moth trap. Our garden isn't massively sheltered and so I tried to place my moth trap in a place where it would minimise the amount of light filtering through to neighbouring gardens. Its also worth considering building your own moth trap, as this can save you hundreds of pounds, Robinson traps are usually between £150-£300 and so if you're up for a project and are good with tools, making a moth trap shouldn't be difficult.

Checking my Moth trap first thing in the morning. Its always best to check the moth trap as the sun is rising, at this time, the moths are still cold and gives you a little time to be able to photograph them while they're unable to fly away.

Bat Detector

All bat species are protected in the U.K and if you are looking to go into ecology to possibly become an ecological consultant, then bat surveys are a must. Companies carrying out building projects will often require the help of ecologists to assist them in understanding the ecological community of a possible construction site. Due to bats being protected certain rules and regulations need to be followed. Bat surveys are a great way to engage with nature, especially at night, each species has its own specific call, which is picked up by the bat detector, over time you'll get used to the clicking sounds that come from the detector. There are many different types of bat detectors, handheld ones, phone application related ones as well as others. Due to the various types of bat detectors available, prices can range massively from £50 to over £1000. Magenta Bat Detectors (the one I own) are great but you need to manually change the frequency in order to locate specific species of bat, so if you're unaware of what species are in the area you'll have to spend a good amount of time ranging between frequencies. Pipistrelles (Common and Soprano) are generally the most common in Heston, and so setting your bat detector to somewhere between 40 and 50Hz is a good place to start. If you're going to Osterley Park then its a great place to witness the remarkable hunting behaviour of the Daubenton's Bat *(Myotis daubentonii)*. These bats will fly over water bodies skimming the surface in search for flies and pick them off, they tend to fly in patterns, often circling a specific area, so they are quite an easy species to find and follow. You'll be surprised with how many bats there are and how often they will turn up in our gardens even in Heston, so its well worth purchasing a bat detector.

Butterfly Net

If you're interested in Lepidoptera or other flying insects, then a butterfly net can be a handy tool to let you get closer to inspect these animals. You'll need lightning reflexes to catch species like Dragonflies, but Lepidoptera are pretty easy to catch once you've got the hang of it. Sweep netting involves fast sweeping of an area close to the ground up to waist height, this works well in grassland and shrubby areas. Be mindful of the fact that much of the time you'll end up collecting more than what you intend to, spiders will invariably be swept up as will Shieldbugs and many other invertebrates that happen to be resting upon grasses.

Pond Net

For those of you that have a pond, having a pond net is essential for clearing the pond of litter, whether that be chunks of soil that have fallen in or leaves that have been blown by the wind into the pond or even removing the odd splodge of algae. Keeping nutrients to a minimum in a pond is really important for keeping it clear of algae which can wreak havoc to submerged plants and also make it difficult for certain organisms which can become embedded within it. A bamboo stick will help for picking out pond algae, but if you want to explore your pond, to have an idea of what species you have in there, then the best way to do a bit of pond dipping is with the use of a net and a collecting tray. Many lakes and streams are becoming increasingly polluted and pond surveys are often carried out by professional ecologists, something as simple as pond dipping in your own garden can help with improving basic ecological skills that can carry over to surveying lakes and rivers. Certain species do better in polluted waters, such as Pond snails, whereas other species require pristine unpolluted waters such as Caddisfly larvae.

R Studio

For those of you that are interested in statistics and mathematical ecology, as well as people that are good with coding, R-studio is a great help in dealing with large amounts of ecological data. Its free software that can be downloaded online and has an endless number of additional packages that can be used for a variety of analyses. Much of my own research is heavily based on count data and some categorical data and so R-studio has been a huge help in analysing and visualising various data and being able to recognise trends. I will admit it can be quite confusing in the beginning trying to get used to the codes, but once you have a code, you can save it, and 'copy and paste' will become a time saving move. There is a lot of scope for creating graphs and figures which suit your own needs and preferences, its a highly flexible tool and one every ecologist should become acquainted with.

Lab Equipment

Certain lab equipment should be purchased as they can deeply enhance many skills required for field or lab work. What I consider to be some of my most important bits of equipment are my microscopes, a compound microscope for examining items which require a high magnification such as cells and spores and a stereomicroscope for small specimens such as insects or leaf structures. Light bulbs of microscopes can become extremely hot so be careful when handling a microscope and always keep the dust cover placed over the microscope when its not in use. With microscopes you'll need slides and a neck wash bottle. A scalpel is always useful for dissecting, along with vials for collecting specimens and a bottle of ethanol for preservation of specimens. Be mindful that 100% ethanol should be diluted with distilled water, and for preserving insects, 70% ethanol is best, higher concentrations can result in structural damage of exoskeletons. A tip for when you're examining insects under a microscope is that they can dry out extremely quickly due to the intense heat of the microscope bulb, therefore having a pipette on hand to keep the subject wet is important. As an insect dries, its exoskeleton can crumple and become irreversibly damaged. Each of these tools are really helpful in the long run and it can be easy to forget how useful small objects like blades and vials are.

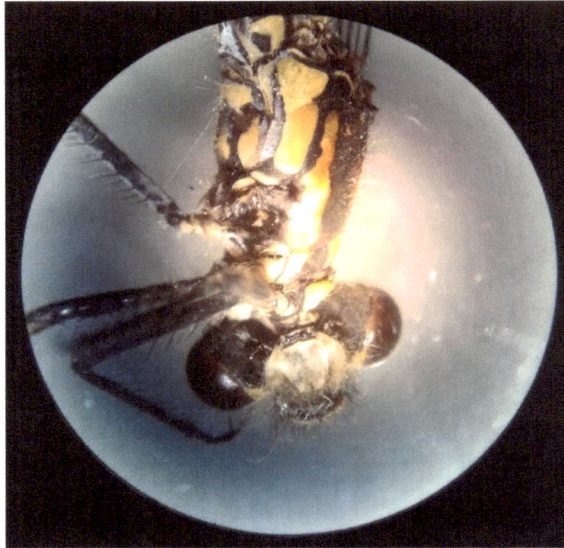

A dead Damselfly I found in the garden, under the light of a microscope.

Reference Books and Guides

Books are important, without my small collection of reference books and guides, much of my ecological knowledge wouldn't exist, being able to identify species is a necessity when carrying out surveys or monitoring an area as data needs to be accurately recorded. The leg work for identifying tons of species has already been done by previous naturalists and is immortalised within reference books. I find myself resorting back to these books just to look through the pictures and also to try and learn about the species and key identifiable features or structures they may have, one step at a time. Its always worth checking out charity shops or old book shops as they may have some good reference books or guides. A good place to look is the old Osterley Bookshop where I was able to purchase a couple of very good bird field guides, one original copy which was published in 1952!

Small Container/Cotton Bud Tub

I had to include a cotton bud tub as an essential piece of equipment simply because of the number of insects and spiders I have caught in mine over the years. I was also able to rear the Angle Shades moths within these tubs, they are just extremely useful and a good size for catching a range of organisms, as long as you don't leave anything in there for too long! I originally only used these tubs for removing insects that had become trapped in our house and I still continue to do so. They are also handy for catching moths if you don't have any other equipment.

Pen, Pencil and a Notepad

The last bit of equipment is what everyone should have on them, yes we have phones that we can use to note things down with, but they can stop working or break, a pen, a pencil and a notepad are always going to work (maybe not all pens). Making notes and making basic drawings are important for engaging your mind with the environment as well as helping with the development of ideas. Bear in mind that if you are completing fieldwork, the weather can dictate what you can and can't use, using a phone during windy rainy days is not the most practical option, whereas a pen and notepad are a lot more reliable. For those of you that have an artistic background, making quick drawings of things that you come across can hone your artistic skills and also be a perfect way for recording sightings in a way that's personal and specific to you, we all have our own style.

Ponds and Ecology

I have come to the conclusion that every garden needs a water body, its a must! Even if its just a small sink basin filled with water and a couple of plants, that's enough, wildlife will still be attracted to it. There's every chance that it will be inhabited by amphibians and insects, as long as it is accessible. The birds will arrive to have a drink and maybe a quick dip to cool off before flying away. Ponds are also great if you want to have an overgrown area, grasses around a pond can be left to grow tall and I would say that maintenance of a pond is fairly minimal with only thinning of pond plants and removal of algae being the main things to stay on top of.

The most basic of ponds, it wasn't very big or deep so I wasn't sure whether it would be used to any great affect by wildlife, but over time it became a magnet for a range of organisms that I probably wouldn't have been able to see otherwise. Its best to top up a pond with rainwater to minimise the availability of nutrients for algae to grow.

I didn't really have any idea of how much wildlife would come to our garden when I made the pond, but that small space turned out to be one of the best spots in the garden for attracting wildlife. The sheer number of birds using the pond during spring and summer was quite staggering, and the fact that newts somehow made it into our pond was even more amazing. Having a pond will only make your garden a more attractive place for wildlife. Without one you're unlikely to find Newts, or Dragonflies or Rat-tailed maggots! Another great aspect of having a pond is seeing how a habitat evolves, from just an empty area of water to a thriving, plant filled pond. Pond Skaters, Mosquitoes and Midges will be the first to colonise a pond and their presence will attract various predators until there's a fully functioning ecosystem that's full of interesting interactions.

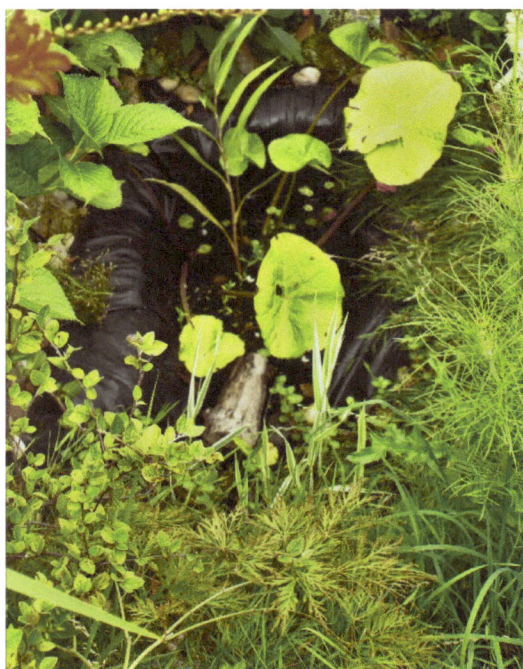

Over time the pond became a lush green area and surrounding grasses and plants added more character to the pond. The pond plants grew larger, and it began to look more like a suitable place for wildlife. Pond edges are important spaces for wildlife and also act as shelters and hiding spots for many insects as well as newts, which may use stones or log piles as areas to tough out the winter.

Looking at water is also really therapeutic for me, its nice to just stare into it and see the range of colours, the ripples and reflections, to witness how lines and shapes become distorted and spot all of the tiny larvae twitching and swimming within it, the aquatic world is full of wonder.

There's also the chance of visiting birds carrying out some gardening for you, by that I mean some species will inadvertently carry seeds of various plants and deposit them into the garden, we had the pleasure of Purple Loosestrife *(Lythrum salicaria)* growing beside our pond, likely due to visiting birds. I cannot stress enough the importance of placing water bodies in our gardens, over the decades water bodies have become less and less frequent and wetland areas are continuing to decrease across the U.K. So, get into your gardens and make that space for water!

The casing of the final moult of a Large Red Damselfly nymph, highly unlikely to be found anywhere else other than beside a water body.

Plants and Ecology

Where would we be without plants, we wouldn't even exist, where else would we get our oxygen from, or food, or timber? This is something that should be embedded into everybody's minds. Not only are plants important for humanity but they shape and create an array of natural wonders, habitats and ecosystems, on a large scale as well as small scale. One mature oak tree will harbour thousands of species throughout its lifetime and its leaves will be utilised by an abundance of invertebrates and fungi. Birds may use leaves and moss as insulation for their nests. Squirrels will cache acorns and feast upon them when the time is right. Its not just above ground that plants are important but underground too, roots help to anchor plants into the soil and helps to combat soil erosion. They provide an underground network for an array of invertebrates to feed upon. Vegetables provide food for billions of people worldwide. Medicines created from chemical compounds found in plants can aid and cure a multitude of diseases and illnesses.

Flowers produce colours and fragrances that can make life seem a whole lot nicer and provide a nice distraction from the tensions of everyday life.

From an ecological standpoint, flowers are essential for thousands of organisms across numerous taxa. Its not just plants found in grasslands or woodlands that are important but also plants that are aquatic or found in ponds, which harbour a great deal of wildlife. Reeds provide stable supports for the nests of many bird species such as the Reed Warbler *(Acrocephalus scirpaceus)* and Bearded Tit *(Panurus biarmicus)*, and many Ducks or Geese will feed from seeds produced by aquatic plants. In the grasslands and hedgerows, seeds and fruits provide an important source of food for birds, mammals and insects.

A *Buddleia* creates a great range of shapes against the sky and attracts many insects.

Plants and fungi will form bonds and symbiotic relationships to transfer various nutrients and water between them. Many fungi will enhance plant protection and defence from predators and in some cases will cause an increase in growth rate[54]. Plants are tremendously adaptable and that is reflected in how speciose they are. Although many plants are beneficial there are also plants that can cause havoc, invasive species such as Giant Hogweed *(Heracleum mantegazzianum)* and Japanese Knotweed *(Fallopia japonica)* can colonise large areas in a relatively short amount of time, these species are able to outcompete native plants and subsequently cause their demise. Invasive species such as the ones mentioned can be problematic and its worthwhile being alert to the fact that plants can also have negative impacts on surrounding environments and associated species.

The world of botany is remarkably complex, plants are found everywhere across the globe in every habitat and there is still an endless amount to be learnt about them. Their importance cannot be understated or oversimplified. Spend time to learn about plants, or even one plant, and start planting seeds and follow their growth from there. Learn about why plants have leaves, the processes that occur for photosynthesis, the different types of photosynthesis, how their roots grow, how plants defend themselves physically and chemically, the triggers for emergence in spring, the hormones that initiate flowering and growth. There are so many aspects of plants to think about, and then there is the topic of how plants interact with the environment and the species that rely on plants in order to live, and the role of plants in succession and development of habitats.

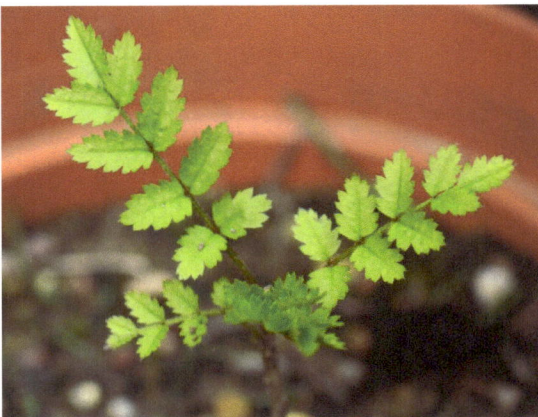

A Rowan I grew from a seed, with its distinctive serrated leaves. One of my planting achievements! I hope this tree will grow for many decades and provide lots of organisms with food and shelter.

Death and Ecology

Specific truths about life should be spoken about and accepted more than they currently are. For example, continuing as a species as we are, will likely result in catastrophe for many species including ourselves. We are NOT indestructible, as a species I believe we will go extinct at some point just as millions of species have done before us and will continue to do so in the future. Death is a natural process, its an essential process, I often think of all the organisms that are required to die for other organisms to survive, a carcass is an ecosystem, sustaining large numbers of invertebrates and carrion feeders. Its a shame that the one aspect of life we can all be certain of is also something that brings a lot of fear, but it shouldn't, its a natural part of life and a great motivator. I say its a great motivator because its a subject that I often think about, at least once a day I remind myself that one day I will no longer exist, so all I am left with is wondering how I should spend my time, what do I want to do or accomplish? There are a few things I want to do, but time is limited and its the same for every organism that exists.

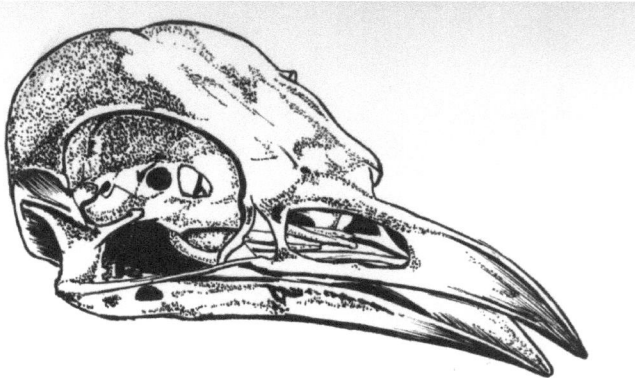

Drawing of a corvid skull that I found during one of my walks through the woodland.

From the hundreds of journals and books that I have read, and the lecturers, ecologists or conservationists that I have listened to, the word death itself isn't used so often, its hidden behind less evocative words such as mortality, predation, expiration, extinction, and of course, its context specific but they all result in the same event, death. Whilst some species are chosen to be protected, others are condemned to die simply by being ignored. Numerous species go extinct every year, and who knows how many species go extinct without ever being discovered. Each of those species had a role to fulfil, just as each person has their own role within the world.

In terms of ecology, the role of death in various processes needs a lot more attention. A great deal of emphasis is placed on the need for planting many trees and wildflowers but the overall usefulness of this can be minimal when the soil is low in nutrients and organic matter[55]. In mature woodlands, plants and animals die, trees rot and an endless number of interactions take place between invertebrates and rotting matter. Log piles and dead tree stumps provide countless numbers of habitats for so many organisms[56]. Preserving these types of habitats for fungi and saprobic invertebrates is essential to maintaining a functioning ecosystem. Decomposers break down matter and subsequently allow for nutrients to be released back into the soil. Soil ecology is extremely important, and the death of organisms is an integral part of sustaining a rich and fertile rhizosphere[57].

The brutal end of a Jersey Tiger moth which appears to have been dismembered by a Common Wasp.

Many of my walks around the woodlands and grasslands have resulted in finding dead animals, mostly from being attacked by predators, I have seen animals die as they have been hunted by birds of prey. I have found the skeletal remains of a range of birds and mammals, leaving me with only speculations of how they may have died. I have watched an endless number of insects be caught and subdued by spiders. The popping sound of a wasp being bitten into by a Garden Spider is etched into my memory. Its easy to focus on promoting life but when the importance of death is lost or disregarded, the complete picture is not accounted for and important information is missed. Thousands of invertebrates are dependent on carrion, as well as mammals and birds. Predator – prey relationships and the understanding of how population dynamics work, revolve around death rates and birth rates, where prey abundances increase and predator numbers increase, which subsequently causes prey numbers to decrease followed by a decrease in predators and so on, although this is highly simplified.

Remains of a corvid amongst the woodland, it was found beside a tree, perhaps it had perished due to disease or harsh conditions during winter.

The human aspect in terms of causing the death of animals can often be unseen. Habitat loss and use of pesticides are carried out with a focus on human requirements, but its hugely detrimental to wildlife. As suitable areas for organisms become smaller, areas become increasingly congested with various organisms and competitive interactions become more frequent, this could result in the death of many organisms, some of which may already be struggling. Walking through the grasslands, I once came across a dead Jackdaw which appeared to have drowned in a water butt but its journey was not over yet, it still had a purpose to fulfil, and that important purpose was to be broken down and decompose, perhaps it may have even been eaten by a carrion feeder, but even in death the body has a purpose. There is no wastage in nature, its organic material for another process, a transferral of one form of energy to another. This simple fact must be remembered, explored and accepted.

The fleeting life of a Mayfly, the entire adult life of this amazing insect can be over within 24 hours.

People, Work and Ecology

After paying attention to my surroundings for years, it seems that the importance of the environment is decreasing to many people in Heston. What may have been common knowledge a couple of decades ago, that relates to the environment, such as being able to identify certain plants, birds or butterfly species, many people now don't seem to have a clue of what is around them or have any identification skills. That's partly the reason for which I am writing this book, it may act as a helpful reference guide for the people that live in or visit Heston, that also have an interest in ecology. From speaking with various people of different ages and backgrounds, the gap in environmental knowledge between generations is quite big. The pressures behind sustaining a good quality of life for people, can make us forget or disregard the environmental aspect of things, which is fair enough, when you have a family or kids to look after and bills to pay, that becomes the focus, not things like recycling or planting wildflower meadows in your garden, although it should be acknowledged that there are still many people that do these things even with a family and bills to pay, but I'm not going to berate anyone for not really thinking about the environment when the pressures of working and family life are there.

Many environmental jobs aren't amazingly well paid considering the work involved, especially at entry level, and it can take a while to move up and get to the well-paid jobs in ecology. This is where a big problem lies when it comes to conservation and ecology, unless you're extremely passionate about the natural world and conservation (as many people are), its unlikely that people will even consider ecological jobs. Ecology encompasses so many disciplines such as public engagement, law and legislation, education, conservation, research, business, and marketing to name a few. Without having an incentive for people who aren't massively interested in ecology, or perhaps don't know much about ecology, then it will be difficult for ecological jobs to become an attractive area of work to get involved in. Conserving the environment is not going to happen with just the help of people that care about it, people that don't prioritise the environment can also help massively provided they're able to benefit from ecological roles financially. Humanity has created this structure in society which revolves around money, so I believe it must be used wisely in a way that is positive for people, the economy and ecology. This is only one of the many issues that is holding back ecological improvement and its a long hard road ahead if anything is to get any better.

No matter what avenue you take in the world of ecology, you have to be able to communicate effectively with people. The abilities to remain open and engage with other people, to understand the various thoughts and opinions that are out there and to voice your own thoughts are all hugely important. It is imperative that knowledge and experiences are shared. You never know who you will end up knowing and the opportunities that may arise, or who you may help. After visiting various events, attending summer schools, having numerous jobs in different sectors and attending University I have met a number of great people and have been fortunate enough to learn a tremendous amount from many generous people.

Field Trip to Millport where I was able to learn a tremendous amount thanks to the people that were there.

Ultimately, a lot of the progress people make is down to their will, conviction and determination to succeed, but no one gets anywhere completely alone. It can be an arduous route to make a living as a fieldworker or conservationist, with long hours and tremendous effort, but it can also be hugely rewarding.

Art and Ecology

Finally, a subject that will forever be special to me is art. Art and ecology go hand in hand and have a rich history of being associated with each other. Where would ecology be without the anatomical and representative drawings that artists have created? Long before cameras were invented, other than written descriptions, painting and drawing was the best way of recording a sighting of an organism. Cave paintings depicting animals that date back thousands of years provide important information about what must have been present for that specific time.

The way in which art has helped me in terms of ecology is that it focuses my attention completely on the object that I would be drawing. I end up spotting morphological characteristics that I would otherwise miss. Spending all that time focusing on a subject also etches the organisms shape into my memory, so when I happen to be in the field or garden during low light and I spot a birds' silhouette I can sometimes tell what it is just by outline alone. A majority of the time when I am looking through books I focus on the illustrations as they help me to identify species more easily than reading through descriptions. The importance of imagery and imagination cannot be underestimated. Being creative is a key aspect of ecology especially when trying to create experimental designs or when asking questions about how certain aspects of ecology work.

A Greenfinch feeding from a birdfeeder.

A Large Skipper with its angled mid lines on its forewings.

I tend to draw in pen more often than pencil and use colour sparingly, this is because I want the form of the subject to be the most important aspect of the drawing, I also like to have strong, clear lines. More than anything, I think my style of drawing is just a reflection of the way I am as a person. I like things to be black and white, I have belief and confidence in the marks I am making when drawing or painting, there's no room for error, and so I don't plan any piece, I just dive straight into it. Creating art for me is a way of staying in the present and its the same for when I am in the garden or fields searching for things. Being able to stay in the present is probably one of the most important aspects of life for me, and art and ecology are the ways in which I can do that.

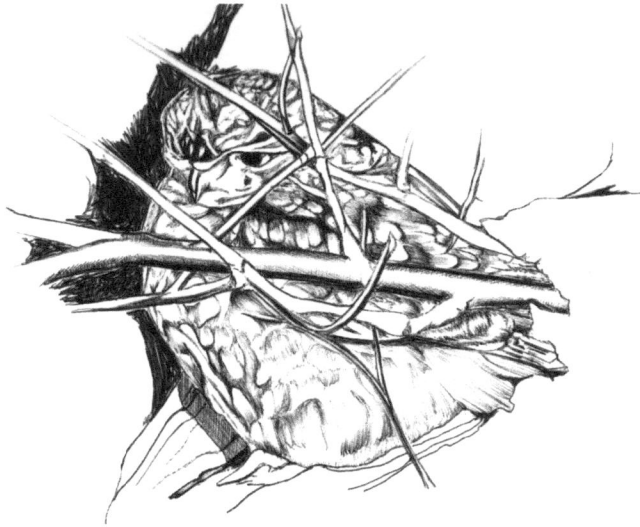

A Little Owl, perched on its favourite tree behind a number of thin branches, this piece was drawn with a biro.

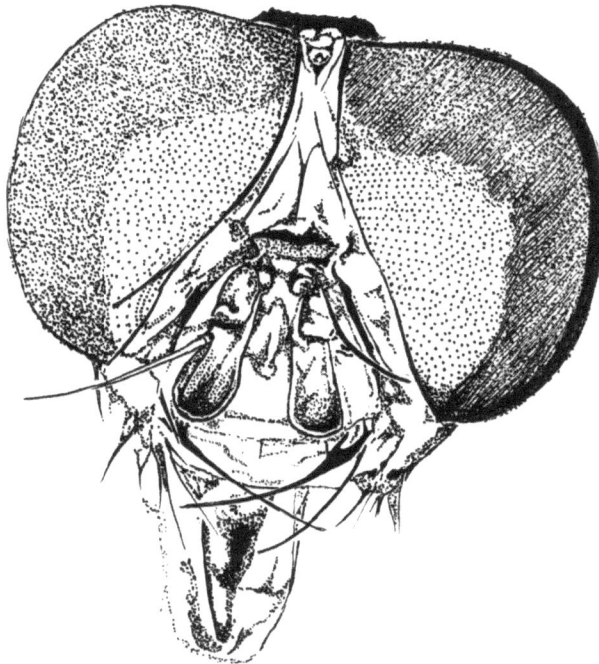

The head of a Dipteran Fly.

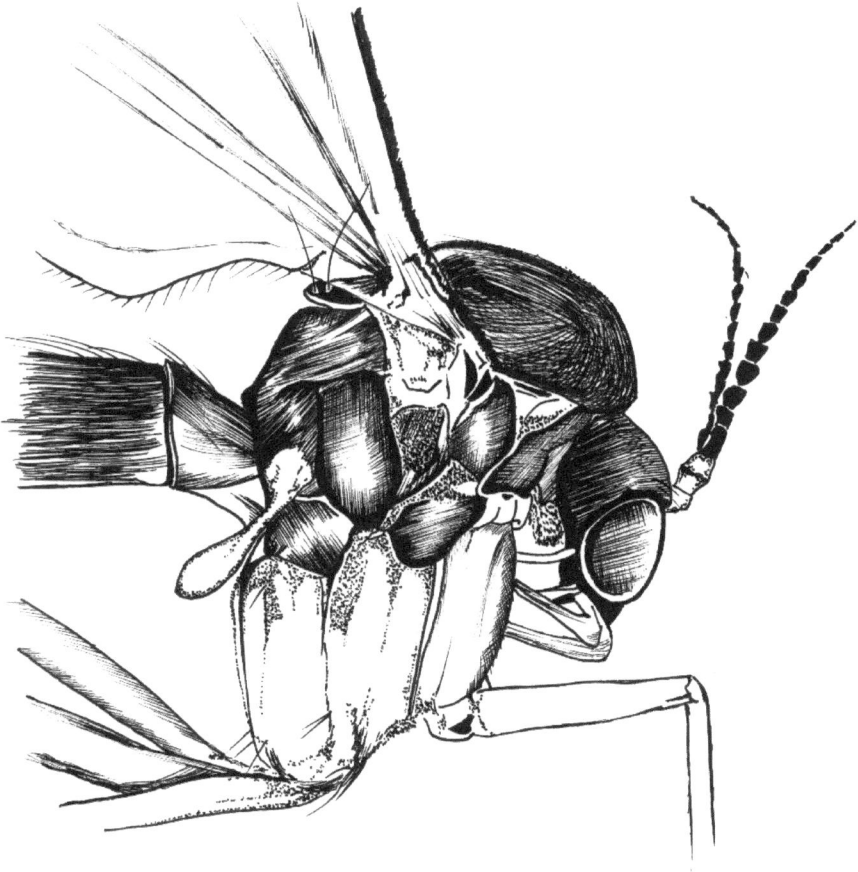

A fungus gnat (Mycetophilid), a member of the genus *Allodia*.
The exoskeletons of flies always have interesting shapes and
structures that are unlikely to be seen on other organisms.
A microscope will be required to truly appreciate the structure
of insect exoskeletons.

Pencil drawing of a Smooth Newt.

Pencil drawing of a Feral Pigeon.

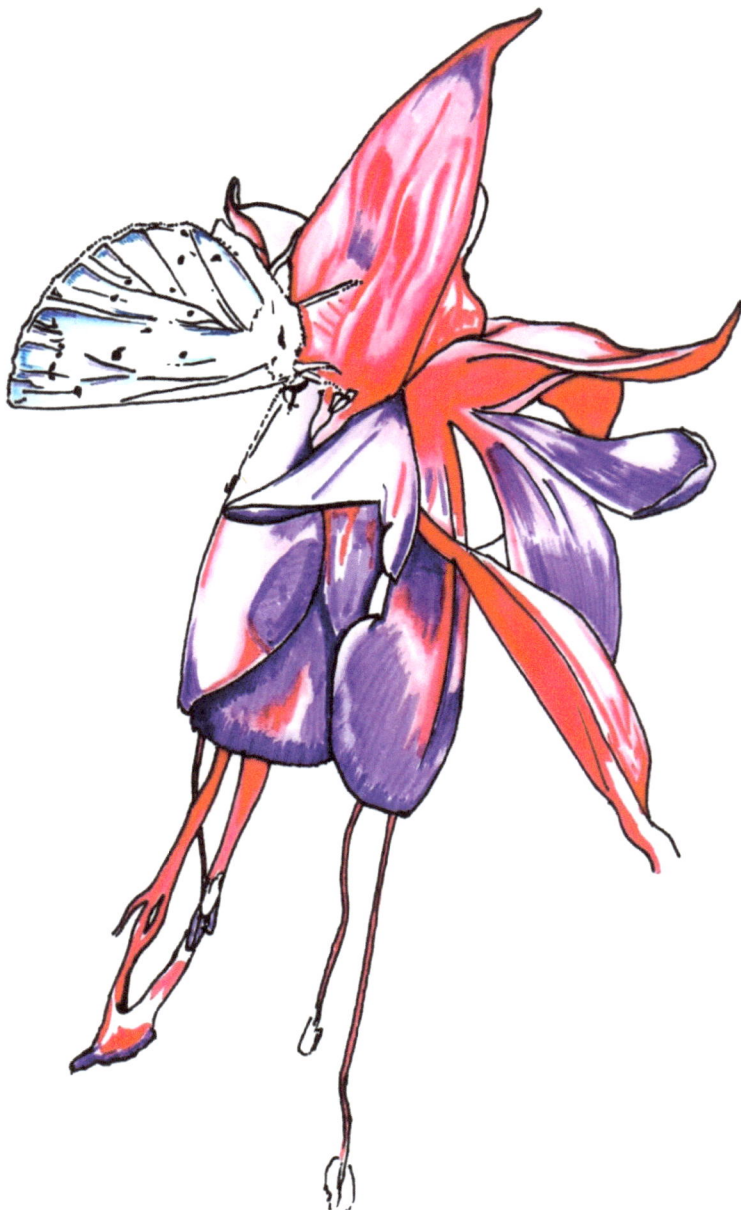

A Holly Blue clambering along a *Fuschia* spp.

Peacock perched upon our wooden garden fence.

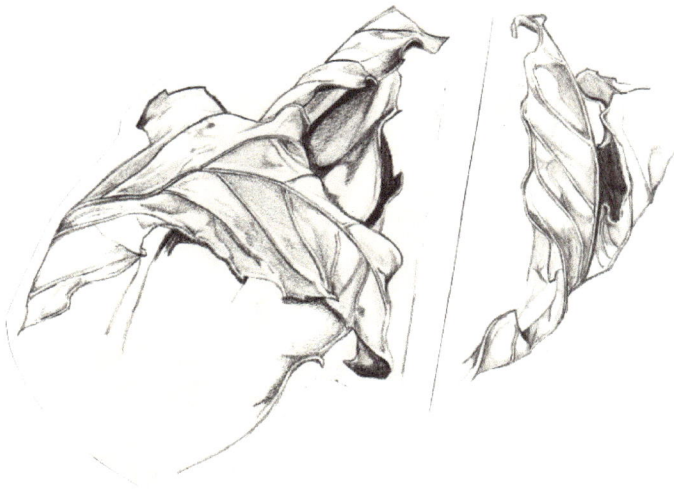

Old and crumpled leaves can be interesting subjects to draw.

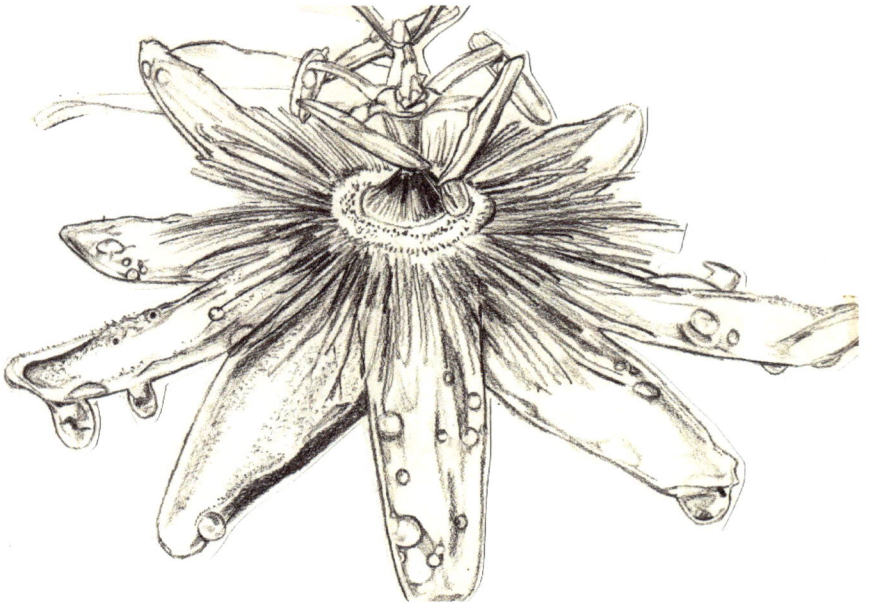

A Passion Flower *(Passiflora* spp.) covered in raindrops

A pair of Magpies perched upon the top of a tree.

Acrylic painting of a Tulip in the garden.

An important member of the fields, Chris walking in the grassland with his tools.

An Endless Journey:
My Final Thoughts

The few years that I have spent monitoring and recording the species in the garden and in the fields made me realise that I could spend my entire lifetime monitoring these areas and I would never be able to learn everything or see everything that there is to see in these places. Even specialising within a subject be it mycology, entomology, ornithology, it would be impossible to know those disciplines completely and so I just wish to explore and see what there is until I am physically incapable of doing so. I believe our gardens will become more and more important over time as green spaces continue to be lost or paved over, and so understanding what attracts wildlife to our gardens and local areas is paramount to the survival of many species.

Another aspect is climate change, and as it continues to impact wildlife, perhaps certain species from abroad will naturally make their way to these shores. As areas become more habitable, migrating species may become resident, perhaps certain insects will make the most of our mild winters and be able to avoid overwintering or entering diapause. Keeping an eye out for invasive and non-native species is also massively important when considering the state of our environment. Change is unavoidable, which is one of the many reasons why monitoring and observing is tremendously important, so any changes that do occur can be spotted and noted.

The garden and fields have been places for reflection and solitude and have been extremely beneficial for my mental state. In a world which seems to be growing and developing at a rapid rate, and life is lived around the clock, being surrounded by nature is immensely important for being able to switch mindset and relieving stress. Various pressures and stresses can be lifted or reduced just by going for a casual stroll in a field and it allows you to notice and take in your surroundings. Being in an office building, a place of work or even within the home can sometimes be suffocating and so what better way to relax and relieve our minds, than by exploring our own gardens and local green spaces.

Garden Species List

Having talked about the many species I have found and come across in both my garden and the fields, I have added a full list of the species I have been able to identify since I began. Beginning with species that I have found in my garden.

Robin	*Erithacus rubecula*
House sparrow	*Passer domesticus*
Blackbird	*Turdus merula*
Mistle Thrush	*Turdus viscivorus*
Crow	*Corvus corone*
Jackdaw	*Corvus monedula*
Magpie	*Pica pica*
Great Tit	*Parus major*
Blue Tit	*Cyanistes caeruleus*
Coal Tit	*Periparus ater*
Long-Tailed Tit	*Aegithalos caudatus*
Goldfinch	*Carduelis carduelis*
Chaffinch	*Fringilla coelebs*
Greenfinch	*Carduelis chloris*
Wren	*Troglodytes troglodytes*
Goldcrest	*Regulus regulus*
Blackcap	*Slyvia atricapilla*
Dunnock	*Prunella modularis*
Pied Wagtail	*Motacilla alba*
Swift	*Apus apus*

Feral Pigeon	*Columba livia*
Woodpigeon	*Columba palambus*
Collared Dove	*Streptopelia decaocto*
Starling	*Sturnus vulgaris*
Kestrel	*Falco tinnunculus*
Red Kite	*Milvus milvus*
Sparrowhawk	*Accipitor nisus*
Ring-necked Parakeet	*Psittacula krameri*
Grey Heron	*Ardea cinerea*
Common Brown Rat	*Rattus norvegicus*
House Mouse	*Mus musculus*
Grey Squirrel	*Sciurus carolinensis*
Red Fox	*Vulpes vulpes*
Common Pipistrelle	*Pipestrellus pipistrellus*
Soprano Pipistrelle	*Pipistrellus pygmaeus*
Green Shield Bug	*Palomena prasina*
Forest Bug	*Pentatoma rufipes*
Common Froghopper	*Philaenus spumarius*
Jumping Tree Bug	*Calocoris nemoralis*
	Heterotoma merioptera/planicornis
Mirid Bug	*Deraeocoris ruber*
Common Nettle Bug	*Liocoris tripustulatus*
Common Backswimmer	*Notonecta glauca*
Lesser Waterboatmen	*Corixa punctata*
Common Pond Skater	*Gerris lacustris*
Eared Leafhopper	*Ledra aurita*
Honeysuckle Sawfly	*Abia fasciata*
Valerian Sawfly	*Macrophya albicincta*
Garden Bumblebee	*Bombus hortorum*
White-Tailed Bumblebee	*Bombus lucorum*
Honeybee	*Apis mellifera*
Leafcutter Bee	*Megachilli centuncularis*

Buff-Tailed Bumblebee Queen	*Bombus terrestris*
Ashy Mining Bee	*Andrena cineraria*
Red-Tailed Bumble Bee	*Bombus lapidarius*
Early Bumble Bee	*Bombus pratorum*
Hairy-footed bumble bee	*Anthophora plumipes*
Moss Carder Bee	*Bombus muscorum*
Gold-Fringed Mason Bee	*Osmia aurulenta*
European Hornet	*Vespa crabro*
Common Wasp	*Vespula vulgaris*
Parasitic Wasp	*Amblyteles armatorious*
Parasitic Wasp	*Protichneumon pisorius*
Parasitic Wasp	*Ophiun minutus (Sub Fam Ophioninae)*
Ruby-Tailed Wasp	*Chrysis ignita agg*
Ornate-tailed Digger Wasp	*Cerceris rybyensis*
Summer Chafer	*Amphimallion solstitialis*
Rose Chafer	*Cetonia aurata*
Lesser Stag Beetle	*Dorcus parallelipidedus*
Dor Beetle	*Geotrupes stercorarius*
Lili Beetle	*Lilioceris lilii*
Sexton Beetle	*Nicrophorus marginatus*
Cereal Leaf Beetle	*Oulema melanopus*
False Oil Beetle	*Oedemera nobilis*
Harlequin Ladybird	*Harmonia axyridis succinea*
Harlequin Ladybird	*Harmonia axyridis spectabilis*
14-spot ladybird	*Propylea 14-punctata*
2-Spot Lady Bird	*Adalia bipunctata*
7-Spot Ladybird	*Coccinella septempunctata*
Bryony Ladybird	*Henosepilachna argus*
Cream-spot Ladybird	*Calvia. quattuordecimguttata*
22-Spot Ladybird	*Psyllobora vigintiduopunctata*

Comma	*Nymphalis c-Album*
Peacock	*Inachis io*
Small Tortoiseshell	*Nymphalis urticae*
Red Admiral	*Vanessa atalanta*
Painted Lady	*Vanessa cardui*
Holly Blue	*Celastrina argiolus*
White-letter Hairstreak	*Satyrium w-album*
Ringlet	*Aphantopus hyperantus*
Small Heath	*Coenonympha pamphilus*
Speckled Wood	*Pararge aegeria*
Gatekeeper	*Maniola tithonus*
Meadow Brown	*Maniola jurtina*
Orange-Tip	*Anthocharis cardamines*
Small White butterfly	*Pieris rapae*
Large White	*Pieris brassicae*
Green-Veined White	*Pieris napi*
Brimstone	*Gonepteryx rhamni*
Small Skipper	*Thymelicus sylvestris*
White Ermine	*Spilosoma lubricipeda*
Buff Ermine	*Spilosoma lutea*
Muslin Moth	*Diaphora mendica*
Pale Tussock	*Calliteara pudibunda*
Gypsy moth	*Lymantria dispar*
Cinnabar	*Tyria jacobaeae*
Straw Dot	*Rivula sericealis*
Beautiful Hook Tip	*Laspeyria flexula*
Scarce Footman	*Eilema complana*
Common Footman	*Eilema lurideola*
Ruby Tiger	*Phragmatobia fuliginosa*
Jersey Tiger	*Euplagia quadripunctaria*
Vapourer	*Orgyia antiqua*
Herald	*Scoliopteryx libatrix*

March Tubic	*Diurnea fagella*
Lunar Marbled Moth	*Drymonia ruficornis*
Buff tip	*Phalera buceuphala*
Pale Prominent	*Pterostoma palpina*
Sallow Kitten	*Furcula furcula*
Hummingbird Hawk-moth	*Macroglossum stellatarum*
Lime Hawk-moth	*Mimas tiliae*
Elephant Hawk Moth	*Deilephila elpenor*
Parsnip Moth	*Depressaria radiella*
Common Flat Body Moth	*Agonopterix heracliana*
	Ethmia quadrillella
Brown Spot Flat Body	*Agonopterix alstromeriana*
Buff Arches	*Habrosyne pyritoides*
Oak Hook-Tip	*Watsonalla binaria*
Chinese Character	*Cilix glaucata*
Angle Shades	*Phlogophora meticulosa*
Old Lady	*Mormo maura*
Lunar Spotted Pinion	*Cosmia pyralina*
Twin Spotted Quaker	*Anorthea munda*
Silver Y	*Autographa gamma*
Setaceous Hebrew Character	*Xestia c-nigrum*
Knot Grass Larva	*Acronicta rumicis*
True Lovers Knot	*Lycophotia porphyrea*
Black Rustic	*Aporophyla nigra*
Mottled Rustic	*Caradrina morpheus*
Common Rustic	*Mesapamea secalis*
Lesser Common Rustic	*Mesapamea didyma*
Vines Rustic	*Hoplodrina ambigua*
Pale Mottled Willow	*Caradrina palvipalpis*
Rustic	*Hoplodrina blanda*
Beaded Chestnut	*Agrochola lychnidis*
Chestnut	*Conistra vaccinii*

Tree Lichen Beauty	*Cyrphia algae*
Marbled Beauty	*Bryophila domestica*
Common Quaker	*Orthosia cerasi*
Hebrew Character	*Orthosia gothica*
Clouded Drab	*Orthosia incerta*
Early Grey	*Xylocampa areola*
Dark Arches	*Apamea monoglypha*
Light Arches	*Apamea lithoxylaea*
Nut Tree Tussock	*Colocasia coryli*
Lesser spotted Pinion	*Cosmia affinis*
Turnip Moth	*Agrotis segetum*
Spectacle	*Abrostola tripartita*
Grey Dagger	*Acronicta psi*
Treble Lines	*Charanyca trigrammica*
Shuttle-shaped Dart	*Agrotis puta*
Heart and Dart	*Agrotis exclamationis*
Heart and Club	*Agrotis clavis*
Flame	*Axylia putris*
Flame Shoulder	*Ochropleura plecta*
Marbled Minor	*Oligia strigilis*
Tawny Marbled Minor	*Oligia latruncula*
Middle-barred Minor	*Oligia fasciuncula*
Lunar Underwing	*Omaphaloscelis lunosa*
Large Yellow Underwing	*Noctua protuba*
Lesser Yellow Underwing	*Noctua comes*
Broad-bordered Yellow Underwing	*Noctua fimbriata*
Lesser Broad-bordered Yellow Underwing	*Noctua janthe*
Copper Underwing	*Amphipyra pyramidea*
White Point	*Mythimna albipuncta*
Pale Shouldered Brocade	*Lacanobia thalassina*

Bright-Line Brown-Eye	*Lacanobia oleracea*
Lychnis	*Hadena bicruris*
Cabbage Moth	*Mamestra brassicae*
Dun-bar	*Cosmia trapezina*
Clay	*Mythimna ferrago*
Common Wainscot	*Mythimna pallens*
Brown-Line Bright Eye	*Mythimna conigera*
Brown Veined Wainscot	*Archanara dissolute*
Coronet	*Craniophora ligustri*
Small Ranunculus	*Hecatera dysodea*
Barred Sallow	*Tiliacea aurago*
Centre-barred Sallow	*Atethmia centrago*
Dark Brocade	*Mnitype adusta*
Toadflax brocade	*Calophasia lunula*
Dusky Sallow	*Eremobia ochroleuca*
Bee Moth	*Aphomia sociella*
Wax Moth	*Galleria mellonella*
Meal Moth	*Pyralis farinalis*
Rose Flounced Tabby	*Endotricha flammealis*
Large Tabby	*Aglossa pinguinalis*
Mother of Pearl	*Pleuroptya ruralis*
Double Striped Tabby	*Hypsopygia glaucinalis*
Twin Barred Knot Horn	*Homoesoma sinuella*
Dotted Oak Knot Horn	*Phycita roborella*
Gold Triangle	*Hypsopygia costalis*
Grey Knot-horn	*Acrobasis advenella*
Plume Moth	*Emmelina monodactyla*
Brown House Moth	*Hoffmannophila pseudospretella*
White Shouldered House Moth	*Endrosis sarcitrella*
Ruddy Streak	*Tachystola acroxantha*
Sulphur Tubic	*Esperia sulphurella*

Golden Brown Tubic	*Crassa unitella*
March Moth	*Alsophila aescularia*
Yellow Barred-Brindle	*Acasis viretata*
Yellow Shell	*Camptogramma bilineata*
Double striped pug	*Gymnoscelis rufifasciata*
May Highflyer	*Hydriomena impulviata*
Oak Beauty	*Biston strataria*
Spring Usher	*Agriopis leucophaearia*
Brindled Beauty	*Lycia hirtaria*
Common Carpet	*Epirrhoe alternata*
Red-Green Carpet	*Chloroclysta siterata*
Spruce Carpet	*Thera britannica*
Cypress Carpet	*Thera cupressata*
Common Marbled Carpet	*Dysstroma truncate*
Broken-barred Carpet	*Electrophaes corylata*
Blue-Bordered Carpet	*Plemyria rubiginata*
Foxglove Pug	*Eupithecia pulchellata*
Green Pug	*Pasiphila rectangulata*
Willow Beauty	*Peribatodes rhomboidaria*
Maidens Blush	*Cyclophora punctaria*
Light Emerald	*Campaea margaritata*
Common Emerald	*Hemithea aestivaria*
Brimstone Moth	*Opisthograptis luteolata*
Riband Wave	*Idaea aversata ab. remutata*
Small Fan Footed Wave	*Idaea biselata*
Dwarf Cream Wave	*Idaea fuscovenosa*
Least Carpet	*Idaea rusticata*
Small Dusty Wave	*Idaea seriata*
Treble Brown Spot	*Idaea trigeminata*
Peppered Moth	*Biston betularia*
Small Blood-vein	*Scopula imitaria*
Clouded Border	*Lomaspilis marginata*

Small Argent and Sable	*Epirrhoe tristata*
Dusky Thorn	*Ennomos fuscantaria*
Early Thorn	*Selenia dentaria*
Lime Speck Pug	*Eupithecia centaureata*
Cypress Pug	*Eupithecia phoeniceata*
Winter Moth	*Operophtera brumata*
Scalloped Oak	*Crocallis elinguaria*
Diamond Back Marble	*Eudemis profundana*
Hook Marked Straw Moth	*Agapeta hamana*
Broad Blotch Drill	*Dichrorampha alpinana*
Light Brown Apple Moth	*Epiphyas postvittana*
Little Conch	*Cochylis dubitana*
Codling Moth	*Cydia pomonella*
Small Birch Bell	*Epinotia ramella*
Brindled shoot	*Gypsonoma minutana*
Triple blotched bell	*Notocelia trimaculana*
Marbled Bell	*Eucosma campoliliana*
Green oak Tortrix	*Tortrix viridana*
Large Fruit Tree Tortrix	*Archips podana*
Yellow Spot Tortrix	*Pseudargyrotoza conwagana*
Barred Marble	*Celypha striana*
Common Marble	*Celypha lacunana*
Orange Pine Tortrix	*Lozotaeniodes formosona*
May Shade	*Cnephasia communana*
Meadow Shade	*Cnephasia pasiuana*
Flat Tortrix	*Cnephasia asseclana*
Maple Button	*Acleris forsskaleana*
Vetch Piercer	*Grapholita jungiella*
Acorn Piercer	*Pommene fasciana*
Red Barred Tortrix	*Ditula angustiorana*
Dark Barred Tortrix	*Syndemis musculana*
Dark strawberry tortrix	*Celypha lacunana*

Lichen Button	*Acleris literana*
Cherry Bark Moth	*Enarmonia formosana*
Rough-Winged Conch	*Phtheochroa rugosana*
Brindled Tortrix	*Ptycholoma lecheana*
Pine Leaf Mining Moth	*Clavigesta purdeyi*
Bramble Shoot Moth	*Notocelia uddmanniana*
Mint Moth	*Pyrausta aurata*
Elder Pearl	*Anania coronate*
Lesser Pearl	*Sitochroa verticalis*
Box Moth	*Cydalima perspectalis*
Elbow Striped Grass Veneer	*Agriphila geniculea*
Small Magpie	*Anania hortulata*
Small grey	*Eudonia mercurella*
Pearl Grass Veneer	*Catoptria pinella*
Ringed China-mark	*Parapoynx stratiotata*
Garden Pebble	*Evergestis forficalis*
Common swift	*Korscheltellus lupulina*
Orange Swift	*Triodia sylvina*
Golden Argent	*Argyresthia goedartella*
Bird Cherry Ermine	*Yponomeuta evonymella*
Yellow backed clothes moth	*Monopis obviella*
Peach Twig Borer	*Anarsia lineatella*
Gorse Case Bearer	*Coleophora albicosta*
Colephora spp.	*Colephora* spp.
Oak Nycteoline	*Nycteola revayana*
Scarce Silver Lines	*Bena bicolorana*
Pied Smudge	*Ypsolopha sequella*
Black dancer Caddis fly	*Mystacides sepulchralis*
Speckled Bush Cricket	*Leptophyes puctatissima*
Bee Fly	*Bombylius major*
Crane Fly	*Tipula paludosa*
Drone Fly	*Eristalis tenax*

Narcissus Bulb Fly	*Merodon equestris*
Marmalade Hover Fly	*Episyrphus balteatus*
Dead Head Fly	*Myathropa florea*
Hornet Mimic Hover Fly	*Volucella zonaria*
Sun Fly	*Helophilus pendulus*
	Syrphus vitripennis
	Syrphus ribesii
Northern Wasp Hoverfly	*Chrysotoxum arcuatum*
Spotted Crane Fly	*Nephrotoma appendiculata*
Bluebottle blow fly	*Calliphora vomitoria*
Greenbottle blow fly	*Lucillia caesar*
Robber/Assassin Fly	
Soldier Fly	*Chloromyia formosa*
Tachinid Fly	*Tachina fera*
Large Red Damselfly	*Pyrrhosoma nymphula*
Common Darter	*Sympetrum striolatum*
Brown Centipede	*Lithobius forfiticus*
House Spider	*Tegenaria domestica*
Cellar Spider	*Pholcus phalangioides*
Woodlouse Spider	*Dysdera crocata*
Cricket Bat Orb Weaver	*Mangora acalypha*
Garden Cross Spider	*Araneus diadematus*
Cucumber Green Spider	*Araniella cucurbitina*
Missing Sector Orb Weaver	*Zygiella x-notata*
Common hammock weaver	*Linyphia triangularis*
Furrow Spider	*Larinioides cornutus*
Buzzing Spider	*Anyphaena accentuate*
Nursery Web Spider	*Pisaura mirabilis*
False Widow Spider	*Steatoda nobilis*
False Black Widow	*Steatoda grossa*
Zebra Jumping Spider	*Salticus scenicus*
Common Crab Spider	*Xysticus cristatus*

White Crab Spider	*Misumena vatia*
Long Jawed Orb Weaver	*Pachygnatha degeeri*
Silver stretch Spider	*Tetragnatha montana*
Stone Spider	*Drassodes lapidosus*
Glistening Inkcap	*Coprinus micaceus*
Crystal Brain Fungus	*Exidia nucleata*
Honey fungus	*Armillaria mellea*
Wandering Snail	*Radix balthica*
Ramshorn Snail	*Planorbarius corneus*
Yellow Cellar Slug	*Limacus flavus*
Smooth Newt	*Lissotriton vulgaris*

Field Species List

Stonechat	*Saxicola torquata*
Robin	*Erithacus rubecula*
Reed Bunting	*Emberiza schoeniclus*
Meadow Pipit	*Anthus pratensis*
Pied Wagtail	*Motacilla alba*
Wren	*Troglodytes troglodytes*
Dunnock	*Prunella modularis*
Kestrel	*Falco tinnunculus*
Common Buzzard	*Buteo buteo*
Sparrowhawk	*Accipiter nisus*
Red kite	*Milvus milvus*
Carrion crow	*Corvus corone*
Jackdaw	*Corvus monedula*
Magpie	*Pica pica*
Jay	*Garrulus glandarius*
Song thrush	*Turdus philomelos*
Mistle thrush	*Turdus viscivorus*
Redwing	*Turdus iliacus*
Fieldfare	*Turdus pilaris*
Blackbird	*Turdus merula*
Pheasant	*Phasianus colchicus*
Green Woodpecker	*Picus viridis*
Greater Spotted Woodpecker	*Dendrocopos major*
Starling	*Sturnus vulgaris*
Great tit	*Parus major*

Blue tit	*Cyanistes caeruleus*
Long-Tailed Tit	*Aegithalos caudatus*
House sparrow	*Passer domesticus*
Goldfinch	*Carduelis carduelis*
Woodpigeon	*Columba palambus*
Ring necked Parakeet	*Psittacula krameri*
Blackcap	*Sylvia atricapilla*
Chiffchaff	*Phylloscopus collybita*
Whitethroat	*Sylvia communis*
Linnet	*linaria cannabina*
Swift	*Apus apus*
Common Cuckoo	*Cuculus canorus*
Spotted Flycatcher	*Muscicapa striata*
Whinchat	*Saxicola rubetra*
Grey Heron	*Ardea cinerea*
Black Redstart	*Phoenicurus ochruros*
Black-headed Gull	*Chroicocephalus ridibundus*
Yellow-Legged Gull	*Larus michahelis*
Lesser Whitethroat	*Sylvia curruca*
Common Pipistrelle	*Pipistrellus pipistrellus*
Soprano Pipistrelle	*Pipistrellus pygmaeus*
Red Fox	*Vulpes vulpes*
Grey Squirrel	*Sciurus carolinensis*
Peacock	*Inachis io*
Small Tortoiseshell	*Nymphalis urticae*
Speckled Wood	*Pararge aegeria*
Orange Tip	*Anthocharis cardamines*
Small White	*Pieris rapae*
Comma	*Polygonia c-album*
Brimstone	*Gonepteryx rhamni*
Common Blue	*Polyammatus icarus*
Holly Blue	*Celastrina argiolus*

Red Admiral	Vanessa atalanta
Green Veined White	Pieris napi
Small Heath	Coenonympha pamphilus
Small Copper	Lycaena phlaeas
Brown Argus	Aricia agestis
Meadow Brown	Maniola jurtina
Large Skipper	Ochlodes sylvanus
Painted Lady	Vanessa cardui
White Letter Hairstreak	Satyrium w-album
Ringlet	Aphantopus hyperantus
Small Skipper	Thymelicus sylvestris
Purple Hairstreak	Neozephyrus quercus
Large White	Pieris brassicae
Marbled White	Melanargia galathea
Gatekeeper	Pyronia tithonus
Essex Skipper	Thymelicus lineola
Common Holly	Ilex aquifolium
Ivy	Hedera helix
Creeping Thistle	Cirsium arvense
Hawkweed spp.	Hieracium spp.
Lesser Knapweed	Centaurea debauxii
Mugwort	Artemisia vulgaris
Prickly Lettuce	Lactuca serriola
Ragwort	Jacobaea vulgaris
Smooth Hawksbeard	Crepis capillaris
Western Goatsbeard	Tragopogon dubius
Yarrow	Achillea millefolium
Hedge Mustard	Sisymbrium officinale
Lesser Stitchwort	Stellaria graminea
Field Bindweed	Convolvulus arvensis
Dogwood	Cornus sanguinea
Birds foot trefoil	Lotus corniculatus

Red Clover	*Trifolium pratense*
Tufted Vetch	*Vicia cracca*
White Clover	*Trifolium repens*
Oak	*Quercus* spp.
Common Centaury	*Centaurium erythraea*
Herb Robert	*Geranium robertianum*
Perforate St Johns Wort	*Hypericum perforatum*
Self Heal	*Prunella vulgaris*
Common Mallow	*Malva sylvestris*
Ash	*Fraxinus excelsior*
Rosebay Willowherb	*Chamaenerion angustifolium*
Ribwort Plantain	*Plantago lanceolata*
Common Bent	*Agrostis capillaris*
Common Crouch	*Elymus repens*
Meadow Foxtail	*Alopecurus pratensis*
Wall Barley	*Hordeum murinum*
Yorkshire Fog	*Holcus lanataus*
Curly Dock	*Rumex crispus*
Creeping buttercup	*Ranunculus repens*
Blackthorn	*Prunus spinosa*
Bramble	*Rubus spp.*
Field Rose	*Rosa arvensis*
Hawthorn	*Crataegus monogyna*
Goosegrass	*Galium aparine*
Elm	*Ulmus* spp.
Hogweed	*Heracleum sphondylium*
Stinging Nettle	*Urtica dioica*
Cuckoo-pint	*Arum maculatum*
Wasp Spider	*Argiope bruennichi*
Crab Spider	*Xysticus cristatus*
Nursery Web spider	*Pisaura mirabilis*
Emporer dragonfly	*Anax imperator*

Common Darter	Sympetrum striolatum
Black Tailed Skimmer	Orthetrum cancellatum
Scorpion Fly	Panorpa communis
Bishops Mitre	Aelia acuminata
Burnet Companion	Euclidia glyphica
Cinnabar	Tyria jacobaeae
Red-Tailed Bumblebee	Bombus lapidarius
Two-Banded Wasp Hoverfly	Chrysotoxum bicinctum
False Oil Beetle	Oedemera nobilis
Six-Spot Burnet	Zygaena filipendulae
Bee fly	Bombylius major
7-Spot Ladybird	Coccinella septempunctata
Buff-tailed Bumblebee	Bombus terrestris
Yellow Barred Longhorn	Nemophora degeerella
Hairy Shield Bug	Dolycoris baccarum
Red Soldier Beetle	Cantharis fusca
Devils Coach Horse	Staphylinus olens
Harlequin ladybird	Harmonia axyridis
Large red Damselfly	Pyrrhosoma nymphula
Meadow Grasshopper	Pseudochorthippus parallelus
Dock Bug	Coreus marginata
Yarrow Plume	Gillmeria pallidactyla
	Aclista spp.
	Allodia spp.
	Allodiopsis rustica
	Bolitophila spp.
	Bradysia spp.
	Copromyza equina
	Corynoptera
	Dinotrema spp.
	Drosophila melanogaster
	Exechia fusca

	Exechia repanda
	Fannia spp.
	Leia bimaculata
	Leiomyza spp.
	Megaselia rufipes
	Muscina spp.
	Mycetophila fungorum
	Mycetophila ruficollis
	Mycetophila spp.
	Myrmica rubra
	Pseudexechia spp.
	Pseudexechia trisignata
	Pseudexechia trivittata
	Spelobia spp.
	Suillia variegata
	Tarnania fenestralis
	Trichocera spp.
	Tricimba lineella
Clustered Bonnet	*Mycena inclinata*
Glistening Ink-Cap	*Coprinus micaceous*
Velvet Shank	*Flammulina velutipes*
Jelly-Ear Fungus	Auricularia auricula-judae
Horse Mushroom	*Agaricus arvensis*
Field Mushroom	*Agaricus campestris*
Wrinkly Peach Fungus	*Rhodotus palmatus*
Ivory Funnel	*Clitocybe dealbata*
Frosty Funnel	*Clitocybe phyllophyila*
	Lactarius spp.
Spring Brittlestem	*Psathyrella spadiceogrisea*
St. Georges Mushroom	*Calocybe gambosa*
Conical Brittlestem	*Parasola conopilus*
	Marasmius spp.

Shaggy Parasol	*Chlorophyllum rhacodes*
Wood Blewit	*Lepista nuda*
	Pleurotus spp.
Sulphur Tuft	*Hypholoma fasciculare*
	Collybia spp.
Honey fungus	*Armillaira* spp.
	Cortinarius spp.
	Tubaria spp.
Dewdrop Mottlegill	*Panaeolus acuminatus*
The Deceiver	*Laccaria laccata*
Stubble Rosegill	*Volvopluteus gloiocephalus*
	Lentinellus
owy Waxcap	*Cuphophyllus virgineus*
Yellow Brain Fungus	*Tremella mesenterica*
Stump Puffball	*Lycoperdon pyriforme*
	Russula spp.
Bay Polypore	*Polyporus durus*
Yellow Fieldcap	*Bolbitius titubans*
Earthstar	*Geastrum* spp.
Blue Roundhead	*Stropharia caerulea*
	Postia spp.
Mealy Funnel	*Clitocybe vibecina*

References

1. Tobias, J. & Seddon, N. (2000) Territoriality as a paternity guard in the European robin, *Erithacus rubecula*. *Animal behaviour*. **60**. 165-173. 10.1006/anbe.2000.1442.

2. Adomako, M., Xue, W., Roiloa, S., Zhang, Q., Du, D.L. & Yu, F.H. (2021) Earthworms Modulate Impacts of Soil Heterogeneity on Plant Growth at Different Spatial Scales. *Frontiers in Plant Science*. **12**. 10.3389/fpls.2021.735495.

3. Plummer, K. E., Siriwardena, G. M., Conway, G. J., Risely, K., & Toms, M. P. (2015) Is supplementary feeding in gardens a driver of evolutionary change in a migratory bird species? *Global change biology*. **21**. 4353–4363. 10.1111/gcb.13070

4. Rolshausen, G., Segelbacher, G., Hobson, K.A. & Schaefer, H.M. (2009) Contemporary evolution of reproductive isolation and phenotypic divergence in sympatry along a migratory divide. *Current Biology*. **19**. 2097–2101.

5. Kelber, A. (2019) Bird colour vision – from cones to perception. *Current Opinion in Behavioral Sciences*. **30**. 34-40. 10.1016/j.cobeha.2019.05.003.

6. Steidinger, B., Crowther, T.W. Liang, J., Nuland, M.E., Werner, G.D.A., Reich, P., Nabuurs, G.J. de-Miguel, S., Zhou 周沫, M. Picard, N., Herault, B., Zhao, X., Zhang, C. Routh, D., Peay, K., Abegg, M., Yao, C.Y.A., Alberti, G., Almeyda Zambrano, A. & Zo-Bi, I. (2019) Climatic controls of decomposition drive the global biogeography of forest-tree symbioses. *Nature*. **569.**

7. Bennett, A. & Classen, A. (2020) Climate change influences mycorrhizal fungal–plant interactions, but conclusions are limited by geographical study bias. *Ecology*. **101**. 10.1002/ecy.2978.

8. Dean, R., Kan, J., Pretorius, Z., Hammond-Kosack, K., Pietro, A., Spanu, P., Rudd, J., Dickman, M., Kahmann, R., Ellis, J. & Foster, G.

(2012) The Top 10 Fungal Pathogens in Molecular Plant Pathology. *Molecular plant pathology*. **13**. 414-30. 10.1111/j.1364-3703.2011.00783.x.

9. Pollard, K.M., Gange, A.C., Seier, M.K. & Ellison, C.A. (2022) A semi-natural evaluation of the potential of the rust fungus Puccinia komarovii var. glanduliferae as a biocontrol agent of Impatiens glandulifera. Biological control. 165. 104786. 10.1016/j.biocontrol.2021.104786

10. Fitter, A. H. & Fitter, R. S. (2002) Rapid changes in flowering time in British plants. Science (New York, N.Y.). 296. 1689–1691. 10.1126/science.107161

11. Breuner, C., Sprague, R., Patterson, S. & Woods, H. (2013) Environment, behavior and physiology: Do birds use barometric pressure to predict storms? *The Journal of experimental biology*. **216**. 1982-90. 10.1242/jeb.081067.

12. Galton, P. & Shepherd, J. (2012) Experimental Analysis of Perching in the European Starling (Sturnus vulgaris: Passeriformes; Passeres), and the Automatic Perching Mechanism of Birds. Journal of experimental zoology. Part A, *Ecological genetics and physiology*. **317**. 205-15. 10.1002/jez.1714.

13. Götmark, F., Post, P., Olsson, J., Himmelmann, D. & Gotmark, F. (1997) Natural Selection and Sexual Dimorphism: Sex-Biased Sparrowhawk Predation Favours Crypsis in Female Chaffinches. *Oikos*. **80**. 540. 10.2307/3546627.

14. Tseng, M., Kaur, K., Pari, S., Sarai, K., Chan, D., Yao, C., Porto, P., Toor, A., Toor, H. & Fograscher, K. (2018) Decreases in beetle body size linked to climate change and warming temperatures. *Journal of Animal Ecology*. **87**. 10.1111/1365-2656.12789.

15. Dunbar, J., Vitkauskaite, A., Lawton, C., Waddams, B. & Dugon, M. (2022) Webslinger vs. Dark Knight First record of a false widow spider Steatoda nobilis preying on a pipistrelle bat in Britain. *Ecosphere*. **13**. 10.1002/ecs2.3959.

16. Vance, J., Williams, J., Elekonich, M. & Roberts, S. (2009) The effects of age and behavioral development on honey bee (Apis mellifera) flight performance. *The Journal of Experimental Biology*. **212**. 2604-11. 10.1242/jeb.028100.

17. Pimm, S. & Lawton, J.H. (1977) The number of trophic levels in ecological communities. *Nature*. **268**. 329. 10.1038/268329a0.

18. Shipley, J., Twining, C., Taff, C., Vitousek, M., Flack, A. & Winkler, D. (2020) Birds advancing lay dates with warming springs face greater risk of chick mortality. *Proceedings of the National Academy of Sciences.* **117.** 25590-25594. 10.1073/pnas.2009864117.

19. de Fouchier, A., Walker, W.B., Montagné, N., Steiner, C., Binyameen, M., Schlyter, F., et al. (2017) Functional evolution of Lepidoptera olfactory receptors revealed by deorphanization of a moth repertoire. *Nature Communications.* **8.** 15709–15709. 10.1038/ncomms15709

20. Zhang, D. & Löfstedt, C. (2015) Moth pheromone receptors: Gene sequences, function and evolution. *Frontiers in Ecology and Evolution.* **3.** 10.3389/fevo.2015.00105.

21. Buniyaadi, A., Taufique, S.K. & Kumar, Vinod. (2019) Self-recognition in corvids: evidence from the mirror-mark test in Indian house crows (Corvus splendens). *Journal of Ornithology.* **161.** 1-10. 10.1007/s10336-019-01730-2.

22. Brown, P., Roy, D.B., Harrower, C., Dean, H., Rorke, S. & Roy, H. (2018) Spread of a model invasive alien species, the harlequin ladybird Harmonia axyridis in Britain and Ireland. *Scientific Data.* **5.** 180239. 10.1038/sdata.2018.239.

23. Brown, P. & Roy, H. (2017) Native ladybird decline caused by the invasive harlequin ladybird Harmonia axyridis : evidence from a long-term field study. *Insect Conservation and Diversity.* **11.** 10.1111/icad.12266.

24. Kindl, J., Jiroš, P., Kalinova, B., Zacek, P. & Valterová, I. (2012) Females of the Bumblebee Parasite, Aphomia sociella, Excite Males Using a Courtship Pheromone. *Journal of chemical ecology.* **38.** 400-7. 10.1007/s10886-012-0100-3.

25. Harwood, T., Tomlinson, I., Potter, C. & Knight, J.D. (2011) Dutch elm disease revisited: Past, present and future management in Great Britain. *Plant Pathology.* **60.** 545 - 555. 10.1111/j.1365-3059.2010.02391.x.

26. Yarger, A. & Fox, J. (2016) Dipteran Halteres: Perspectives on Function and Integration for a Unique Sensory Organ. *Integrative and Comparative Biology.* **56.** icw086. 10.1093/icb/icw086.

27. Townsend, M. (2013) Oak Processionary Moth in the United Kingdom. *Outlooks on Pest Management.* **24.** 10.1564/v24_feb_10.

28. Claridge, M. (2005) Insect sounds and communication-an introduction. Insect Sounds and Communication: Physiology, Behaviour, Ecology, and Evolution. 3-10. 10.1201/9781420039337.pt1.

29. Lessio, F., Picciau, L., Gonella, E., Mandrioli, M., Tota, F. & Alma, A. (2016) The mosaic leafhopper Orientus ishidae: Host plants, spatial distribution, infectivity, and transmission of 16SrV phytoplasmas to vines. *Bulletin of Insectology.* **69.** 277-289.

30. de Raad, L., Lurz, P. & Kortland, K. (2021) Managing forests for the future: Balancing timber production with the conservation of Eurasian red squirrel (Sciurus vulgaris). *Forest Ecology and Management.* **493.** 10.1016/j.foreco.2021.119164.

31. Visser, M. & Holleman, L. (2001) Warmer spring disrupt the synchrony of Oak and Winter Moth phenology. *Proceedings of The Royal Society B. Biological sciences.* **268.** 289-94. 10.1098/rspb.2000.1363.

32. Robertson, P., Mill, A., Rushton, S., Mckenzie, A., Sage, R. & Aebischer, N. (2017) Pheasant release in Great Britain: long-term and large-scale changes in the survival of a managed bird. *European Journal of Wildlife Research.* **63.** 10.1007/s10344-017-1157-7.

33. Mikkola, H. (1976) Owls killing and killed by other owls and raptors in Europe. *British Birds.* **69.** 144-154

34. Carter, I. (2019) The Red Kite Reintroduction: thirty years on. *British Birds.* **112.** 422-426.

35. Gange, A., Gange, E.G., Sparks, T. & Boddy, L. (2007) Rapid and Recent Changes in Fungal Fruiting Patterns. *Science* (New York, N.Y.). **316.** 71. 10.1126/science.1137489.

36. Jakovlev, J. (2011) Fungus gnats (Diptera: Sciaroidea) associated with dead wood and wood growing fungi: new rearing data from Finland and Russian Karelia and general analysis of known larval microhabitats in Europe. *Entomologica Fennica.* **22.** 10.33338/ef.4693.

37. Hågvar, S. & Krzeminska, E. (2007) Contribution to the winter phenology of Trichoceridae (Diptera) in snow-covered southern Norway. *Studia dipterologica.* **14.** 271-283.

38. Renou, M., Conchou, L., Lucas, P., Meslin, C., Proffit, M. & Staudt, M. (2019) Insect Odorscapes: From Plant Volatiles to Natural Olfactory Scenes. *Frontiers in Physiology.* **10.** 972. 10.3389/fphys.2019.00972.

39. Hounsome, T., O'Mahony, D. & Delahay, R. (2004) The diet of Little Owls Athene noctua in Gloucestershire, England: Capsule Little Owls take a wide variety of food, most of which is made up of earthworms, but also includes bats. *Bird Study.* **51.** 282-284. 10.1080/00063650409461366.

40. Jakovlev, J. (2012) Fungal hosts of mycetophilids (Diptera: Sciaroidea excluding Sciaridae): a review. *Mycology.* **3.** 11-23. doi: 10.1080/21501203.2012.662533.

41. Braschler, B. & Hill, J. (2007) Role of larval host plants in the climate-driven range expansion of the butterfly Polygonia c-album. *The Journal of Animal Ecology.* **76.** 415-23. 10.1111/j.1365-2656.2007.01217.x.

42. Moorcroft, D. & Wilson, J.D. (2000) The ecology of Linnets Carduelis cannabina on lowland farmland. In Ecology and Conservation of Lowland Farmland Birds (eds Aebischer, N.J., Evans, A.D., Grice, P.V. & Vickery, J.A.), pp 173–181. British Ornithologists' Union, Tring.

43. Wickman, P. & Wiklund, C. (1983) Territorial defence and its seasonal decline in the speckled wood butterfly (Pararge Aegeria). *Animal Behaviour.* **31.** 1206-1216. 10.1016/S0003-3472(83)80027-X.

44. Boddy, L., Büntgen, U., Egli, S., Gange, A.C., Heegaard, E., Kirk, P.M., Mohammad, A. & Kauserud, H. (2014) Climate variation effects on fungal fruiting. *Fungal Ecology.* **10.** 20-33. 10.1016/j.funeco.2013.10.006.

45. Gange, A., Gange, E., Mohammad, A. & Boddy, L. (2011) Host shifts in fungi caused by climate change? *Fungal Ecology.* **4.** 184-190. 10.1016/j.funeco.2010.09.004.

46. Jaworski, T. & Hilszczański, J. (2013) The effect of temperature and humidity changes on insects development their impact on forest ecosystems in the expected climate change. *Forest Research Papers.* **74.** 10.2478/frp-2013-0033.

47. Kauserud, H., Stige, L., Vik, J.O., Halvorsen, R., Høiland, K. & Stenseth, N.C. (2008) Mushroom Fruiting and Climate Change. *Proceedings of the National Academy of Sciences of the United States of America.* **105.** 3811-3814. 10.1073/pnas.0709037105.

48. Fürstenberg-Hägg, J., Zagrobelny, M., Jørgensen, K., Vogel, H., Møller, B. & Bak, S. (2014) Chemical Defense Balanced by Sequestration and De Novo Biosynthesis in a Lepidopteran Specialist. *PloS one.* **9.** e108745. 10.1371/journal.pone.0108745.

49. Clark, C., Piane, K. & Liu, L. (2020) Evolution and Ecology of Silent Flight in Owls and Other Flying Vertebrates. *Integrative Organismal Biology.* **2.** 10.1093/iob/obaa001.

50. Maurice, S., Arnault, G., Nordén, J., Botnen, S., Miettinen, O. & Kauserud, H. (2021) Fungal sporocarps house diverse and host-specific

communities of fungicolous fungi. *The ISME Journal.* **15.** 10.1038/ s41396-020-00862-1.

51. Guevara, R., Hutcheson, K.A., Mee, A.C., Rayner, A.D.M. & Reynolds, S.E. (2000) Resource partitioning of the host fungus Coriolus versicolor by two ciid beetles: the role of odour compounds and host ageing. *Oikos.* **91.** 184-194. 10.1034/j.1600-0706.2000.910118.x.

52. Kumschick, S., Fronzek, S., Entling, M. & Nentwig, W. (2011) Rapid spread of the wasp spider Argiope bruennichi across Europe: A consequence of climate change? *Climatic Change.* **109.** 319-329. 10.1007/ s10584-011-0139-0.

53. Buxton, P.A. (1960) British Diptera associated with fungi. 3. Flies of all families reared from about 150 species of fungi. *Entomologist's monthly Magazine.* **96.** 61-94.

54. Song, Z., Bi, Y., Zhang, J., Gong, Y. & Yang, H. (2020) Arbuscular mycorrhizal fungi promote the growth of plants in the mining associated clay. *Scientific Reports.* **10.** 10.1038/s41598-020-59447-9.

55. Van Geel, M., Yu, K., Peeters, G., Van Acker, K., Ramos, M., Serafim, C., Kastendeuch, P., Najjar, G., Améglio, T., Ngao, J., Saudreau, M., Castro, P., Somers, B. & Honnay, O. (2019) Soil organic matter rather than ectomycorrhizal diversity is related to urban tree health. *PLoS ONE.* **14.** e0225714. 10.1371/journal.pone.0225714.

56. Leather, S.R., Baumgart, E.A., Evans, H.F. & Quicke, D.L.J. (2014) Seeing the trees for the wood - beech (*Fagus sylvatica*) decay fungal volatiles influence the structure of saproxylic beetle communities. *Insect Conservation and Diversity.* **7.** 314-326.

57. Barton, P., Cunningham, S., Lindenmayer, D. & Manning, A. (2012) The role of carrion in maintaining biodiversity and ecological processes in terrestrial ecosystems. *Oecologia.* **171.** 10.1007/s00442-012-2460-3.

Index

www.ingramcontent.com/pod-product-compliance
Lightning Source LLC
Chambersburg PA
CBHW040933030426
42336CB00006B/63